WINDWARD

TO

FANTASIA

WINDWARD

TO

FANTASIA

ADVENTURING UNDER SAIL

ANDREW STRANSKY

Dedicated to my girls, Carolyn and Mara

who made this all possible.

WINDWARD TO FANTASIA

CONTENTS

CHAPTER 1

THE JEWEL OF ZABARGAD ISLAND

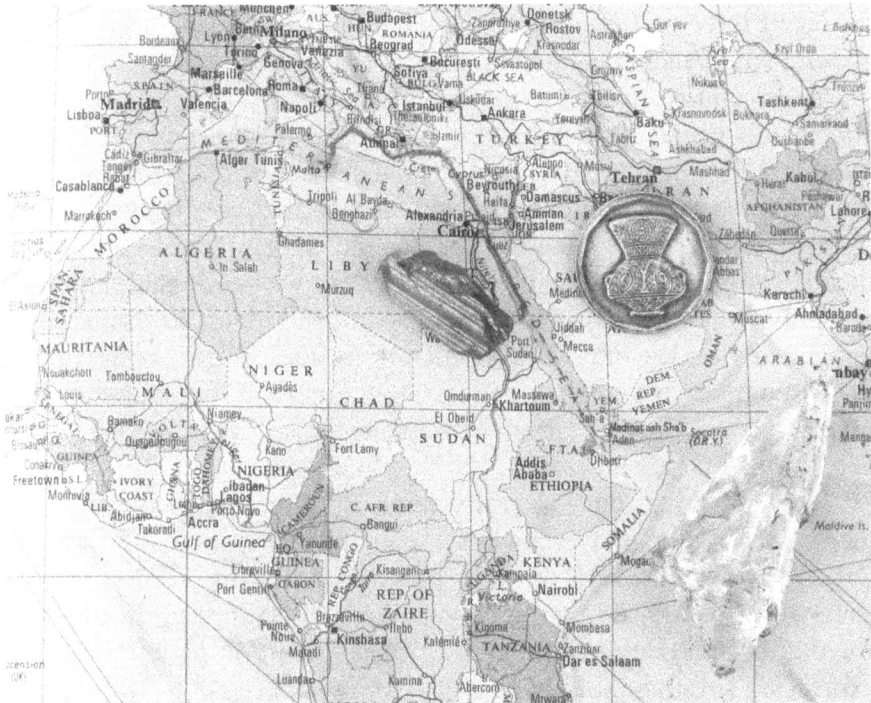

Imagine yourself flying, high above the world, fluffy clouds below, the bright sun beaming down and a great sense of freedom in your heart. Now the clouds begin to thin, revealing the vast sparkling blue ocean that stretches out to the red deserts of the Horn of Africa. Gliding over the bleak, black mountains of Somalia you pass the Straits of Bab al-Mandab and enter the Red Sea. You'll be wondering where it got its name as you soar over the brilliant cobalt blue expanse, its edges speckled with a maze of reefs like turquoise jewels.

In contrast to the sea's illustrious beauty you observe the harsh, arid mountains and plains of Eritrea then Sudan. Passing the Egyptian border you begin to descend, the sea shows its true self, ruffled by a steady north wind, waves cresting occasionally, a vast remote expanse. The air pressure increases, giving you refreshing oxygen and the friendly smell of salt, seaweed and plankton, borne on desert flavoured sea-mist. Now what's this up ahead? Looks like a creamy white yacht beating into this otherwise deserted sea.

Soon you're up close enough to make out a modern looking yacht, sails deeply reefed down to handle the fresh headwind, heeled over at 25/30 degrees, the name *LONGNOSE* painted boldly along the narrow bows. Gliding down you land aboard, an invisible being. Immediately you are taken aback by the uncomfortable angle the boat is sitting at, occasionally hitting waves awkwardly and throwing up spray, while an unusual stainless steel contraption steers the long laminated wooden tiller. Sitting happily in the cockpit, oblivious to the discomfort, a youngish couple lounge peacefully, studying *The Red Sea Pilot Book,* peering forward every so often to look at an island ahead on the horizon.

"Hey Carolyn, do you really think the breeze will die off like they're predicting so we can anchor in this fairly exposed reef off Zabargad Island?" says the tall, blond-haired, wiry fellow, whose somewhat freckly skin is deeply tanned. He's dressed scantily in weather beaten denim shorts and a green T-shirt on its last legs, his expression soft, thoughtful and slightly nervous.

Carolyn heads inside this bucking yacht, intrigued you follow, struggling for balance in the weirdly slanting interior. She casually flours up steaks of fish, with a frying pan of oil heating on the outlandishly swinging stove.

"Well, the forecast has been pretty right every other day and we're due for a break in the weather, seeing it's been blowing 20 knots and more for the last two weeks." She gracefully slips pieces of fish sizzling into the oil, swaying easily with the movement. Her medium height allows headroom in the low cabin, but you wonder if the chap could stand upright.

For such a long boat the cabin seems minimal, the galley bench is barely two feet wide, the navigation-table cluttered with paper charts and instruments, the lounge/bed brightly covered in an exotic Asian weave. Teak trim is finely varnished giving it a well loved look while an eerie ebony mask adorns the centreboard case, where a narrow passage leads to the forward saloon.

"So, what do you make of the pilot book's warnings about the island being out of bounds?" he asks, anxiety showing on his pleasant face. She weighs this question carefully, a hint of doubt flashing over her sun-bronzed features. Energetically she pops out through the companionway, dark brown hair ruffled by the breeze, beaming happily, her strong, curvaceous, supple body completely at ease aboard this bucking vessel.

"That book's probably out of date anyway. It's most unlikely, but if we do get an official visit, we'll just be nice and tell them we have engine problems." She gives him a bright encouraging smile then slips back inside to tend the fish, whose delicious aroma now fills the cabin.

Welcome to the unusual lives of our two adventurers, now deep in their pursuit of an escape from typical suburban life. It's May 1998, the 20th century winding to its conclusion, you're invited to join them as they explore the wonders of the world, searching for their life's purpose, for adventure, friendships and the simplicity of nature's beauty. Spared the bucking and rolling motion of a yacht, you'll enjoy their life unfolding from the comfortable pages of this book.

*

Zabargad Island lies offshore in reef-strewn Foul Bay, deep in the heart of the Red Sea. More than two thousand years ago the Pharaohs sent slaves in feluccas to mine the foothills of this remote island for peridots, the olivine green gemstone formed deep in the earth's mantle. Despite the promise of precious stones, sailors rarely visit this foreboding, mountainous island. Unfortunately, its lack of protected anchorages allows only calm weather visits. For many yachts calm weather is considered a gem for easy motoring, a welcome respite from the relentless headwinds. Being keen sailors, we choose to use the calm as a perfect opportunity for a crack at this treasure.

"We may not have any money in the bank but at least we have *Longnose*," I reflect as we row ashore in our canoe like dinghy, looking back in admiration at our fine 13m yacht lying gently at anchor. Her sleek modern lines strike incongruously with the barren, rugged island, faded white gel coat contrasting starkly with the clear, blue sea beneath. "If we'd waited until we had 50k in the bank we'd still be back in Sydney, working for someone else!"

The topography of the pilot's detailed chart proves very inaccurate, yet the green tinged diggings stand out clearly against the dark hills of uplifted mantle. In searing heat, armed with lunch and makeshift digging tools in our backpacks, we trudge over the rough ground that leads up to the ancient mine. "When I was a little boy, growing up in Grenada, all our cruising friends scraped by on day to day earnings and they had a tremendous time," I say to Carolyn, defending our low budget, rugged lifestyle.

Descending deep into a hopeful looking trench, we scratch about ineffectually at the hard, black earth with our machete and hardwood stick. "Why is it that we always find ourselves searching for something, striving to grasp that thing just beyond our reach?" I philosophise, working steadily.

Without a cooling breeze, our clothes are soon drenched in sweat. Imagining the poor slaves who toiled down here day after day, year after year, conjures a vivid image of hell. After a few hours the novelty of this labour has totally worn off, bits of rubble our only reward. "Oh well, no treasure for us it seems! Let's go off exploring elsewhere."

Trudging through heat mirages over the stark barren plain, we head back down to the building ruins near the shore to eat our lunch. Munching ships biscuits and swigging water in the shade of the decaying stone shed I notice a glimmering in the dirt. "Hey, Carolyn look what I've found!" I cry out joyously, "they must have processed the peridots here!" Half an hour of excited scrambling about in the burning black sand produces a handful of ancient, olive-green peridots.

Buoyed by our success, we set off to explore more of this desolate island. Climbing over the loose, yellow, metamorphic rock on the ridge leading up from our anchorage I'm thrilled to find a clear, tear drop shaped stone, over an inch long. Holding it in my rope-calloused hand, its rugged magnificence mesmerises my heart.

"I think I've found a diamond!"

Carolyn, happily scanning the strangely placid Red Sea, keeping an eye out for the approach of any official-looking vessel, comes over to inspect my find. "It's beautiful, but what makes you think it's a diamond?" she says in her down to earth fashion. Not being particularly knowledgeable on precious stones I cast aside my hopes and continue exploring.

Having rowed back out to the boat, tired and dusty, we don our snorkelling gear and dive into the inviting clear water to cool off. It being 32 days since we last took on fresh water in Al Mukula, Yemen, our water supply is so frugal, this is our method of taking a bath. An enormous Mauri wrasse, almost 2m long hovers under *Longnose,* he's been there all day like our guardian. His eyes, as big as tennis balls, seem to reflect deep compassion. We marvel at his vibrant green scales and purplish green patterns, his powerful bumphead and vast rubbery lips. Finning along in such clear water feels like we're flying over the coral reefs below. Taking deep breaths, we push down deep below the surface, cruising through the maze of corridors and caves until a huge, ferocious looking barracuda blocks our path in a menacing fashion and we retreat back to our ship.

Drying ourselves in the warm sun, we crack open one of our plentiful supply of coconuts from the Chagos Archipelago, scrape out the moist white meat and squeeze out the milk using a clean tea-towel. Carolyn artfully mixes the ship's cocktail. From the markets of Madagascar, powerful local rum seeped with vanilla beans blended with our fresh coconut milk. The heady spirit regales our energy, as I sit at the chart table excited again by the wild looking jewel in my hand. I have this strange feeling of finding something magical.

Yet it's later this night, after few more cocktails and a delicious baked fish dinner, under the sheets of our saloon bed that the real jewel is formed. A gentle wind caresses the rocky wildness of Zabargad, barely touching the tranquil sea. This is as remote as it's ever felt sailing the world, 500 miles from Cairo and 8000 miles from home.

Departing Zabargad Island we continue to push into the relentless headwinds, at times our travelling home falling off waves with a jarring crash. In the stark light of a fresh new day, the wild stone seems to have lost some of its lustre and I begin to think it is only topaz or some common gem. During the day the biggest dolphins we have ever seen fall in with us, grown plump on the rich sea-life of this rarely visited body of water. Dolphins have always signified good luck for us, so we take these whale like creatures as a fine omen. Little do we know of the changing currents of our future prospects.

*

Having lived aboard our trusty sailing boat for 14 years, this feels the pinnacle of our adventures. Tackling the infamous Red Sea, travelling the world under sail, doing it the hard way with barely a penny to our names. While the glories of a Mediterranean cruise lie before us, I constantly feel a gnawing pressure upon myself to find my life's inspiration, other than just gaily swanning around from one magnificent port to the next. "You know Carolyn, I think leaving university to take on the school of life has proved my stumbling block!"

"Well, look where we are now," she replies, gazing out at the stark beauty of our anchorage in the Gulf of Sinai. "Making lots of money doesn't always lead to a better life."

As our yacht's bow slices through the pristine blue sea, I ponder my life's direction as something of a Jack of all trades. I feel a pressure from the modern world to become specialised in order to thrive. Somewhere along the sea lanes of this voyage I hope desperately to discover a solid direction to pursue on our eventual return to Australia.

Longnose's 20 year old motor, splutters and blows white smoke, making us feel ill at ease. It must take us through the Suez Canal, without fail. Sailing won't be allowed as a back-up here and the cost of a breakdown will put our cruise in jeopardy.

*

Exiting onto the wide blue Mediterranean we toast the last of our Madagascan rum to celebrate our Canal transit. It's straight into the next adventure though as we must now make a mad dash to rendezvous with my mother in Turkey.

In the ancient stone-walled harbour of Antalya, the early spring chill is being washed away by a warm golden sunshine, which has a special, almost magic quality in the Mediterranean. We're sitting in *Longnose's* modestly spacious cockpit, rigged with a makeshift table, enjoying the luxury and novelty of being moored up in a 2000 year old harbour. Our lunch, a fine spread of the crusty Turkish bread 'Ek-Mek,' sharp sheep's cheese, fresh black olives and spicy Sujuk salami is being happily consumed with a fresh garden salad and glasses of a slightly disappointing Turkish red wine, a point which does not slow its consumption. With my mother here we can afford to live it up a touch.

Promenading Turks are providing us with endless entertainment. One unusual vendor in fancy embroidered costume and funny peaked hat, is yodelling and banging bells as he twirls about his mad stretchy ice cream on a long stick. It's at this moment Carolyn drops the bombshell which is to blow my complacency out of the water.

"Isn't this a lovely lunch! It's so nice to have you with us Robbie," she says, taking a delicate sip of wine. "I have a bit of an announcement to make and this seems an opportune moment. I've known from the beginning, but didn't like to mention it, the time not being right," she ventures, heightening our interest. "I'm pregnant!"

A nervous electric thrill courses through my body. It's a life changing moment that puts a whole new dimension on my need to discover a proper direction in life. Having Mum aboard for the best part of our cruise up the Turkish coast, takes the burden off our insufficient budget and for the time being we enjoy life without care for the future.

Of course all things come to an end, so after my mother flies home from Marmaris, we must decide our new course. "We've seen the best of this Turkish Coast, don't you think Carolyn? The yodelling entertainer selling stretchy ice-cream on a stick in Antalya, the ancient Lycian Sarcophagi of Kekova Lagoon, the delicious Ek-Mek bread, turquoise coves full of beautiful Gulets manned by amusing Turks and now the bass drum pumping discos of Marmaris Bay. I just think it's time we head out into the Aegean and tackle the Greek Isles, don't you?"

"Sure, I'm ready when you are!" replies my faithful companion, basking happily in the golden glow of evening sun.

Back in the time peridots were first mined on Zabargad Island, the 35m high Colossus of Rhodes stood over the entrance to Mandraki Harbour on Rhodos Island. Now, as *Longnose* enters this Greek clearance port, a small bronze deer will have to do, for us modern seafarers. From here, galleys of the Knights of St John harried the powerful Turkish fleet, attracting the wrath of the mighty Ottoman Empire who turned upon them in one of history's greatest sieges.

The cobblestone alleys and ramparts of the great crusader fortress are now alive with buskers and the aroma of charcoal grilled octopus. Piles of huge stone cannonballs lie about, stirring the imagination. Strolling in the warm night air one can easily feel the terror of having them whistling past one's head, as awesome siege machines gradually reduce the castle walls to rubble.

We shop around for what's cheap in the Greek stores. Olives, bread, goat's milk, feta cheese, thick creamy Greek yoghurt, almonds, dried figs and apricots, local produce that is both fresh and economical. All set to depart, we spy the collector of port fees doing his rounds. Calmly, yet quickly we cast off and pull up our anchor, slipping out past the harbour walls with a few extra drachmas in our pockets bound for Simi Island.

In the relative cool of evening we sit in the cockpit, refreshing ourselves with Ouzo after a demanding day working sails and ropes. It being Carolyn's birthday we trek over the ridge to the town waterfront. Striding along we ponder on the Greeks passion for building their villages on such steep inclines, marvelling at the marble steps worn smooth by centuries of foot traffic. No wonder old Greek men and women are such hardy people. Perhaps most remarkable is Carolyn's cheerfulness to undertake such a strenuous walk on her birthday, savouring the adventure.

As a rare treat we decide to dine out at one of the typical waterfront tavernas. We order glasses of wine but as we are now very thirsty, gulp it down like water. In a drunken state we ravenously await our meal. Gentle lights twinkle on the placid sea as we sit bewitched by the glorious aromas that drift about this peaceful night, fascinated by the elegant manners of these cultured Europeans. When our delicious meal arrives, we do our best not to appear like famished sailors. It's been a big day and the food and wine bring on tiredness. As we trudge back, tipsy in the moonlight, to our faithful yacht, even though our bank balance is lamentable, it strikes me that the adventurous sailing life is the richest one, and for me nothing else will do.

Where more appropriate than sitting in a yacht below the whitewashed villages of Greece to tackle Homer's *Iliad*? The local Gods Zeus, Aphrodite and Poseidon, to name a few, sound a fearful lot, full of evil cunning. I begin to fear lest their eyes should fall upon us strangers, so gaily waltzing across their arena. Even as I read, I am sure they are plotting challenges upon our course.

Under the hot airless lee of the Turkish mountains we had been sceptical of reports that the Meltemi blows force 7/8 regularly, that's up to 75km/h. As we leave Simi heading west across the Aegean to explore the southern Cyclades, the north-west Meltemi delivers us a blow to cast any such doubt out of our minds.

Carolyn is always keen on voyaging to the remotest islands. Her choice of Ioannis Island is to prove particularly wild. On this afternoon the Meltemi is gusting near enough force 8 to have me fearing the ship's safety. Waves are washing over *Longnose's* low bows, threatening to rip the dinghy out of its lashings. The sea can be so sublimely peaceful, yet when it flexes its muscles a sailor on a small yacht can find themselves suddenly up against an adversary who is more powerful in every way.

We peer grimly forward into the wild sea, focus totally on steering a safe path through the regular violent sets of waves, praying our equipment is strong enough to handle this battering. Senses keen on finding shelter under the island, the anchorage on lonely Ioannis looks most uninviting, with a host of white horses galloping out from the entrance to greet us. It takes us a good hour to moor ourselves into a tiny cove with countless anchors and warps, Tierra del Fuego style.

At last we have an element of peace aboard ship, the wind whistling overhead, wafting down the pleasing wild herbal aromas so prevalent on these islands. The cove's clear water looks so inviting, we slip in to refresh our tattered nerves. Even here, on the highest peak of this savage windblown island, the hardy Greeks have built a monastery. Its fresh whitewash, glowing under the stark Aegean sun. In our brief visit to this rugged island we glimpse not a soul, only goats that come to inspect us.

Thus, the Aegean reveals its character. Steep boarding waves, driven by powerful winds, which begin to shriek like enraged sirens as one tries to gain an islands lee. It's this very harshness that gives one such a euphoric feeling when finally secure in a snug haven. The islands are rocky and devoid of trees, stripped bare in the days when wood was the world's key resource for smelting and shipbuilding. Yet at the same time this starkness has a remote beauty which enthrals the visitor.

Skala, the main town of Astipalia, proves one such snug haven. A conglomerate of blue trimmed, whitewashed dwellings cling to the steep hill, crowned by a fortress. Local history has it that a successful defence of this fortress involved throwing beehives on the invaders. Merely to awake in a port steeped in such history is nectar for the soul of a sailor.

In the quiet of morning we brew a pot of freshly ground coffee, savouring its smooth energising flavour. A bowl of rich creamy Greek yoghurt topped with freshly scrumped figs and black grapes, plus of course a generous drizzle of honey, seems a healthy economical breakfast. As the sun begins to warm up the village, chords from Zorba drift out from a nearby waterfront taverna, where a bleary-eyed waitress is sweeping up, getting ready for another day.

"We have our concerns," says Carolyn, licking her spoon. "Cruising the world on a shoestring with virtually no income, yet it's times like this, we seem to be living the best life imaginable."

Legendary Santorini Island lies on our path. It offers no snug anchorage, only intrigue. Was it the fabled lost Atlantis, still thriving into the 21st century, where an advanced civilisation once lived in the time of the Pharaohs, destroyed by the greatest volcanic eruption in recorded history, three times greater than Indonesia's powerful eruption of Krakatoa? Was this Atlantis sunk into the sea only to rise up again with shades of its great past?

As we sail into the crater entrance, a puff of smoke bursts from its volcanic cliffs. With persistence and luck we find a tiny shallow ledge to anchor on, amongst a few scattered local moorings. Backed by towering cliffs, a village looming above our mast, we have shelter from the driving Meltemi, evident by the clouds rushing overhead. Diving on the anchor some 18m down, assures me of its capricious grip on some rocks just before the ledge drops away into the black depths of the crater.

Securing our dingy on the stone wharf we set off up the cobblestone path that zigzags its way to the village. Wealthy or lazy tourists can hire a donkey to take them up, but we are neither. Catching our breath high above the blue sea we find ourselves amongst the chic European glitterati. White-washed shops and houses are moulded and carved into the steep caldera cliffs, aesthetically shaped and decorated as though everything is a work of art, surely the Atlantis touch. Perched on the rim of an active volcano would certainly make one value the beauty of each day.

We shape our course around the Peloponnese, trying to keep off the tourist trail and avoid paying the $200 US Corinth Canal fee. By now Carolyn, in the full bloom of pregnancy, is becoming most concerned that she should visit a hospital to have tests done. Finding a public phone she sets about making enquires and immediately finds the language barrier is a serious issue. It seems her only option is to go to Athens, 300km away, almost an eternity on public transport. Worst of all the hospital fees are phenomenal and all but booked out. What with the associated travel and related costs, we would be just about broke if she tried to have tests done. Bravely Carolyn makes the decision to trust that our baby is healthy. After all, these tests can present their own dangers, we console ourselves.

Even though our money is running very low by now, we cling to the positive approach that's been our hallmark, enjoying the beauty of each day. Anchoring off the town of Koroni, we walk up to the grand fortress once held by the Venetians when they dominated this trading route. Fig trees and grape vines grow wild about the crumbling stonewalls. We savour some of this delicious fruit, content in the warm sun, the clean air still and heavy with the aromas of wild oregano.

Sated by nature's booty we stuff our packs to the brim and return with this harvest to our boat. As the sun begins to sink low in the sky, the town livens up. Mouth-watering restaurant smells waft out on the warm breeze, while a tinkling bouzouki charms diners. Looking for our dinner I slip into the cool clear sea with my spear gun.

The harbour is fairly open to the sea so the water is fresh, visibility good. Gropers like to come out and hunt at this time of day so I search keenly amongst the weed and rocks for my quarry in the fading light. After a while I spy one but it escapes into a hole. Feeling cold, the urge to catch a fish pushes me on. Then I see a good-sized fish cleverly camouflaged in a clump of brown swaying weed. He thinks I can't see him, but he is wrong, and he is dinner.

Scrambling out of the cold water with the speared fish, the last rays of golden sun warm my chilled skin. Carolyn pours me a glass of Greek retsina, the smooth pine flavoured alcohol warming my soul. Before long we have our own magic aromas floating from our oven. With slices of potatoes and onions, sprinkled with olive oil, oregano and salt, the fish roasts gently. Sipping more of the fine Greek table wine and nibbling on fresh market olives we savour our challenging yet rewarding lives, which we know are about to change in a big way.

Diesel is very expensive on the shores of the Med, double what we pay down under. With the wind being so variable on this land bound sea, pure sailing is very demanding. Our budget forces us to rise to the challenge, and we keep our fuel expenses at one dollar a day. This dollar takes us in and out of the crowded harbours, charges our batteries, ices up our fridge and even pumps up our dive tanks. Rightly so, we feel this good value for our money.

With the Aegean behind us the local landscape offers more trees to greet the eye. Reaching the Ionian Islands, the towns have a more Italian pastel hue, and although lacking the remote beauty of the Greece we have just cruised, the protected waters amongst these islands are a welcome haven. Now we are back in the crowded circus of Mediterranean yachting, with cruisers, charters boats and flotilla fleets crowding the anchorages.

We enter the Ionian regatta, a race of some 25 miles with a huge mixed fleet of over 100 boats. After a good start *Longnose* holds a narrow lead and begins to pull ahead. Yet the Gods will not have some Australians taking the honours and deliver a huge wind shift. In a matter of moments the greater part of the fleet is ahead of us. We still have some fun making up tremendous ground and rushing past a great number of fancy yachts.

Trying to get one's anchor to hold on the weedy Med sea-floor is infamously difficult. One dark night in Levkas with autumn gales setting in, we look out through the rain at a yacht struggling its way to anchor. "Poor devils, fancy being out in this," I say, rather smugly. Yet only minutes later I realise we're dragging and almost out to sea. It's entirely unpleasant to find the engine won't start due to flat batteries. Our anchor chain, now becoming old and rusty will not grip on the gypsy as we try to haul the full weight of chain and anchor, now dangling free in the deep sea. Desperately we hoist sail and sweat up the anchor with lines to a genoa winch.

Vivid sunrise sees us safely back at anchor, nursing the grim realisation that there is much work demanding attention. The splendid summer is behind us, holidaymakers are heading back to work and I begin to feel very uncertain of the future. Carolyn heads ashore to phone up her parents, which she does regularly, a costly but necessary business. I set to work sewing up a seam in the mainsail with palm and sail thread, which came apart during our wild night. Before too long she comes rowing back with a loaf of fresh Greek bread.

"Well Andrew, Mum and Dad have offered to pay my airfare so I can fly home to have our baby in Australia. I know we could manage somewhere here, but what do you think?" I give her a big hug, my heart taking a huge dive, a sad destiny unfolding.

"It's a very generous offer and as much as I will miss you terribly, I do think it's the most sensible thing to do. It will be a wonderful chance for you to be with your family," I manage, trying to sound brave, but feeling vulnerable and small. A few days later she is booked to fly out of Rome in a month's time. This leaves me with the question of where to spend the winter alone.

Feeling pressed to decide a suitable destination for Carolyn to depart from, we head on, almost out of habit. Across the Ionian Sea for 200 miles to the toe of Italy lies the Roccella Ionica marina.

"Well, it's great being free of charge and all, but it's rather bleak!" I say to Carolyn as we stroll past acres of empty concrete pontoons on our way to town. Some hours later, our shoes dusty from the long walk, crusty bread and rather expensive Italian produce in our backpacks we trudge back to the marina. Large waves are beginning to roll into the harbour entrance.

Our lone neighbour, a rather scruffy Aussie on a rusty steel yacht, greets us as we return, lounging with a beer in hand. "Hey mate, once the sea builds up here it can be weeks before it's possible to leave! They ran out of money building this place and the entrance is silted right up. Looks like you guys are going to be staying here awhile, we'll have plenty of drinks together no doubt!"

Back aboard we both express our alarm over this situation. "It's getting too dark to leave now. We'll just have to be all set to depart first thing and hope the seas don't get much worse," I gloomily conclude. We spend a pensive night, listening to the increasing sound of waves crashing on the breakwater, sleeping fitfully. We desperately don't want to spend these final days together, holed up here.

A crowd of onlookers rush up to claim a good vantage point on the entrance wall as we motor towards the white wall of breakers. It's not a prudent thing to do, but I've always taken the risks needed to make adventures flow. Timing a hopeful lull in the swells, I gun our feeble 13hp engine and hope for the best. Charging out of the harbour mouth a big breaking swell rolls towards *Longnose* and we brace ourselves. A wall of white water cascades over our bows, covering our ship in a blanket of foaming sea, all but stopping our forward momentum. With painful slowness we begin to move again, fearful another such wave will come and hurl us back upon the jagged concrete blocks. *Longnose,* our vital shelter and transport holds straight, carrying us out into the relative calm of the open sea.

Feeling a bit shaken I feel the urge to come up with a destination. "Well, we could make for Malta, I suppose! That's the place cruisers go to winter over!" Now we happily cruise down the Sicilian coast, content with our heading. There can be few more stunning landfalls on earth than the extensive stone fortifications that surround the town of Valletta, golden in the first light of dawn. In the 15th century Malta was attacked by the Turks, in one of the most hard fought sieges of all time. The ancient fortification of the main harbour still rich with this dark history. Memories flood back to me from my childhood days, living here aboard our family yacht *Yanda* in the winter of 1968.

*

Carolyn smiles happily, her skin a firm rich amber brown in the golden glow of afternoon light. Standing against the yellow Maltese sandstone, her dark glossy hair frames a face full of positivity. It's a poignant moment on the eve of her departure and I can only hope the baby in her firm tummy will be strong from its healthy origins. Half the world will stand between us in the many months to come.

Feeling surreal I accompany her to the shipping terminal on the other side of Valletta. Putting on a brave, carefree face I wish her great personal power and luck, with all the energy I can muster. Watching the boat steam slowly out of the harbour from a cold stone bastion, my heart feels rather low. A little rain begins to fall from the dark sky as I set off back to the boat alone, the wet streets sparkling like some sad dream.

Winter is closing in, a chilling westerly wind is ransacking the streets. I have to walk briskly to keep warm, buffeted by unruly gusts, laden with the scent of wet sandstone. Back aboard, *Longnose* feels very empty, yet I must plunge courageously into my new life. Here I am on the far side of the world, with scant resources, knowing I must survive this European winter and make some success for the future of my child.

CHAPTER 2.

WINTER ALONE

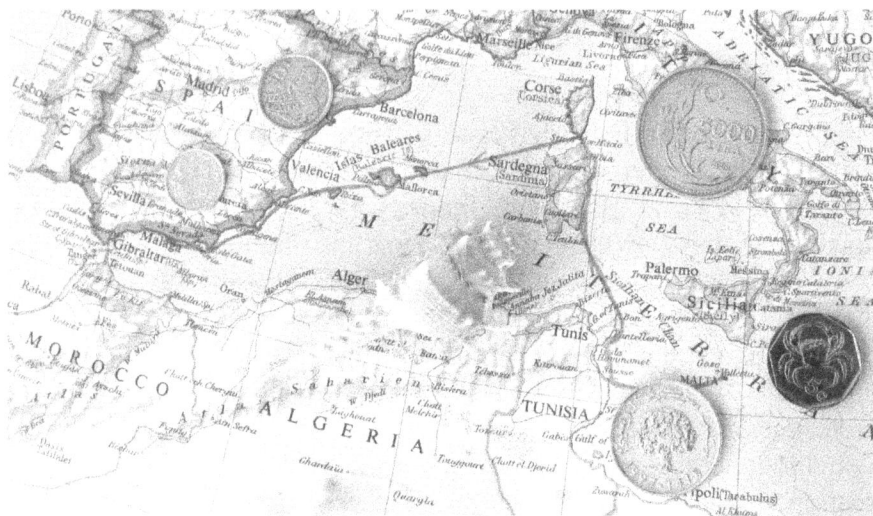

"What to do now?" I mumble to myself, busily sweeping the bare teak sole. "I can't afford to stay in Malta and really, I'm in the mood for adventuring!" Pouring over my charts and guides the Islamic land of Tunisia promises those third world prices and relief from the Med's cold winter. Across the gale ridden Libyan Sea the thin bows of the Adams 13m dive and crash as I make my way alone towards this strange foreign shore.

Safely moored up in Mahdia, the hypnotic call to prayer swirls through the ancient town as the mosques demand worship. Surrounded by rustic fishing craft, the vile stench of rotting fish hangs over the port so thick you could cut it with a knife. A scum of black oil pollutes the harbour, lapping up onto my once clean topsides, splashing onto the ropes and fenders. Fleeing north to Monastir, I'm forced to moor up in the fancy marina where prosperous sailors happily while away the days tinkering with their already perfect yachts. I had planned on hauling my ship out of the water for some much needed maintenance, but the yard proves much less affordable than hoped.

Pushing on across the Gulf of Hammamet, Kelibia, a traditional fishing port greets me with that same powerful odour of fish. My hopes of hauling out are dashed as the slings are not suitable for yachts so I busy myself with other jobs. Each morning at first light, huge fishing boats of 100' and more, manned by 20 odd crew, return to port. Rough, unsmiling characters swing their rust stained and weather worn craft uncomfortably close to the handful of yachts sharing their wharf. "Such is the price of adventure!" I console myself, sipping steaming coffee in the icy morning air, as the powerful Mistral blows unceasingly from the cold north forming snow on the nearby Atlas Mountains.

Gearing up, I climb the mast to change a blown anchor light bulb. While enjoying the view, my hands begin to feel numb in the chill wind. "This isn't what I imagined being on the edge of the Sahara would be like!" I cry out, hurriedly fumbling with the abseiling ring I need fit to the descending rope. Losing feeling in my fingers, I battle to push away horrible thoughts of being stuck up here with frost bitten fingers and nobody to help me.

Wrestling the thick rope through the icy alloy ring I'm able unfasten the ascender and whiz down to the safety of the deck. Feeling intensely relieved I retreat into my cosy cabin, urgently lighting the gas stove to boil the kettle. Reflecting on the difficulties of life alone, my hands thaw out on a hot cup of cocoa.

Some mornings I make the long walk into town, strolling briskly to warm up. Heading for the traditional markets, hard working donkeys rest easy before their carts of fresh cauliflowers, onions, tomatoes, apricots, pomegranates and so much more - all organically grown and sun ripened. I'm enjoying the rough charm of the place, but one day I decide to depart Tunisia and try my luck in Italy.

Marching purposely into town to exchange my dinar for Italian lira, any hope of escaping this country is halted at the bank. The tellers will not change my dinar back into foreign currency and annoyingly they are useless in any other country. "Can't you just spend it before you go," they suggest. It's a tidy sum so I decide to return the 70 miles back to Monastir and haul out there after all!

Gale force winds often sweep through the yard, shaking *Longnose* about on her wooden props. During the night a guard comes around every so often and belts in the wedges with a huge mallet. While it is nice to know the props are not working loose, it does little for one's continuity of sleep. To save on expensive new paint I adopt a rather unusual method to refresh the topsides. I strip off the failing paint and polish up the original gel coat to a new finish. Likewise, what's left of the old anti-fouling is stripped off leaving the hardy, but only modestly effective copper in epoxy antifoul.

Strolling up to the medina quarter, I make for the market, honing in on bargain priced local produce. Newly picked bunches of yellow dates still on their stalks, flood the stalls offering a crisp texture, something like an apple, before they settle into their soft sticky maturity. Abundant fresh chicken, raised naturally, prove the best I've ever tasted. Great mounds of vivid red Harissa, the spicy paste of Tunisia, enlivens any meal. Back aboard I munch happily on fresh French bread with butter and Harissa, before getting back to work.

Ten days on a Belgian local with a yacht in the yard kindly asks me back to his place for dinner one afternoon. "Alone is alone, you must be very bored here all by yourself!" I am not, but agree to come anyway. It's to prove an ill-fated visit.

Many years ago, when my dad was skipper of *Longnose,* returning from a cruise of the Solomans, we hit a reef with *Longnose's* centreboard, breaking it off and damaging the centreboard case. Ever since then it has proved the bane of the ship, leaking water into the enclosed keel area. It would be a great achievement to repair this, yet to access it from inside, all the floors must be pulled up, which turns the living area into chaos. I'm using a nasty little kerosene heater, which poisons me each day with its fumes and barely warms the cabin but it's all I have for drying work.

On this day I am hovering over it, working on the centreboard case down in the bilges, sandpaper, tools and rags strewn about. In a hurry to finish my job and be ready for this diner date, I stretch down to sand a particularly awkward area under the chart table and manage to knock over the heater. It falls onto an acetone rag, which bursts into flame and the kerosene spills out to instantly build a powerful fire. I quickly toss my bucket of washing-up water at the flames, already licking the cabin top. To my horror the water has little effect and I seriously begin to fear *Longnose* will tragically burn.

Trembling with dread, I frantically unclip the dry powder extinguisher from the oilskin locker and aim it at the flames. Pulling the trigger overwhelms the fire with white powder, suffocating it. Shaken but relieved I stare down at the mess that has been my day's work. Carefully cleaned, sanded and dried surfaces now coated in kerosene, washing up water and a thick layer of white powder.

Reluctantly I leave this mess and take a shower. As the sun sets over the white-washed marina buildings lined with palms, the Belgian man's wife picks me up in an old BMW, accompanied by their very scary dog. This large dark mongrel commands the front seat, barking at me viciously as I cower in the back, rather alarmed by this beast. "Don't worry about the dog," she manages between his nasty growls "He's never hurt anyone!" Somehow I don't feel comforted!

When we get to the house this dog rushes through the gate to guard his home. As I arrive his welcome is to leap up and snap at my face, his sharp teeth slice clean through my lip chipping a tooth on the way. There I stand, blood pouring from my lip, any hope of a refreshing meal and good company forgotten. Holding onto my mouth we drive around town for quite some time, trying to find a doctor who will do a careful job, hoping to avoid stitch scars. Finally a respected physician carefully tapes it together. This is a night memorable for all the wrong reasons. Returning to my poor messy yacht, all bandaged up, having missed dinner altogether, my spirit has sunk to an all time low.

Barely able to move my mouth the next day, I walk up to the markets and buy a fresh chicken. Normally I am too busy with my work to bother much with food, but now I need something really wholesome. I put the whole chicken on to stew with lots of vegetables and begin tidying up the mess. Sipping at the hot broth my strength begins to ebb back. I can't afford to slacken off in my work and I feel too low to simply sit about resting.

Doggedly continuing my constant labour, a week later things are looking brighter as I stroke on the final touches to *Longnose's* newly painted name. Next day *Longnose* is lifted back into the water and I set off sailing north with a fair wind. It's a relief to be back at sea again, topsides gleaming and hopefully the centreboard case no longer leaking. A new Tunisian house battery is fitted, so 'touch wood', no more dangerous dead flat situations to deal with. Gentle seas help the stress of being on the hard slip away, my lip mostly healed, although I am quite upset with the scar left by that nasty dog.

Back in the port of Kelibia I make final clearance from Tunisia and wait uneasily for my chance to cross the notorious Sicilian channel. It's the middle of winter and even big ships report foundering here in bad weather. One night a 50-knot wind rips through the harbour, causing havoc. A 60' yacht snaps one of its mooring lines, and a trawler breaks free altogether, just missing *Longnose.*

Tunisia has been a rewarding place to visit, still retaining much of its old world charm, yet I feel relieved and excited to depart, eager to get this difficult crossing under my belt. Setting off at a good speed, by nightfall Cape Bon, the north-east corner of Tunisia, lies astern. Sickness tugs at my mind, but I force it aside to deal with the busy shipping channel. Pressing on at full speed, close hauled into a north-north-east breeze I am constantly dealing with ships passing quite close and the lingering smell of diesel fumes is worse than a highway.

This shipping lane seems never to end and well after midnight ships still hound the course. Fatigue begins to overcome me and I struggle to keep awake. By 2.30 am the horizon is empty of these menacing monsters so I tune up the trusty radar detector, a tiny gadget which I fit behind the dodger. Now that it feels safe, I snuggle down into my warm bunk, quickly getting into the single handed sailor's cat napping mode.

Morning light reveals gentle long swells barely ruffled by a peaceful breeze. Not being the best sea cook, the conditions are perfect to whip up a Spanish omelette to refresh my energy. As the day wears on a powerful westerly breeze kicks in, so I must pull on the 3rd reef and battle steep rising seas. By midnight Cape Carbonara on the south-east tip of Sardinia offers its protective lee. Dropping anchor in the sheltered bay, protected from the tiring westerly seas, the wind now whistles harmlessly in the rigging as a warm bed beckons.

Landing upon the pristine beach, desolate and wildly glorious on this bright winter's day, the most beautiful murex shell lies glistening in the sand. "Surely this must be a good omen," I exclaim to the wind, thinking of the imminent birth of my child on the other side of the world. Stretching boat bound legs I stroll up to the village, sucking in the fresh herbal aroma of the land, savouring warm sun on my body, With the tourists gone, life is quiet in the streets and I feel distinctly alone with none of the action and fanfare of summer holidays to make one feel part of the scenery.

Purchasing a loaf of bread, the lady charges me by weight, which seems novel, then I must have some mortadella, pepper cheese and Sardinian wine. Forcing back money concerns I head back to my ship. Munching rich cheese and meat on real Italian bread, sipping spicy red wine, the flavours fulfil my dreams as I bask in the satisfaction of having crossed the Sicilian channel mid winter.

Day hopping up this wild east coast, the vast bulk of Sardinia takes the brunt out of the chilly, penetrating wind and keeps the seas low. *Longnose* is a lone craft on this stretch of pristine blue water, the greater populace safe behind walls.

One evening I anchor up peacefully in the port of Arbatax and in the morning men from the port authority are waving at me to come to the main dock. Dutifully I obey, welcomed by a band of mad Italians from customs who are very friendly and inquiring about the status of my clearance, for want of anything better to do. They troop me up to the main office and clown around with forms for a time until the boss comes back from his morning coffee break. "Leave him alone," he gesticulates, "he doesn't need to fill out any papers and he is free to stay in the port, you boys look after him," he commands.

I am pleased to find no charge levied, but just at that moment a man comes running up from the dock. "Mr Andrew, the northerly wind has sprung up, you'd better move your boat now or it will be smashed on the wharf!" he says in an urgent manner that has me running for my life. A powerful breeze is blowing straight through the harbour entrance and waves are already starting to jostle *Longnose* up against the heavy wooden piers.

"Why did you guys make me moor up here?" I cry out in despair, as I can see escaping the dock before the swell builds up and begins to smash the topsides in, is going to be very difficult with only a 13hp motor. Wasting no time, I enlist the aid of two sturdy fellows, crisp and neat in their handsome uniforms but eager to help this wild Australian. I battle the increasing wind rowing a kedge anchor as far out as possible, then we gradually winch the bow off the wharf, praying the anchor will hold, while the remaining gaggle of Italians manfully do their best to fend off the stern.

Hauling and pushing, engine struggling, *Longnose* breaks free of the danger. My makeshift crew haul up the kedge and direct me across to the safe side of the harbour, which is tranquil in the now howling wind. "You can stay here as long as you like!" they inform me generously, while a wave of relief stems my flow of adrenalin.

The afternoon finds me busily tidying up the boat, enjoying the warm winter sunshine coiling ropes on deck. A car drives up and I see a beautiful young Italian woman appear on the dock above. "Hello you are Australian?" she calls down to me, which is rather a surprise.

"Yes, but I love your country more," I reply in way of a compliment.

"If you like you can come to a party with us tonight," she suggests, which sounds very attractive. "I'm Rosa. My house is up on the hill there," she gesticulates waving a tanned arm at the heights above Arbatax. "We can go now if you're ready and I'll show you about my town." This is an offer to good to refuse and we set off at a great speed in her little Renault.

That night Rosa takes me to a local gathering. There's a tremendous amount of eating to be done, a welcome relief from my own thrifty efforts. Traditional lasagne, cheeses, meats, olives and salads all washed down with local Sardinian red wine and Peroni beer.

Sated with fine food we return to her house and sit overlooking the harbour lights drinking small glasses of mirto. She pours me a second and heads off to take a shower while I enjoy the myrtle flavour. Rosa floats back in dressed in a loose black dressing gown wafting the fresh aroma of cherries. She reaches over and pours herself another liqueur, her large firm breasts revealed as she lingers over the bottle, nipples erect. Leaning back joyously she casts me a mischievous smile.

"You can share my water-bed tonight if you like?" she offers shyly, looking away and presenting her Sophia Loren like profile. Feeling amazed, I grapple with my emotions. I've always been a faithful, kind person and any day now I'll be a father. I tactfully decline and she happily drives me back to the quiet dock, where I kiss her gently goodbye.

Driven to move on, as though somewhere on the distant horizon lies my true purpose, I sail north, bound for the large town of Olbia. Creaming along happily before a fair wind, suddenly a fierce northerly headwind blocks my path. I'm forced to retreat into Port Brandinchi, a wild and partially enclosed bay whose entrance proves to be scattered with nasty submerged rocks. Navigation is stressful with vicious bullets of wind, whistling down over the sparsely vegetated hills. A pristine white sandy beach lies at the head of the bay, decorated with granite out-crops. Dropping anchor, I work to sooth my shaken nerves, yet the wind continues to attack my ship, leaving me pensive.

During the night the wind starts to blast across the bay, ripping up spumes of sea and hurling them at *Longnose,* heeling my ship over in a fearsome fashion. Deeply concerned the anchor can not withstand these brutal assaults I deploy the storm anchor, only managing to toss it over the bow, praying it will dig in if the main anchor begins to drag. This action produces no sense of security.

I sit up all night nervously taking bearings, for those nasty rocks that scatter the bay await, if *Longnose* loses her hold on the sandy bottom. Little do I know that on the other side of the planet the labour pains have begun and Carolyn is heading for Mona Vale hospital.

After a miserable, sleepless night I'm keen to leave this scary bay, so with the storm seeming to have eased I begin hauling in the anchors. The main anchor has dragged because all the loose rode of the storm anchor is now under load. With the primary anchor winched aboard the storm anchor must be brought in by hand. Having pulled the rode halfway in, a savage squall descends out of the hills, blasting *Longnose* with spume and laying the gunnels right down to the sea. The vicious intensity of the wind scares me to work frantically in the lulls, hauling aboard anchor tackle. Savage gusts swoop down the hills throwing *Longnose* about like a flag as I hang on fearing for my life.

Fright and desperation give me great strength to pull up the last of the tackle quickly and secure it aboard. Adrenalin now pumping I dash back to wrestle with the helm. Under bare poles alone I am able to bear away and run off at 8 knots, the wind screaming about the rig. Peering ahead the sea is blown white, lit up by the morning glare. Charging into this I must sight rocks to navigate out of this maze. On the knife edge of doom I con my vessel, straining to pick up any tell tale signs. "Why did I go and leave that anchorage?" words ripped from my mouth as *Longnose's* glass skinned foam hull whizzes close by cruel black teeth of the sea bed.

Peering into the dark cabin the sounder shows the depth has increased, so my pulse moderates, yet incredible gusts blow spume high into the air, making rainbows in the bright morning. Still in the grips of danger, there's an undeniable majestic beauty in this power nature is unleashing. Pulling myself together I set the storm jib in order to edge back towards the coast in hope of escaping this tempest.

For several hours the wind-vane smashes down with each tearing squall, shaking the whole boat as *Longnose* battles in towards the port of Caletta. Entering the small harbour, I'm very nervous, as fearsome gusts swoop regularly down from the high mountains and will overcome the meek 13hp engine while trying to moor. Right at the wharf a harrowing gust drives through, but a heavy line is cleated by some friendly line-handlers. They are almost pushed into the water as my nylon line stretches alarmingly. Next lull a spider web of lines secures my home. "Woohoo, thank you Gods!" I cry out in relief.

Ringing home I discover that during all this battle to survive the elements, our daughter has sprung into the world. Mara Peridot, child of the sea, like Captain Nemo's daughter in *20000 leagues under the*

Sea, conceived on the island of peridots. I check the date on my calendar, February 13ᵗʰ 1999, pour myself a small glass of dry Sicilian marsala and drink a toast to my child, who's birth so far away seems to be having a powerful effect on my life. A deeper sense of responsibility creeps over me. Taking another mouthful of the rich spicy alcohol I thank my lucky stars for getting me through this testing day without losing *Longnose* on those evil rocks, the dark amber liquid settling my nerves as I crunch away on some special Mordica chocolate, enjoying this small celebration of life's richness. There's a deep feeling this day marks an epic change in my life but I can't quite see how.

Pressing on north with renewed caution I finally make Olbia, where some locals tell me the airport reported 75 knots and that housing in the area has suffered much damage. Grand stone buildings line the main streets making me feel rather poor as the locals strut about in their fancy winter designer wear, looking smart and sure of themselves. I roam about in scant clothing unable to afford a decent jacket, feeling cold and envious of those sitting about the delicious smelling cafe's, warm in their ubiquitous thick black coats. Yet I comfort myself knowing they don't have such challenging adventures to test them.

Back in my snug cabin I turn on the VHF to hear the latest weather report. My friend the robot weatherman has the same old story "Bo-ni-fac-i-o st-r-ai-ts Nor-ther-ly w-in-ds for-co oc-ho." Force eight, a fresh gale up to 45 knots! I am not looking forward to tackling this notorious strait. For now, sailing by the Costa Esmerelda is an undeniably stunning affair, the most expensive real estate in all of Europe. Its white sandy beaches lapped by translucent waters and granite geology sculptured by millennia of driving winter winds and sun baked summers, its fields of macchia scrub, perfumed by wild herbs such as rosemary and oregano. Anchoring overnight in Porto Cervo, the Aga Khan's lavish development lies deserted for the winter, lacking the energy of its jet set clients.

Ten miles on, Isla Maddalena lies at the mouth of the Bonifacio Straits, happily alive with the charm of locals so it's a joy to stroll about in the warm sunshine, drinking in real Italian character. Ancient cobblestone streets, busy fish-markets, elegant women and the constant aroma of fine food, which I can only afford to look at and savour the mouth watering smells. I must content myself with cooking a fish stew, which warms the cabin a little in the chilly night, while a cheap local red wine warms my soul.

Feeling driven to face my challenges, I sneak across the mouth of the Bonifacio Straits, on a glorious sunny day, catching the boisterous Mistral in a gentle mood. Approaching the south-east coast of Corsica the citadel and fortifications of Bonifacio perch magnificently on steep vertical white limestone cliffs and I sail into the fully sheltered ravine, anchoring in a small wild bay just short of the commercial harbour. After a pleasant day of sightseeing I pluck up courage to tackle the greater part of the straits and the wide expanse of the Mediterranean Sea, taking on the full brunt of the Mistral.

Nerves on edge I set three reefs in the main and reach nervously west through the Straits with gale force winds on the beam. A busy traffic in ships add to my difficulties, but having passed Cape Scorno, the funnelling effects die off and the pesky ships head off in all directions leaving my new course to the south-west deserted. A dark moonless night has fallen now, yet I feel safe to catnap in the snug cabin once again, letting the miles slip by.

Two days of fair wind takes me across 340-miles of blue Mediterranean. The sea's wild beauty is left behind as *Longnose* enters the Mediterranean's largest natural harbour, the port of Mahon, cutting deep into Menorca Island. Wandering this town, I feel a powerful seafaring history emanating from the bricks and stone, happy to be part of this moment in time. There're far less people wearing thick black coats, so the worst of the cold is hopefully weathered. Looking around happily at the grand colonial buildings, faintly warm sun on my skin surges pleasure through my body, the heady aromas of coffee, fresh bread, fried fish and feminine perfume all blend into that delightful scent of town living.

"Well, what now?" I wonder, gazing out at my fine sailing machine. "A nice cruise through the Balearics for starters, but I need to find a nice warm, economical place to await the return of my girls! I'll have to be more careful, now that I'm a father, try to avoid wild adventures. Yes, I'd better stick to the coast of Spain, much safer than heading over to the Moroccan coast," I reflect, running my hands over several days of stubble on my chin. "Sounds way cheaper in Morocco though! Mmmm?"

CHAPTER 3.

PIRATES AND CONTRABAND

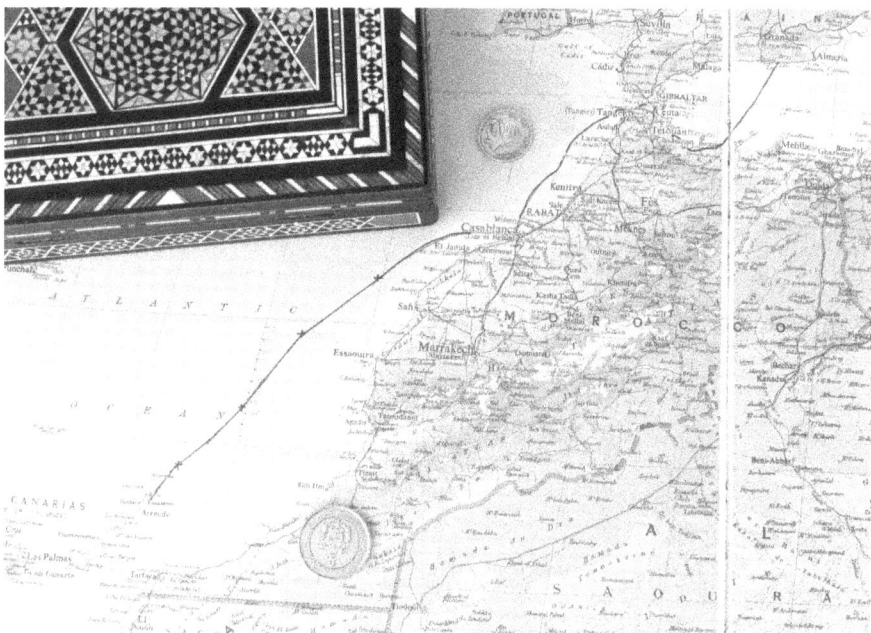

It's late morning, ghosting along under full sail with the Riff Mountains visible ahead, crisp and clear in the spring air. Peering through the binoculars a small black boat can be made out, coming towards me. The weather is mild and easy, much warmer now being further south, so the acrid scent of my nervous sweat hangs about the cabin.

Feeling uneasy I decide to start motoring, altering course a few degrees in the hope of subtly avoiding them. Yet this does not help as they slowly gain. Before long the naked eye reveals three bedraggled men with dirty white turbans set upon heads, clearly fixated on my yacht.

Morocco, the ancient kingdom of north-west Africa promises old world towns, dusty roads, ancient characters in traditional garb, donkeys hauling carts to market, life unscathed by tourism. Yet virtually every sailor I talked to said it would be madness to think of sailing to Morocco. "The officials are all corrupt, they will confiscate your boat!" they warn in the most off-putting tones. Yet I have grown wary of such negative talk and over time developed an unusual philosophy. 'The worse warnings people give about a country the more exciting it will be.' Morocco has me intrigued.

In Tunisia, fate sent me a Swiss single-hander sailing an old gaffer. "They are the good people, Morocco is a special part of the Med, with the freshest, tastiest food. There is nothing to fear," he assured me, while we sat exchanging yarns and sipping Tunisian fig liqueur in his travel worn cabin. Even so it was one man's word against virtually everybody else's, but Spain proved expensive, tipping the scales in favour of adventure.

The small wooden motor craft with its fearsome looking crew is close to now. Loading my spear gun, dive knife tucked into my pants, adrenalin pumps my senses into a state of super alertness. Standing poised, fingering my razor sharp knife, I'm fully prepared for this meeting. It's all very well to be tall and strong from sailing, but they will be tough and wiry from hard living. The talking inside my head turns off, I am animal, fully alert to every instant.

Weapons aside, my first order of defence is to put on a welcome smile and wave a cheery hand. When I can see them more closely they strike me as honest, perhaps it's their eyes or the hard-working look of their craft. I back off the engine and let them come alongside. Showing handsome grins they call out "Cigarettes, have you any cigarettes sir?"

Adrenalin abating, I feel rather sheepish with my weapons. Relief floods over me as I give them a pack from the supply we had purchased to tackle the Red Sea. They are very happy and hand up a couple of handsome silver snapper, which I accept with genuine pleasure, for a fish is an expensive prize in the Med. This first contact puts me at ease somewhat and I begin cleaning up to be ready for port.

Having just finished shaving, a large patrol boat roars up, standing off while an officer is sent over in a zodiac to search me. Amused by this situation I ask the fellow what I would be smuggling into Morocco, a country so famous for its export of hashish. "Would it be cocaine?" I suggest cheekily. He laughs in a friendly manner, but gives *Longnose* a thorough search just the same.

Arriving in the port of Al Hociema my nerves are set on edge again. Fishing craft of all shapes and sizes crowd the wharfs and it's not at all comforting to see several confiscated yachts rotting at their warps. My heart sinks as they signal for me to berth with these sad looking relics. Five officials greet me as they march aboard and in a jolly manner crowd into the cabin. They have me working furiously with a pen, filling out the usual cascade of forms. Feeling relieved by this friendly arrival I make a foolish mistake.

From our supplies for the Red Sea voyage I still have half a carton of cigarettes purchased in the Maldives for only 20 cents a packet. On a whim I generously hand out packets all round. They are delighted but I detect surprise, and a touch of suspicion enters their eyes as they troupe off. Feeling a trifle perplexed I cast the question aside to fry up my fish.

On this first evening I feel tired, some young fellows are chatting away at me in a bothersome fashion, giving me a headache. A handsome fisherman approaches shooing them away to my relief. "Welcome to Al Hociema sir. We are very honoured to have you here," his smile is genuine and I take an instant liking to him, inviting him aboard. "My name is Hassan. I am living here all my life," he says, crumbling up hashish with tobacco and rolling a joint as if its the most natural thing for a man to do. We sit, cool as can be, smoking in the fresh evening air. It seems a decidedly dangerous thing to be doing, but when in Morocco do as the Moroccans do. "Ok, I must go now, fishing for the night on my ship," he says, setting off. "Tomorrow I would like to take you to see my town."

Awaking to the powerful aroma of fish, men call out as boats return from their night's work. Sipping steaming hot coffee in the cockpit, I am a touch on edge as a rustic looking 100-foot trawler turns on its own length stopping only feet from my transom, yet the crew cast me reassuring glances. Hassan comes aboard after his night out on the cold windblown Med, bringing me fresh sardines.

He dusts the fish in flour and fries them in hot olive oil. Sitting in the sunshine together we savour the crispy skin sardines with salt and lemon juice. "Mmm, these are the freshest, tastiest sardines I've ever had," I tell my new-found friend with genuine feeling. He helps me clean up and then we stroll off to town. Immediately I sense how at home he is, feeling quite envious of his oneness with the local community. I am very proud to walk the streets with him, obviously so well respected. For his part, he obviously enjoys parading me about like some interesting curiosity from the sea.

Typical of Moorish North Africa, the town is a cluster of whitewashed dwellings. They sprawl across the high rocky hills looking down upon the busy harbour. Al Hociema is rather messy but gives one that priceless 'foreign' feeling. Hassan takes me to one of the many cafes, where the local men seem to spend their leisure hours sipping "Moroccan whisky". We sit down to this delicious sweet mint tea served in a tall glass and I lounge back taking in the easy atmosphere.

Titanic is playing on a big screen TV, enthralling everyone in the café. My friendly neighbour hands me a long wooden pipe. "Try some of this my friend, it's very relaxing." Smoke curls gently into the cafe's high ceiling, putting me under its spell. Gradually the epic power of *Titanic* overcomes me. My whole life becomes titanic, like Leonardo de Caprio's struggle against all odds to survive and live with his love Rosa. At this point a bolt of realisation hits. I have my own love that I must fight to keep, my own life on the abyss of survival. The thought Carolyn may for some reason not return grips me with an uneasy fear. This drama soars through my head, poignant with emotion.

Eventually emerging from this café I'm a transformed being. I have a new strong drive in my life and a building desire to reach more settled tropical waters. As Hassan guides me home he stops to buy a packet of cigarettes, where to my surprise he pays the equivalent of $4US for a single pack. "Wow, cigarettes are very expensive here! You know I gave each of the customs men a pack when they gave me clearance, they must have thought me very generous!"

"Oh Andrew my friend, that is not a good thing! They will be thinking you are a drug dealer, handing out packets of cigarettes like that. You must go and explain this situation to them!" he suggests quite sternly with a worried look. I shall never forget his good friendship.

The next day, palms sweating, I visit the head police officer to explain. He is quite amused by my concerns, "Don't worry, this is Morocco, every thing's OK," he reassures me in a friendly manner.

One must clear in and out of each Moroccan port visited and typical of Al Hociema's hospitality the policemen insist I share Morocco's traditional dish of couscous with them before I depart. It comes in a large ornate wooden bowl, a huge mound of couscous sits in the middle soaking up the juices of a lamb stew. My teeth sink into the deliciously tender meat, the flavours of this exotic land seeping into my system with every mouthful. Smiling appreciatively at my hosts, their fine features show a hint of satisfied pride.

Next morning customs officials insist on another full search, which puts me on edge, yet I'm soon on my way with papers in order. It's a pleasant day sail in fine sunny weather, past the rugged, dry rocky coast speckled with grey sandy beaches to the port of El Jebha.

Wharfing up astern of the patrol boat, I immediately attract a huge crowd of about 100 wild looking locals. In awe I smile and gesticulate, trying to entertain these lively people who now surround *Longnose,* jabbering and pointing in fascination as though the circus has come to town. Suddenly the customs officers roar up in an old Citroen and one leaps out and shouts at the crowd to clear off in a rather brusque and alarming manner. These officers are dressed in the smartest of uniforms, heavily adorned with lavish gold jewellery. I look on amazed and a bit shocked by this whole spectacle.

Coming aboard the officers prove to be very friendly which is a relief. Patiently I endure another full search as well as the usual paperwork and before too long I am all cleared in. The courteous head officer's final remark "If you need anything, don't forget to ask us," leaves me wondering, what he means. After this disquieting arrival, I begin to tidy up and settle my nerves with a glass of cheap Spanish box wine. The crowd has cleared off but one fellow remains, approaching me in the twilight.

"Hello Sir, my name is Abdullah. Yes, listen to me I have very good English!" He's a big burly, scary looking chap. "I am the only one in town who can speak." This claim seems possible so I am friendly to him even though he makes me nervous. Locking up I venture off to town with him. "Mr Andrew, I am very happy to be back in my town after being in goal for three years," he announces as we eat our dinner in a rustic café. "You have come to the right town to buy hashish my friend. I can get you as many kilo's as you want! The police have been very strict so demand is down and I can get you best price!" He states, openly, sending me into a cold sweat.

El Jebha is a step back into the olden days of this ancient kingdom. A small fishing port, it backs onto the high green foot hills of the Riff Mountains and to my delight boasts barely a car. As much as I try to tell Abdullah dealing hashish is not my business, he continues with the hope he will make a sale and spends his time showing me much of interest about the town.

We climb up into the dry, rocky hills, where like apparitions out of a fairytale, a family of goat herders dressed in the most stunningly colourful traditional clothes appear, tending their animals. Their impeccable cleanliness and beauty strikes a magical note out on the dusty land.

On Tuesdays the market comes to town, bringing wild highland characters from all over the district. A farrier shoes horses, working busily in the warm sun. Under faded, patched tents lies abundant produce of a quality and taste I have not experienced before. I wander about most impressed by these traditional scenes. "This is the best season for fresh hashish," Abdullah mutters in my ear over the somewhat discordant cacophony of this bazaar.

We return to his dingy room with some friends, were Abdullah insists I partake of his water pipe. The aromatic resin from the cannabis plant heightens my feeling of nervousness, but I somehow feel it will aid my search for direction in life. Of course it's an illegal stimulant, made so by its competitors the alcohol and tobacco companies. Throughout the afternoon and into the night I partake a little too deeply of the smooth hashish. My mind goes into a deep spin, lost in another world, it becomes extremely late and I am totally lost. Demons haunt me, chasing me as I blunder back to the port, eerie and slightly chilling on a dark moonless night.

The patrol boat guard appears out of the darkness, smiling knowingly. "Where you been?" he quizzes me as I stand there starry eyed, fumbling, unable to formulate a decent answer. He barely suppresses a smile and kindly guides me to my yacht.

Life is so peaceful in El Jebha that I am sad to depart. I do however feel a certain paranoia due to my associations in the town. I have a lurking fear this adventure could lead me into bad trouble. When I turn up to clear out, the head officer dispatches a man to check that I have made no deals. I speculate they are quite disappointed I have not done any business, as they humbly grant me port clearance.

My next port of call, M'Diq proves a stepping-stone back into the 20th century. It even has something of a marina, but in my usual penurious manner I raft up with a fish-farming barge. Here I merely clear in at the port office in the usual fashion.

Once again a fine lad turns up to be my friend. He takes me to the nearby University town of Tetouan, where craft shops, crammed full of the most intricate and unusual artefacts, open my eyes to the rich culture of this country. Greatly excited I carry away a hand-crafted box, inlaid with over a thousand pieces in which I plan to stow my treasure. This rarely visited coast is to prove the gem of my Moroccan voyage.

Gibraltar seems too famous to pass, so I sail across the straits for a visit, but its ordered streets seem so lifeless in comparison to the creative culture in Morocco. Filling up with duty-free diesel I sail for Tangier after only one day. Passing the fabled capes, the "Pillars of Hercules," *Longnose* enters the Straits of Gibralter, gateway to the Atlantic Ocean.

Tangier seems worth a visit, though I feel like a tourist again and have to pay for a berth in the port. Walking up to the old town my "friends" only want to lead me to their cousin's carpet shop or the like. Stocking up on the local bargains of dried fruit, nuts, fresh fruit and vegetables, I depart for Casablanca, in search of a more romantic town.

Dusk off Cape Spartan, doorstep of the Atlantic Ocean, *Longnose* sails gently along. It's been a busy day clearing out, so feeling weary I boil the kettle for tea and smoke a little of the hashish which I could not avoid buying from my friend Abdullah. In the past I had found the occasional use of this legendary and controversial herb to have a beneficial, calming and enlightening effect. On this occasion things turn out quite differently.

Peaking out from the dodger to see if all is clear, my heart misses a beat. A dirty black craft, bristling with rough looking men, shouting in a frightening way is roaring straight towards me. I panic, fire up the engine and drive it full ahead, then grab the HF radio mike and hit 2182. "Tangier Coast Guard, Tangier Coast Guard, this is the yacht *Longnose,* Victor Juliet 2427, I have PIRATES after me, can you send assistance." Only the crackle of static noise answers so I dash on deck to find the vessel truly in hot pursuit, her crew sounding even more hostile.

"This is Brest Radio, Brest Radio calling the yacht *Longnose,* we receive you loud and clear, can we be of assistance?" Tearing myself away from the fascinatingly unwelcome sight I stumble inside.

"Brest Radio this is *Longnose.* I am being pursued by a very suspicious vessel, who I believe intend to pirate me. I am two miles east of Cape Sparta, can you help me in any way?" It seems futile talking with someone up in the north of France, with this vessel in such hot pursuit, it also feels foolish to be on the radio with so much else to tend to.

"*Longnose, Longnose,* this is Brest Radio, we are trying to call Tangier to see if they can assist you...," but my attention is suddenly diverted, when the engine stalls, stopping dead.

"Oh no they've put a rope out to foul my prop! I should have listened to my father and become a dentist." Rushing outside I peer into the twilight, the craft is now idling close by my stationary yacht, the men calling out angrily in harsh, guttural Arabic, pointing into the water. Looking over the side, a fishing net is drawn up along the hull and it slowly begins to dawn on me. "So perhaps they are fishermen and were simply shouting at me to avoid their net? Oh no!

And I shoved the engine on full and raced straight into it. I am simply trapped in these poor fishermen's net!" A fool must face the music. First I must get on the radio and explain my folly as by now I have involved three stations in my drama, with Cadiz radio now offering help.

Making matters worse the sun has set and the twilight is rapidly fading. In the gloomy cockpit I count 15 desperately poor fellows staring down on me from the high topsides of their weather beaten trawler, which stands off very close, in the roly ocean swell, a great deal of animated gibbering coming from the crew. I have to act fast, grim as it may sound, I must don mask and fins, then armed with a torch in one hand and knife in the other, jump into the chilly heaving Atlantic.

It feels like a scene out one's worst nightmare as I dive under, *Longnose* rolling back and forth above my head, threatening to knock me unconscious, the torch beam waving madly illuminates crabs and fish swirling about in the inky sea. Struggling not to become trapped in the net myself, I dive down several times, savagely cutting the mess away from the propeller. Having freed it I scramble out of the dark and scary water feeling shaken yet relieved.

Still the angry fishermen loom over *Longnose*. "You come back with your boat to Tangiers! Pay for our net mister sailor!" demands one fearsome looking fellow. I stand, dejected and shivering in the cockpit, lost for what to do.

At this moment a fair breeze springs up and *Longnose* begins to run away at a good speed. I can barely believe this stroke of good fortune allowing a possible escape, so set a course to clear the cape, quickly outrunning the heavy trawler. Whizzing through the darkness, dozens of dim flashing lights can be seen all about the horizon. I'm trapped in a maze of nets. What can I do but run on? Suddenly *Longnose* comes to a slow halt, caught in a second net.

Looking over the side I can see the heavy net rope has caught the centreboard. I have no choice but to cut the rope. Now I am free to pass out into the Atlantic Ocean. Feeling exhausted and guilty for cutting those poor fishermen's nets, I spend the rest of the night haunted by shipping, getting little rest. The next day smoggy Casablanca greets me. The port is a huge commercial shipping facility, polluted and reeking of rotting fish. My romantic illusions are shattered.

Smog blankets the busy metropolis, which even the tropical sun fails to pierce, giving it a dull and gloomy appearance. I want to cut away the last of the netting from the prop, but the port waters look like a thick brown soup. I notice some local kids swimming about, which gives me courage, so braving the murk I dive in, cutting off the netting. Quickly I rinse in fresh water and bask in the bleak sun. Soon the port authorities arrive to clear me in and I set off on the long walk to town.

By now the fog has mostly burnt off although it still gives the sunshine a pallid, disappointing glow. Strolling down the grand palm lined boulevard in the city's newer district, a fresh energy ebbs back. Before long I discover the old town area, which is ramshackle and poor but by far the most interesting part of the city. Street wise as I consider myself, I seem to walk into the hands of one trickster after another.

Adjacent to the old town with its squalor and poverty is Africa's largest Mosque, the Hassan II, tallest in the world. This prominent landmark of Casablanca lies just south of the port, a marbled masterpiece reflecting grand extravagance, unjust politics and a depth of culture barely glimpsed.

While admiring this spiritual wonder, I meet a couple of nice fellows, who impress me with their friendly talk and I join them walking towards the old town. 'Good friend, please do us the honour of coming to our sister's wedding," the taller fellow asks me, a toothy smile lighting up his dark features. Quite excited to see some local culture I accept happily.

"Oh, we haven't any money with us! If you could just lend us some to buy some flowers for the wedding, we'll take you there straight away," my friend suggests. Now suspicion begins to rise in my heart with every step. My two "friends" chat away in Arabic as we make our way through a crowd of locals. Seeing my chance, I duck behind some large ladies and run for my life. I hear them calling but soon I am safely lost in the crowd.

Should I take the Marrakech express or explore the ancient capital of Rabat? Pondering my dog-eared passport, overcrowded with Moroccan clearance stamps, I feel a certain stigma attaches to these stamps. The trade winds and tropical climates beckon, a force I can rarely resist.

Much shipping is on the move sailing from Casablanca. All of a sudden thick fog falls upon the sea, restricting visibility to no more than 60m. Ships bleat their horns, *Longnose* races along through this foul gloom while I make meek fog signals on a pea whistle and pray for safety. A radar would be a comforting piece of equipment right now. Any moment a ship could swoop out of the fog and send me to Davy Jone's Locker. An hour of worry passes contemplating this fear, then as unexpectedly as it arrived, sun bursts through the fog as a fair wind blows it away.

Charging south-west off the coast of Africa, the Atlantic Ocean stretches out endlessly. Oh what joy to be once again falling in with the sunny trade winds. I feel most delighted to be leaving the horse latitudes behind, with their fickle and variable winds, their gales and treachery. Now though, there is the 430 mile voyage to the Canary Islands before me and having been unable to come upon a chart for this ocean trip I have only the *Times Atlas* to navigate by, so I am hoping the publishers Mr Bartholomew and Sons have not left out any ocean reefs or rocks from their fine world maps.

On a voyage of discovery such as this, the next anchorage always feels like something of a lucky dip. People, ports and weather being such capricious things at times. I would dearly love to find a pleasant and safe anchorage, where it would be easy to stay for a longer period. I'll need a lot of luck if things are to fall into place, but for now there's just the steady rush of the sea passing by. Making a cup of tea I lay down in my bunk contentedly, settling into a nice book, letting the miles slip by.

CHAPTER 4.

THE SHIP'S KID

It's late March 1999 as *Longnose* glides before the wind, fleeing the Mediterranean winter. True to the latitude and longitude of *The Times Atlas of the World,* and to my deep relief, Lanzarotte Island appears on a clear sun drenched horizon. Sailing in close to this dry volcanic island I dig out a tattered, coffee stained photocopy of an old Canary Islands guide to navigate *Longnose* into Lanzarotte's protected inner harbour. Clear blue water over sand looks most inviting and finding a mooring I make fast to it, happily savouring the warm trade wind on my skin.

Fitting the cover over the mainsail I admire the black volcanic rock used to build the harbour walls, a small fort and bridge to the town. Dragging the drifter and No3 jib bags into the forepeak, bright sandy beaches and the whitewash of the town buildings contrast vividly with this ancient stonework. Coiling stiff salty ropes the desert landscape beyond the town is mostly devoid of greenery, stark and unpretentious but charming all the same, with barely a cloud disturbing the pristine blue sky.

Pulling the dinghy onto a small, windblown sandy beach, I stroll excitedly along the 17th century stone mole, the black rock radiating welcome warmth. Gateway to the town is a drawbridge, built to repel pirate attacks that plagued this settlement in days gone by. Roaming about, people are smiling, well tanned and dressed in quality holiday clothes, an air of leisure about their actions. The shops are crammed with all the latest white goods, fine foods and designer clothing, yet the prices make me cringe.

I treat myself to a gelato, licking luxuriously on coconut and mango while strolling the expansive paved waterfront boulevard. Looking out over clear blue water my fine yacht lies securely moored amid a handful of other cruising yachts. Drinking in the ease of tropical weather I feel a fragile contentedness. Over the last three years we've visited on average, one whole country per month, a cracking pace. Constantly on the look out for a change in the weather which could make an anchorage dangerous, adjusting to so many new languages, customs and currency has been quite testing and tiring. Yes, this will be the place to spend a little time, I decide!

Returning aboard with a bag of groceries I sit down at my typewriter, a 1930's *Royal,* that belonged to my great grandmother. Dreams of earning money through writing articles for a cruising magazine have been curtailed by an editor who seems to delight in rejecting a number of my best stories. "Because they had been, 'done before,'" he claims, while publishing his own stories of chartering in the Whitsundays. Tapping out a letter to Carolyn, I praise the town, encouraging her to come as soon as they are ready. Deep down I am quite concerned she will not wish to return to this wild and frugal life.

Having posted this important letter I begin to contemplate my situation. The mainsail leach is worn away and needs replacing, the refrigeration system needs re-gassing, baby proof netting must be fitted under the lifelines right around the boat, the list goes on and on. Evidently there is a lot to achieve with scant resources.

"What will it be like having a baby aboard?" I wonder, working away at my list of tasks while still tending to all the cooking, cleaning and washing. Taking a jaunt ashore I swim and bask on the sand. Sun dried I stroll leisurely around to the fishing docks, hunting for fishing net that may be suitable for baby netting. Returning with a smallish piece of suitable netting I decide to make the remaining 25m. For this I make a net shuttle and a gauge block, procuring a roll of 2mm braided cord.

Having knotted up 1.5m of net I brew a pot of plain black tea. Laying back on the settee, I open Joshua Slocum's classic, *Sailing Alone Around the World*, letting my mind drift off into a good adventure. Getting up refreshed after a prolonged read I ponder my situation. "Surely having a baby aboard won't change life all that much?"

I check for mail at the Post Restante counter each day as the weeks slip by. Finally a small letter arrives, ripping it open urgently my eyes flit to the key words, "Arriving June 14th." Excitement and relief flood my chest, 3 weeks to get sorted!

It's late in the day as I happily walk several miles to the airport, saving a taxi fare. Lounging in the comfortable foyer seats, idly relaxed, I'm blissfully ignorant of my approaching fate. Then my two jet-lagged crew emerge, ashen faced from 48 hours travelling half way around the world.

They are both exhausted and need transporting to their new abode, quickly as possible I gather, aided by Mara's nerve shattering bellow. Keen to halt this racket, a taxi is hastily called up and she calms down as we enter the plush interior. Mara's strong little body crowned with a mop of white hair, bristles in her papoose. A complete new person, packing way more punch than one would expect of a being so small.

"Oh it's so lovely to be back aboard," says Carolyn, while Mara curiously takes in her surroundings. "It was the right thing to go back to Australia to have our baby, but I've deeply missed the simplicity of our life afloat. I just hope we'll be able to manage with this lively new creature."

Over the coming days, in a feeling akin to being hit with a cattle prodder, I'm indignantly booted out of my relaxing ways. "We'd better set up all the lee cloths Andrew. So Mara won't fall out of the bunks!" Pulling out the sections of canvas normally stowed under the bunks I tie them up into place. They conjure up a feeling of stormy weather at sea, making in harbour lounging and access to food and tools under the bunks very difficult. They do however form excellent baby cots all around the boat.

The cockpit bed is rigged up with the awning making it a perfect playpen. "She's a lot of work!" I remark, forced to lay about tending to this demanding creature, unable to tackle the multitude of pressing jobs. Mara works herself up into a sitting position, smiling gorgeously at my constant attention. She begins to examine the rope used to tension the backstay, absorbed by its braided texture, the flecks of blue, white and black, the way it snakes about as she flicks it, the taste of salt on her tongue as she senses it on every level. Observing this baby fascination for such a commonplace object, one can't help but begin to reassess the world afresh, through baby eyes.

"Gosh, you did a great job with the baby netting!" says Carolyn as Mara charges up the side decks, hemmed in by my handiwork. Following her on my hands and knees, I begin to feel it's time for a nice lie down but now I seem to be on watch 24hrs a day. "Wow, so your mum's offered to pay for a watermaker! That's one benefit of having a baby! I was feeling pretty distressed at the prospect of having to use disposable nappies and now we'll have enough water to wash proper cloth ones."

A few weeks later the boxes of watermaker pieces arrive, ordered from the US. Mara's having a wonderful time, chewing at pipes and making games of the maze of parts and tools spread about our cramped yacht. Carolyn lifts her up onto the tiny galley bench, involving her in the lunch making process. With our boisterous creature briefly entertained I must make use of every second. Holes must be drilled, pipes wrestled into place and wiring threaded home through awkward looms. It'd be nice to sit back and contemplate this work more, but that luxury is gone.

After lunch Carolyn begins to tidy up the galley, while Mara plays happily with a winch handle. "Gosh, the hardest part of this watermaker installation is fitting the high pressure water pump to the engine!" I grumble, trying to hold its heavy weight up in the position it needs to be mounted.

"I'm sure you'll manage," says Carolyn. "You know, I think it's really good having a baby aboard a boat, they're always close by." Yet it seems Mara isn't close enough. Hearing us chatting happily away inside, the insatiable beast sets off a deafening bellow that halts any form of normal human thought.

"OK, OK, Mara! How about a shore going adventure?" I suggest, seeing that Carolyn is bursting to make some order aboard. Rowing with the stroller perched in the bows, Mara sits with remarkable aplomb in the stern, eyeing the sea suspiciously. It seems she comes pre-loaded with a mind full of various common sense.

Frolicking in the shallow sea refreshes us both, allowing contented basking in the sun. Thus sated we zoom off to town, gay and carefree, doing wheelies down the streets with Mara still in her swimmers. I'm quite ignorant of convention when it comes to babies, so a pair of Spanish grandmothers stop us with beaming smiles. They "tut-tut-tut" away at Mara, feeling her cool skin. "Oohh, baby she cold," they repeat in their scant English, while pulling out Mara's clothes from her bag. Mara is delighted under all this attention. "Belle Bambina," they agree still worrying about her cold feet.

"Gracias senoras, no problema, bebe est bien," I manage in my pitiful Spanish, before we rush off gaily once again in search of novelty.

How it happens I don't know but Mara seems to take over my life in the blinking of an eye and an altogether new chapter begins. From Zabargad Island on the 5th day of May in the blistering sun, to Lanzarotte Island there is a strange connection. Both are barren volcanic islands yielding peridot gems from their mines. Yet such mystic connections help little in the demanding work of looking after this baby girl.

As it turns out Mara's first sail is a local race out of Arrecife; quite a big affair with helicopters buzzing over the start line and a good fleet of flash racing yachts. We have plenty of keen locals aboard yet even they can't understand the Spanish race committee's instructions and we lose some minutes being late for the start in our confusion. Hard beating into the fresh trades sees us back in 8th place with half a dozen yachts hot on our heels. *Longnose* is no witch upwind in a breeze, her narrow beam letting her fall over without developing much power.

Approaching the windward mark, we begin shaking out our reefs. Suddenly there is a loud 'BANG' as the main halyard breaks and folds of Dacron flop sadly down the mast. It looks like the race is all over for us, still to leeward of the mark, only a half dozen boat-lengths from the rocky lee shore. Holding onto a slim hope, still making a little way under the jib alone I quickly call out for our makeshift crew to use the boom topping lift in order to hoist the main. Jumping to exceptionally, they soon have the main climbing back to its mark without too much drama from the now unsupported boom.

Setting off under full sail and running before the blustery breeze, *Longnose* shows her remarkable downwind speed, her narrow beam and flowing lines slicing along effortlessly. We start to pass yachts at a cracking pace and our nerves settle. Carolyn brings Mara on deck, bubbling with baby excitement. She hands out our lunches and we all enjoy this turn of events while munching hungrily on crusty bread rolls with chilled grilled chicken and salad. Spirits rise as we race past the town in sparkling sunshine and by the leeward mark we are in 5th position.

Reluctant to reef we must feather our giant main, edging up high to the wind, allowing it to spill some of this fresh trade breeze. We pass another yacht by catching a favourable lift of wind along the shore, just managing to hold 4th place to the windward mark. By now we have cracked a few Coronas to settle the hangovers of our Spaniards, thoroughly enjoying ourselves pegging back the yacht ahead. Mara is very happy, enthralled by all this action and suspense.

Just outside the harbour walls we move into 3rd place, then to our surprise we realise the other two yachts, which flew spinnakers, have to round the leeward mark again. So we actually come into the harbour first, gaining line honours. "Well, having a baby aboard certainly didn't slow us down," says I swigging on a Corona in the warm afternoon sun. "Perhaps she will become a great racer, our daughter!"

Our previous busy pace of one new country a month, grinds to a standstill. Five months *Longnose* spends in the Canary Islands. Patience replaces adventure as we slowly get used to having a lively ship's baby aboard. It's a pleasant change getting to know a place really well, our lives filled with that peculiar satisfaction tending a new being can create.

"So Carolyn, do you think we're ready enough to get on our way?" I broach the subject close to my heart. "I know there's a lot of jobs that still need tackling, but I fear we'll never get going if we wait until everything's perfect!"

"Well yes, I think we're sorted enough to make a start. We can always get more jobs done on the way and the sailing will show us what really needs doing," says Carolyn in her sensible, adventurous fashion.

Sailing south down the coast of Fuerteventura, we fall into the company of some young Brazilian/Americans on the ex-racing yacht, *Coeur de Lion*. They seem to enjoy hanging out with the wild Australians whose strikingly fair haired baby seems to have a passion for sailing at barely eight months of age. Off the SW cape, anchored over a delightful sandy bottom, with the sea so clear one feels to be floating in space, we head off together hunting fish in the fresh Atlantic water.

"Hey Andy, how do you manage to catch these cunning devils so easily, all the while towing your baby girl around in her life ring!" exclaims Lucas as he lounges in the Zodiac, having already given up on his attempts to spear a rock groper.

"Haha, she does seem to love it and gets so excited when I come up with a fish. Hey this'll do for dinner don't you think?" I suggest as Alex swims up waving a nice Sole on his spear. Back aboard their sleek vessel, the western horizon is alight with the warm glow of sunset. Our relatively wealthy friends pop open two bottles of fine red wine and we all sit happily savouring the rich liquid and the last of the day, while Mara sucks contentedly on her bottle of milk.

As the mouth watering aromas of roasting fish fill the cabin, Alex patiently minces up an entire knob of garlic for their signature rice dish, rich with olive oil and garlic. "Hey team *Longnose,* so where are you guys heading from here? You should come to Brazil with us, you'd love it!'

"Ahh, wouldn't we love to! Realistically though, we haven't got enough money to even dream about spending a year cruising South America. Also we're a little concerned about about the high levels of Malaria around the Amazon, especially with a baby aboard," pipes up Carolyn.

"Brazil sounds the coolest place on earth! The best music, liveliest people, exciting food....Yeah, we'll sail for Las Palmas on Gran Canaria Island, then head South to the Cape Verde Islands for our crossing to the Caribbean. We're homeward bound for OZ, hoping to find a decent way of making money." I add, torn to be missing such a special part of the world.

"Well I reckon you guys have the best life already. We've got to get back home and finish our studies. Our families have been very generous, helping us pay for this European trip, but I suppose we'll have to make our own way sooner or later," laughs Alex, opening another bottle of expensive Spanish red.

"We're sailing direct to Brazil from here," puts in Lucas, "so this is really a farewell party for us all. Here's to happy days, cheers."

Rowing back to our ship, the sky is so clear, a blanket of stars covers us tight. Bellies rich with fish and garlic rice, minds slightly intoxicated by fine wine and life, Mara instantly asleep in Carolyn's arms. "It's one of the drawbacks of the cruising life. One meets such nice people, then promptly must bid them farewell, often forever!" I say, laying into the oars.

"Yes that's true, but the beautiful thing is, there are always more special people to meet at the next anchorage," replies Carolyn, always so positive.

Las Palmas, home of the famous ARC rally, affords us free shelter in the outer harbour, the water a murky green with occasional rainbow oil slicks, the city bristling with activity. Having employed the services of a refrigeration mechanic to re-gas our fridge we sail off on the first fair wind. The Cape Verde Islands, 900 miles on, will hopefully give Mara a pleasant taste of ocean crossings.

After several serene days of smooth seas, late in the afternoon the breeze begins to build, a huge long swell starts to run, boding more wind to come. By nightfall the deep blue sea has turned an eerie green, a strong wind has us deeply reefed with a small head-sail poled out to balance our course for the reliable windvane self steering. During the night with a gale of wind hurling us south, up and down the hills and valleys of an uneasy ocean, great schools of flying fish whiz about our ship. When we venture on deck their slippery bodies slap into us painfully, the boat reeking of their strong fishy odour.

By morning the decks are strewn with the unlucky ones, trapped by Mara's lifeline netting. Great seas and fatigue have me feeling a little green under the burden of my responsibilities, while Mara, crawling out of her bunk after a comfortable night's sleep, greets me cheerfully. Unlike me she is innocent to any danger, full of zest and joy for life. Mara loves seafood so I begin frying up a batch of flying fish, her eyes wide with wonder and thrilled by all the action going on. Freshly caught, these fish are one of the tastiest of all, their succulent flavour and crisp skin goes down easily, grounding my queasy stomach, setting us all up for the day ahead.

Bleak morning light struggles its way through a thick overcast sky, revealing our landfall, the most northern Cape Verde island of Il de Sal. As we approach, the distant harbour looks very uninviting, awash with surf, yachts anchored inside rolling madly. The guide had promised clear water and excellent protection, so this wild murky green sea is quite a let down. Sadly we put off the luxury of anchorage and going ashore, sailing on before this fierce wind. Late that night *Longnose* gratefully gains the sheltered lee of Sao Nicola, and we anchor off Porto Tarrafal feeling distinctly worn out.

Our open roadstead anchorage is surprisingly calm, the water delightfully clear, with the main beach a concoction of red, black and yellow sands. Landing the dingy we set off to explore the town. With her pram clattering unevenly over the cobblestone roads, Mara soon attracts a large following of Afro-Portuguese ladies and children. They jostle each other, eager to goggle at this white haired baby, being whisked about the streets by a tall, wild looking man.

Soon we're hemmed in by a tight ring of bright smiling faces, white teeth standing out from their dark skin, luxurious frizzy hair, the true smell of humanity unmasked by deodorant, all eager to impress by making baby noises. Even Mara who seems to lust after social gatherings finds this all too much and bursts into fearful tears with all these strange faces peering at her. Naturally they are all very concerned and sensitive, quickly backing away to give us space, laughing happily.

We take a winding scenic bus ride over the mountainous island, descending a valley to the colourful town of Riberia Brava which nestles about the river bed. Exploring the narrow cobblestone streets we find a distinctly local shop, with wooden boxes stacked full of local produce. Always loving to try the local food we purchase a bag of sweet coconut cakes rich with brown sugar.

"Ohh, Carolyn, I'm feeling a bit sick. I can't help being adventurous with local food. Must have been those cakes," I moan as we ride the ancient bus back.

"Yes, you do look a bit sweaty and pallid," she replies. "Mara's looking a bit similar and she's been very quiet."

We stay on in Porto Tarrafal, recovering from the flu, protected from the prevailing trade winds by the arid red earth mountains that back this busy fishing village. Each day I drag myself out to the nearby point and hunt for fresh fish, hoping to blow away this local bug. On the weekend dozens of the local kids swim out to visit us on rafts made up of plastic bottles lashed together with scraps of old rope. Mara joins them in her yellow swimming hoop, splashing about happily amongst these joyous third world kids.

Strong, adverse currents make our trip to the capital, Grand Harbour on Mindelo very trying. Battling to stem the tide all day we struggle into port, close after midnight, feeling frazzled to finally anchor amongst the huge fleet of cruising yachts, all preparing for the big Atlantic crossing.

Daylight reveals a dusty African style port, the waterfront lined with dilapidated Portuguese buildings and grand old palms, harking back to its colonial days. Landing ashore, a handsome African fellow greets us in an easy friendly manner. "Hey mon, we friends will look after your dinghy. You just give me whatever you think is fair." It seems a decent offer and there doesn't seem to be a choice anyway.

The waterfront road bustles with colourfully dressed locals, the fish market a great show for Mara, with a bizarre array of sea creatures laid out on tables and in buckets on the streets. We come away with a kilo of cheap fresh caught, big-eyed sardines, which all the local people are buying in great quantities.

Back aboard we fry them for lunch, eating the crispy fish with fresh lemon juice and salt, accompanied by a tasty garden salad of local produce. Later that day our dinghy minder is very helpful and together we wander the dusty streets for hours hunting up a Morse cable for the gearbox, which luckily had broken, just as we anchored. To our amazement we find one in some unlikely shop lost in the back-blocks of this sprawling town.

Preparing to depart we head over to dock up at the commercial ship's wharf in order take on our meagre 40 litres of duty free diesel. A strong blustery wind threatens to make mooring very difficult. Approaching the high wharf, much more suited to ships than yachts, we feel quite nervous. Mara, clipped on to the mast, starts bellowing for our attention, which she often does during tense moments. Of course it is now very hard for us to concentrate on this difficult task, but like a ships bell, Mara's cries bring African wharfies running by the score. Gruff characters coolly take our lines, their weather-beaten faces cracking bright smiles for Mara, who is now wearing her most angelic baby face.

A friendly German couple persuade us to visit them on the nearby island of Santo Antaao, where they claim to be building their dream house in paradise. Unfortunately when we arrive their beach is awash with surf crashing onto boulders. Not daring to land us all in the dinghy, Carolyn puts Mara in her inflatable ring to swim through the surf. Before I can question the wisdom of this feat they are emerging from foaming white water, happily ashore. Landing the dinghy is no mean feat either and just as I tow it desperately over the slippery rocks a great wave pounds the beach at my heels, washing me high up the beach, dinghy and all.

The grey rocky foundations to this house in paradise do not overly impress us, yet the attraction of the simple village does. "You have a wonderful spot here!" I say to them, even though they're rather superior about the whole business. Not feeling at all envious, we are glad to leave the roly anchorage and get cracking across the Atlantic.

To cross any ocean is a big task and soon after our departure the breeze falters, wafting in with just fickle zephyrs. Only a disappointing 80 miles is chalked up on our first day out. The 2160 miles to the Caribbean island of Grenada seems an eternity away, with Mara simply itching for action and demanding entertainment. This does not promise to be the our usual languid ocean crossing, lounging around reading books and eating fine meals. No, it bodes to be an altogether new challenge.

CHAPTER 5

INTO THE 21ST CENTURY

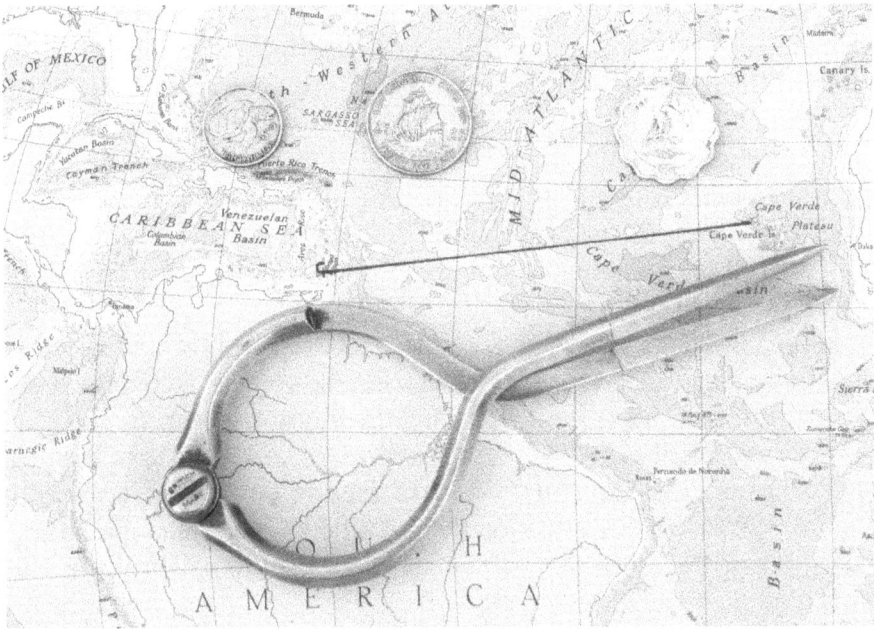

Longnose surges and rolls along, driven by the unusually fickle trade winds. Weeks of endless ocean stretches out before us. Lying back on the settee I grab a moment of rest, then Mara crawls out from the quarter berth, enthusiastically brandishing her only book, *Koalas, Kites and Kangaroos*. Groaning inwardly, I take her battered book and begin reading it to her. It's only the tenth time we've read it to her today, and while she seems enthralled with every page, I'm fit to scream if I have drag through it once more!

"Well, she's far from spoilt with toys!" says Carolyn, as Mara clambers past me and begins to entertain herself with the navigational dividers. "She does love Kerry Mousey, but she seems equally at home with a rusty spanner or a screwdriver. Of course she spends hours playing with the shell collection, I suppose because it's so handy for her along the back of the bunk," continues Carolyn, busily kneading some bread dough.

Welcoming sleep begins to drift over my consciousness, mmm, nice. Suddenly I'm dragged back into the present, as Mara crawls over me, tugging at my shirt to show she wants me to play with her. She lowers herself onto the floor and I follow, obeying my new master. "There's to be no relaxing on this voyage," I murmur, challenging my hazy mind in the undefined world of babies games.

"Let's get that spinnaker up Carolyn! We've got to sail as fast as we can to get this crossing over as soon as possible. I mean, Mara seems fine with all this sailing, but since we can't really relax, we may as well charge along at full speed," I say, hauling the large bag out of the forepeak.

So sparse is our contact with the outside world on this voyage, that for nightly entertainment we tune into Herb's Net, broadcast from the US. It is a long and rather tedious weather forecasting service with Herb giving great amounts of specific advise to anyone who calls in. Listening in to other's reports does paint a general picture of the weather situation in the Atlantic, yet I also brave the rather bossy fellow to test out our HF and of course to ensure our stretch of ocean remains docile.

An unusual hurricane is active in the Caribbean and Herb has everyone terrified that it will swoop out into the Atlantic and cause havoc amongst the huge fleet of passage-making yachts. One evening Herb is being particularly dramatic about the possible movements of this hurricane, which prompts a frightened sailor to log in. This wealthy Austrian lies becalmed 100 miles east of the British Virgin Islands, with engine trouble. He becomes so scared by Herb's various predictions that he requests to immediately be air lifted by the coast guard. We can hardly believe it is happening, as Herb dutifully arranges for the airlift. Ironically the hurricane never comes near this patch of ocean.

With a fine file I fashion a fishing hook to razor sharpness. Next I cut up some white fabric to make a squid skirt. Mara, who loves the tackle box has pounced on the freshly sharpened hook, fingering the needle like point, surprisingly without harm. Suddenly there's a rattle of bells outside.

"It's the fish alarm!" calls Carolyn as I rush out to start hauling in the line. Hand over hand a spectacular Dorado is hauled in, its great golden body whizzing into the cockpit, revealing the amazing green and blue hues of these remarkable fish.

Sadly the magnificent colours of the Dorado fade to a deathly grey as it expires. Mara loves the entire spectacle, pawing all over me during the gory job of cutting up such a big fish. She is strong and firm just like a cat, only content to smell the aroma of fish steaks sizzling in oil, as she hurries along each step of the fish's progress, then scrambles to get at it before it can cool off.

"That's our best day's run so far, 180 miles. It's certainly not your usual trade wind sailing, having to work so hard with such variable winds." I reflect, while Mara climbs all over the chart table, mimicking my work with the dividers and pushing any button within reach."

"It's a long time for an active baby to be at sea," says Carolyn, frying up some floured Dorado pieces. "In the night she loves best of all to crawl onto the top of the dodger and look out at the sea. With her harness on and me holding her of course."

On our final day, 15 days out, our senses have been heightened after such a long time at sea. We are bursting to reach our destination, yet at the same time sad it will all come to an end. With our white, purple and black spinnaker flying nicely, Mara sits in her green babies bath on the foredeck, enjoying the fruits of our water-maker. Barbados is 20 miles north, the joys and toils of land will be on us within a day.

"It would be nice to have a more spacious boat so life is not so cramped! A decent galley and saloon table and and a nice big chart table. Also it would be great to have space for a proper workshop. Hopefully this new catamaran I'm designing will have all of this and be fast also!" I rehash my mantra to Carolyn while grabbing some time to work on the drawings and plans of a new boat which has begun to obsess my every spare moment. This is the direction I feel drawn towards, to build a special boat, on which to continue enjoying this wonderful life on the sea.

"Yes dear, whatever you think," replies Carolyn absent-mindedly, as a new boat is far from her thoughts at the moment. What with the demands of being a mother and our meagre financial situation, I can well understand her reluctance to get excited about my dream.

Our landfall is St Georges Grenada, the commodious, heart shaped harbour said by many to be the most beautiful in the Caribbean. For me it's a return to the island of my boyhood, where we lived for 3 years during our cruise out to Australia on my family's 35' steel sloop *Yanda*. I feel a certain satisfaction to be returning, master of my own ship.

The stone walled waterfront Carenage is the historic business centre, lined with impressive red tiled colonial buildings. Last time I was here it was busy with wooden sail powered banana boats, yet now the tourist trade is king, the banana boats replaced by cruise ships. We anchor on the lagoon side of the harbour with the other cruising yachts, where we used to leave *Yanda* while we rented a house a short walk away.

It feels strange to be back in our first English-speaking destination since Kenya, where we laid anchor two years ago. Wandering about the familiar old streets, it's odd to be suddenly comprehending the baby-related advice. "Put she head straight!" insists one island mama and even though we swelter in tropical heat, the slightest shower brings comments like "She catch she death" and when the rain stops "Dat white baby out in de burnin sun". In the market place "Buy green coconut for she bottle, good for baby." Well meant to be sure, nevertheless we are wistful of our blissful innocence of Spanish and Portuguese, where we could just smile assuming the comments to be about our baby's charms.

Many things have changed about the place, the old cricket field where we used to fly kites is now a built up stadium but the house we rented when my dad practised dentistry in town looks much the same. "Carolyn, that looks just like the old wooden house of my West Indian friends, and that lady, she looks just like the mother, Mrs La Mothe." Lo and behold it is her, as though time has never passed.

She is equally amazed to see me after 27 years. Unfortunately all the children have moved out. My best friend Andy has moved to Sweden, his brother Albert has become a wayward scallywag and their sister, Angela lives on the other side of the island. Before I know it Mrs La Mothe has me renovating her kitchen, which is a worrying business, as she has nails poking out all over the floor, yet Mara seems to negotiate them happily enough. "Dat gal, she happy every-place. Now see dis cubard, tink you can fix dis, praise de lord if you can. You ain't changed much all dese years Mr Andrew, still handy wid a hamma. Just now, I'll fix you some real West Indian bates, wid honey." Her speech enthrals us and seems fair payment for helping her.

One day I return to the boat and find Carolyn distraught. "He came by in a borrowed boat selling stolen green mangoes, wanted $5 for 3 so small they would never ripen. Because I wouldn't buy any he was so rude to me, hexed me something terrible, now my mind's all confused!"

"Carolyn, it's OK, they don't really voodoo people here in the Caribbean. You're just annoyed." She aims a wild looking glare my way, while Mara chews calmly on a piece of coconut. "I'm going ashore to get something for dinner," hoping she will settle in my absence.

Striding along I breath in the wonder of this amazing tropical rainforest island. Shaded by coconut palms, vast tamarind and breadfruit trees, the road is scattered with cotton wings from the devils tree and the magical red and black Jumbee seeds. "Hexed by an innocent mango seller, voodoo nonsense," I laugh to myself, enjoying the warm scent of wild blossoms in the air.

Returning to the small wooden dinghy dock a lanky, languid local confronts me. "W'ap'nin? Here, look mister rich man, dis a special rabbit's tail to protect you from evil spirit. I sell it to you for 10 dalla," he chants dangling a scrappy bit of tail from a string.

"Look, I'm very sorry, but I can't afford to buy your charm." I manage as politely as possible.

"Study your head mon! It's ok for you Whitey, you've got chicken for yo dinner, but what about my family?" he challenges me fiercely, eerily knowing it's chicken in my bag.

Feeling unfairly treated, as we so rarely buy any meat, and could certainly not afford any magic charms, I return to the boat feeling drained. That night after our special chicken dinner a strong flu strikes me down for a whole week. Carolyn's sure evil Voodoo is the cause. In fact I should just have paid him for his magic charm but our finances are so strained.

Luckily I can't be sick for too long with Mara demanding action. Keeping our baby entertained really boots us out of any previous cruising laziness. Shrugging off my voodoo flu, we cruise north through the Grenadines as far as the pristine Tobago Cays, crowded with hundreds of yachts. Racing along in cruising overdrive, we up anchor early, sail like crazy to reach anchorage in time to whisk our baby girl ashore for swimming and exploring.

On the tiny deserted sand island of Carib, off the north-east coast of Carriacou, Mara experiences her first Christmas. Her only present a toothbrush, yet the clean blue Caribbean Sea and island covered in coconut and beach almond trees is her true gift.

Planning to see in the new millennium anchored peacefully off our island paradise, I tune into the local radio for some Rastafari tunes. The melodious tinkling rhythms of a steel band uplift the sun setting on the last day of the 20th century as we sip a spiced rum cocktail from a freshly picked green coconut. "Dread mon! You tunin to Fresh FM 102.7. Praise Jah, tonight on di Carenage in St Georges, dere be fireworks and dancin'. Com on down bredren and sistren, feel irie in town tonight, tanks." Bob Marley, *Exodus* strikes up and we look at each other, clogs ticking. Moments later the anchor is hauling up and *Longnose* rushes off before a fresh trade wind, bound for the capital, 40 miles away.

Off St Georges two huge, anchored cruise ships light up the dark sea as we slip by creaming along in the island's lee. After negotiating a suspicious police boat we anchor in the lagoon. Together with some friends off the *Lady of Spain* we swan around to the Carenage, happy to be in town to celebrate this momentous night. Carolyn and Mara share a soursop and golden apple smoothie, while I crack a Red Stripe Jamaican lager. The girls so love their smoothie they are off to order another. Before we know it the amphitheatre like surrounding hills of St Georges is reverberating with the boom of fireworks.

"This is it, we've entered the 21st century, the "Age of Aquarius" is upon us," I call out, high on life and Red Stripes. "Let's make this new millennium happen, maybe this can be the age of sail! Only problem is me hearties, first up we'll have to brave the Spanish main, notorious for drug runners and pirates!"

CHAPTER 6.

PANAMA BOUND

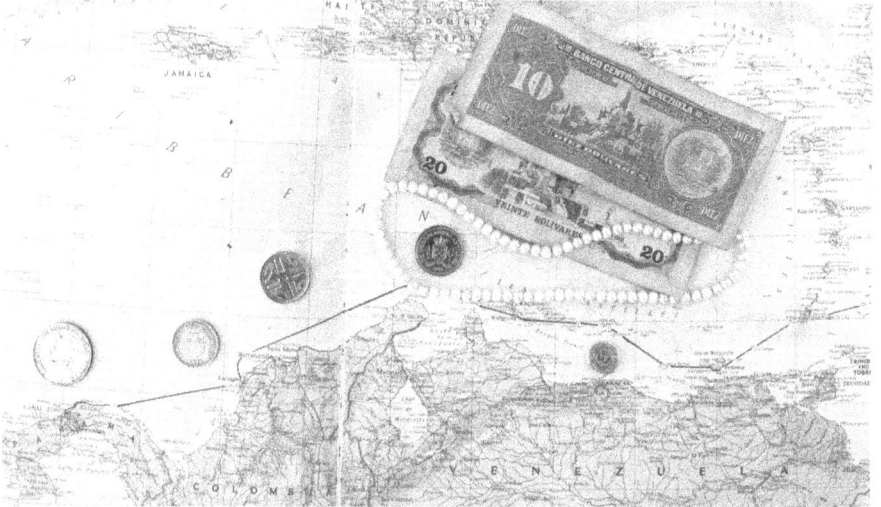

"Venezuela! Guys, why would you want to head that way? There are so many reports of robbery and corruption coming from down there. It's very dangerous, and you have to muck around organising a visa from the consulate here, before you go, which is daylight robbery at $80US," warns a conservative yachtie. We keep on asking around, yet this seems the mainstream attitude towards our next destination. Then we meet a chap who's just been there.

"Yeah, yeah, I know that old story. Complete nonsense and ignorance. I mean the place is safer than the Caribbean. Have you listened in to those HF skeds and noted the number of muggings and robberies reported each morning around the Carib? Venezuela is a beautiful place and very affordable. As for the visa bit, they issue them on clearing in, it's way cheaper. Go there guys, you'll love it!" Armed with this kind of real knowledge and enthusiasm, we have our heading.

Departing at the crack of dawn we make Los Testigos Grande, 90 miles on by late afternoon. Sinister black frigate birds wheel over our wild anchorage, while some local fishermen swing by and toss us 3 nice lobsters in exchange for a fan belt. "You know, it won't be easy to replace that fan belt," I comment a little ungenerously, while we feast on morsels of lobster, dipped in aioli sauce, rich in garlic, olive oil and fresh egg yoke.

The sea continues to demonstrate its abundance as we lure a huge dogtooth tuna before our arrival at Porlamar the clearance port on Margarita Island. "Hey the bay is so full of cruising yachts, I very much doubt the local authorities will notice us. We'll save $150US if we take this little risk of not clearing in!"

From our anchorage the town looks touristy and modern, fronted by high-rise buildings, yet landing on the sandy foreshore, lined with palm trees, quaint wooden houses of a quieter era nestle about the modern concrete foundations. Brightly painted with lush gardens, these houses reflect the true character of the place.

"Yes Hola, a mango and custard apple jugo please then a papaya and guava one, both sin azucar please." Carolyn hands over some fresh Bolivar notes to the beaming young street vendor, a beautiful dark skinned girl who sets to work with her blender. Soon we are replenishing ourselves from the still, tropical heat with these iced juices, Mara greedily gulping down more than her fair share. "We'll try some of those corn cakes too."

Feeling wholesomely refreshed we press on to the town centre. "Best news of all, look! Bottles of rum for $1US," I call to Carolyn, waving a bottle of the golden liquid, carrying a clinking bag, feeling a bit too much like Captain Haddock. She's got Mara in her arms, immersed in a street vendor's wares. Hooking up my swag to the pram I join them, marvelling at the glorious strings of pearls laid out on the wooden table. Pure white pearls, rich rose hues, deep glossy black pearls all full of real character. "What, only $2US a necklace! Let's buy lots!"

With our wake stretching away from the fascinating town of Margarita, we wish we'd bought more pearls and more rum! "In days of old people sailed around the world in search of wealth. They wanted to trade, steal or exploit, driven by greed for money." I philosophise to Carolyn as Mara happily cuts her teeth on a salty sheet rope. "The first recreational sailors voyaged the world to prove it could be done. Now this odyssey of ours is about discovering ourselves through these travels. All we seem to have found so far is Mara?"

Our lack of clearance sees us a bit nervous as we cruise on to the pristine Ilas Los Roques, a vast coral atoll 70 miles off the mainland coast, yet at the same time this fear makes us feel more alive. While wandering the wild beaches of Los Roques we find a poor doll washed up with the drift wood, her legs gone, "probably eaten by sharks". Carolyn and Mara rescue her for she has beautiful eyes and carry her aboard to her new life. Carolyn makes her a mermaid's tail out of an old thong, sews on a new skin and gives her a tiny shell necklace.

In Curacao, an island of the Dutch Antilles, Mara celebrates her Ist birthday. "Mermaid", who came to us from the sea, is her present. Such is the simplicity and economy of life afloat. To this day we still have "Mermaid."

With a fresh trade driving *Longnose* at a cracking pace we set off for Cartegena, the major port of Columbia. "Back in 1973, when we did this passage on Yanda, we got hit by a gale, so we'd better be well prepared." I warn Carolyn. Near the northern tip of South America, where the Andes meets the sea, the trades once again accelerate well over 30 knots. Snugly reefed down we race along, making the approaches to this famous city by dusk on the second day.

Several hours later we pass the entrance between Bomba and Draga island. From here it's a long way to the anchorage, gliding along in the protected waters, peering into the moonless night for dangers. The powerful, dark history of Cartegena sets my imagination running. Slave traders, pirates, cocaine smugglers, all lurk in the very fabric of this place and we feel nervous and suspicious of every vessel that plys these waters so late into the night. Fear and coffee keep us awake. It's 3am when we finally drop anchor in the safety of the cruising fleet and can give in to sleep.

It feels like we've just gone to bed when Mara awakes us at first light, full of beans after her long sleep. Trooping into the fresh morning air, we can see the ancient walled town in the distance, once the stage of mighty battles in its sordid history. Now the approaches are overgrown with a modern concrete sprawl. We set to work making things shipshape and then enjoy a relaxing breakfast of tropical fruits. Eager to explore, we lock up carefully and put ashore.

Clearance is cheaper here and we dare not continue our voyage without some official paperwork. As usual it takes the better part of the steamy morning trudging about the various offices in order to clear customs.

Midday sees us arrive at the main entrance to the old walled city. Clustered about the grey stonework are dozens of street vendors offering Columbian specialities. Hot and hungry we buy coladas, cool, thick, sweet drinks made from oats and fresh potato empanadas. Finding a place in the shade we enjoy our food and begin to feel our energy ebbing back.

"Hey, check out these amazing bottles of sweets! That's dark guava jelly and those are solid condensed milk babies. Lets buy some and head for the old fort," I say reaching for my peso's.

"Mmmm, these are delicious coconut sweets," I declare, as we march up the great stone steps to gain the bastion of the 17th century fortress. "I just hope they don't make us sick also!" Upon the weather-beaten stone ramparts there's a curious feeling with not a soul about. Stowing the bag of candy delights in Mara's pram, I look about cautiously. A huge Columbian flag cracks lustily in the strong afternoon breeze while the Caribbean Sea looks wild and windblown far below us. One can almost see Francis Drake's ships running in to sack the city. Vividly I recall an impressionable eight year old, dashing about this same fortress, wide eyed at this amazing world unfolding before my eyes.

We carry Mara down a creepy passage, enjoying the cool still air. It leads downwards and darkens as we go. Picking our way along the sound deadened passages, my feeling of nervousness grows. "We could head back out now if you like?" I suggest, reluctant to be the one to chicken out.

"Oh, but it's so lovely and cool down here, so exciting!" Carolyn says, pushing deeper into this underground maze.

Perhaps it's my nature to feel a place too deeply, sensing the effort to stay alive and defeat the enemy, the great stones of this fierce strategic fortress fairly reeking of history. Images of canons, swords and armour flit through my mind as we wander about this great stone creation, a monument to the lust for gold in South America.

Dim light somehow filters down into these deep tunnels, so it is not completely black. The steps begin to lead upwards and in the eerie quiet we hear footsteps ahead of us. Alarm is upon me at the thought of who may inhabit such a place. Columbia has a poor reputation in the guidebooks, my every fibre is on edge.

The passage gathers brightness as we come upon a timid pair of German tourists, poking carefully down the steps. I smile quizzically at them as we pass, laughing at my own fears. Back out in the dazzling sunshine a number of tourists now swan about the ramparts forcing me back to reality.

Miles and miles of walking and exploring sees us arrive back aboard in the darkness. Mara is whimpering in hunger and tiredness. Mixing a couple of rums we all hoe into the spicy beans Carolyn had prepared that morning, the fresh chilli more powerful than expected. More rum is needed to cool our mouths, while Mara is too tired to cry out at her burning mouth and falls asleep instantly.

Having spent a week enjoying Cartagena the novelty of city life begins to wear thin and the lure of coral cays beckons. Running again before the fresh Caribbean trades we race westwards and in just over 24 hrs *Longnose* lies suspended in the crystal clear waters of Holandes Cay in the San Blas Islands.

With a day's rest under our belts, some Kuna Indians paddle out in their wooden canoes, loaded with piles of intricately sewn Molas they want us to buy at inflated prices. We smile and try to buy something affordable and small to please them, then Mara crawls out and their faces light up. These weather beaten, natural people insist we come ashore, presenting Mara with a beautiful Mola dress of intricate appliqué.

Waves lap gently on their white sandy beach, while coconut trees sway in the persistent trade wind. They sit us at an old rickety table, the pleasant acrid aroma of smoke drifting about from cooking fires, their traditional life uncluttered by modern paraphernalia. Two giggling, beautiful young Kuna girls bring us plates of food. Iguana stew on rice, an alarming looking lunch! Their beaming smiles, give us no choice but to eat up. It is a peculiar thing to find a section of lizard, looking so familiar, garnishing one's rice. It proves quite mild in taste, bland even, yet a meal to remember.

We're in heaven exploring the coral reefs, living well on lobster and fish. Each day we work on fine sanding our ships bottom in the hope she will slip easily through our next hurdle, the Panama Canal. Eventually though, we have to hoist our well-worn, patched sails, grateful they can drive us on to yet another exotic destination. "Look at Mara's determination to try and walk! The boat rolling about so much makes it testing for her, but she's getting close," says Carolyn as we cream past the thickly wooded coast of Panama. By early afternoon we are anchored in historic Portobello having averaged a swift 8.9 knots.

Dashing ashore we visit Portobello's strange tourist attraction. Washed ashore in the 17th century, the life sized statue of "Black Jesus" is held in high esteem by the people of Panama. That night after our most popular meal of fried fish and chips with salad, we lounge in the cockpit, sipping rum cocktails. A live band strikes up ashore, soothing us with haunting, beautiful melody's. Mara, sated by her day of action falls asleep, leaving us deeply contented under a vivid stadium of stars. Cool night air washes away the days heat, the wholesome smell of jungle mixes with the aromas of town cooking as we savour this special night, our last in the blue Caribbean.

Peaking from the afternoon heat the accelerated trades whistle about *Longnose's* rigging as we enter the port of Colon. Bearing down rapidly on the crowded anchorage, we drop our head sail then round up into the wind and pull down our mainsail. Carolyn sets up the anchor and we pick our spot amid the fleet of yachts. "Ok, anchor away," I call and *Longnose* begins to pull back on her tackle.

Tackling the Panama Canal promises to be a big challenge. I rummage through my special books and secret hiding places, pulling out the last few stashes of cash, hoping we'll have enough. Five hundred US dollars for the canal transit plus an eight hundred dollar bond, then clearance fees as well. "It was much more fun passing the canal when I was a little boy, free of all these concerns," I whimper. With our bank balance now also cleaned out it's vital that we transit the canal without issues to recover the bond and allow us funds to cross the Pacific.

"Cruising boats with children aboard are always on the look out for playmates," suggests Carolyn as we nervously wait in the road-stead for the day of our transit. It seems a wishful remark yet a short while later a curious visit occurs. The sunset has burnt away in the hazy air that hangs over Colon, when a zodiac approaches. A mad looking fellow zips alongside confidently handling his outboard.

"G'day, Stingray, it's your old mate Shakedown. Hey, remember all that spear fishing we did together in the Red Sea, good to see you mate," he begins. I grope fruitlessly in my mind for any possible memory of this chap, inviting him aboard regardless. He looks almost Egyptian with wild black hair, which on closer examination appears to be a wig!

"You're having me on Shakedown! We've never met before!" I eventually confront him, yet he patters on in a disarming fashion admitting nothing. Carolyn is very impressed by his mad humour, reminiscent of Steve Irwin in his enthusiasm.

"Hey, you know how all the yachties listen in to yer private conversations on VHF?" he asks. I nod, for we too will sometimes follow people to their chosen station to see what's going on.

"I dare you Stingray, ring up my missus on *Amaroo*, and complain that her mad husband is aboard drunk and you can't get rid of him!" By this time even Mara is amused by the twinkling devilry in his eyes.

"Go on Andrew," urges Carolyn. So pouring some tumblers of rum to give me courage, I hit transmit.

"*Amaroo, Amaroo*, this is *Longnose*, do you receive me?" I call on the contact station 16. After a few moments comes the answer.

"This is *Amaroo*, Jerry speaking."

"Hey Jerry, I don't mean to bother you, but... your husband is on our boat, and......Well he's kinda getting out of hand, he's had quite a lot to drink you know. Hey we'd better go to 72." At this point the entire anchorage would have leaped up and changed to 72 and there are at least 40 boats swinging in wait.

"Yeah I'm sorry, just send him home, he's harmless really." Jerry continues as though she's used to such calls, obviously pretty good at this game.

"But we've tried that, and we're trying to get our baby girl to bed. He's on the floor now," I manage, holding onto a chuckle at the thought of all the yachties listening in.

"Well I know what you mean, I've got our baby boy I'm trying to put to bed. Just toss Alan into the dingy, he'll find his own way home," she counters, as cool as you like.

The next day you can imagine the number of people who come up to us at the Colon Yacht Club. "Did you manage to get that fellow off your boat last night?" they question in a caring fashion. This fun is nice relief from our usual cares and worries of the canal transit and the upcoming Pacific crossing.

Mara takes her first strides on the stable earth of the Colon Yacht Club, yet her presence is about to make us famous in a less than desirable way. Only a couple of boats get to transit the canal each day, so I must continually plunge into the murky waters to ensure the bottom stays clean. On our 12th day of waiting we finally get the word it's our turn to transit the next day. For the two-day trip through the canal, we have to arrange four line handlers, extra food and dozens of extra fenders, a rough set of car tyres that circulate amongst the yachties.

The big day dawns and our pilot arrives on a launch, a sour looking negro fellow who is not at all amused by my attempts to be jolly. Carolyn emerges from below carrying Mara on her hip. "Ahhhh! one, too, tree... seems yo is one line handler short, as dis woman will be looking after dat baby! You need anoder line handler or you can't go!" he states gruffly.

Motoring desperately about the fleet looking for an extra hand we luckily find a volunteer and wait while they get ready. Unfortunately they cant find their passport and our time runs out, so we have to cancel our transit for the day. This attracts great sympathy from all the other yachties. "What was wrong with the fellow. We've heard of lots of other boats going through with the mother being a line handler as well!"

The next day we set off again, figuring the worst should be behind us. The first lock is going nicely as we moor up securely behind the super tanker *Cosmic Venture*. We have eight aboard now including the four dedicated line handlers and the pilot, so everything seems under control. That is until the *Cosmic Venture* engages their propeller to motor out of the lock.

Directly behind the giant propeller, like moths in a spider's web, with our network of ropes lashing us in place, the thrust comes like a low wall of surf, awesome in its churning power. *Longnose* reels over violently and we are thrown about. It's like being in a washing machine. Our stern line stretches hugely and begins to actually smoke in the cleat.

"Quick, let's try to ease that line a bit," I cry, rushing over to help my line handler control the danger. On our starboard side we have to rely on the lines of another Australian yacht *White Rose,* who we are rafted together with. If a rope explodes we'll be smashed on the steel lock walls. Fortunately luck is on our side. After this scare, the pilot pleads with the ship's captain to take it easy in the next lock.

On day 2 we are all admiring the amazing work done to cut this passage through the mountains when out of the blue our trusty old Volvo Penta slows down, coughs and stops. With a deadline to keep and our bond on the line, I'm distressed by our helpless drifting. No one knows quite what to do and our hearts are sinking fast. Luckily Poseidon is looking after us, and within minutes we sight a big powerful yacht, motoring through at great speed, which we wave to frantically.

"Oh please, our engine has stopped. Please can you tow us through," I plead to the skipper and before long we are rafted besides our buddy, *Ultimate,* feeling very relieved. Actually our trusty engine only needs a few more cups of oil to recover so things look up. Carolyn has everything under control and as we pass through the final locks, serves up fresh baked pizza with salad and cans of icy Balboa beer. Even the crew of the fancy *Ultimate* cast jealous glances at our fare as they sup on packets of crisps. Rarely have I felt so relieved than when we farewell our crew and head for the anchorage under our own steam.

"Hey look it's *Amaroo*," calls Carolyn from the bow, ready with the anchor and keeping her usual sharp lookout. Joining them for sundowners, Mara can happily relate to her new-found friend Rowen a fellow sailor of her own age.

Glasses are raised to the mighty Pacific Ocean, "Here's to having the Panama Canal behind us and successful crossings of the Pacific for us all," I blurt out, enjoying Shakedown's rum and coke, feeling remarkably happy.

Shakedown is quite keen for me to "Drop the sump," on our engine to check that the bottom end is OK. This sounds way to difficult, with babies to cope with, so I settle for changing the oil. After a day's rest we set off for the Las Perlas Islands in company with *Amaroo*. The world's biggest ocean lies before us, 7750 miles to Australia. In one way this seems an eternity of distance, yet at the same time I'm painfully aware that the clock is running down, and I must decide a path for my future before this journey's end.

CHAPTER 7.

ACROSS THE PACIFIC

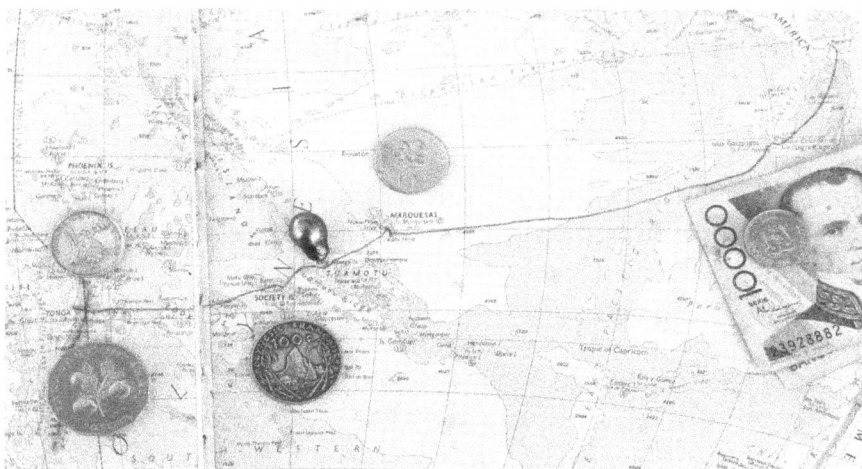

Fickle winds and flotsam greet us on route to the enchanted Galapagos Islands. "Look at *Longnose* creaming along in this light wind," I exclaim easing the sheet which controls the lofty, powerful mainsail. "It's so nice having a performance boat, otherwise we'd have the "iron topsail" rattling away now, spoiling this gloriously peaceful day. A lot of yachts in Panama were taking on 500 litres of fuel and planning on refuelling in the Galapagos!"

"Motoring isn't half as much fun," says Carolyn, dragging the spinnaker bag up to the bow. "We do have to work pretty hard adjusting our sails though. It's good healthy work, especially on a smooth dreamy sea like this." She heads back inside for the spinnaker sheets, while keeping an eye on Mara, busily pulling all the fishing lures out of my tackle box. Life afloat seems almost to good to be true.

The northbound Humboldt current brings cool water up from the Southern Ocean which swirls into the Gulf of Panama. Prolific amounts of flotsam are borne along by this life giving force. We sight many turtles, large trees and vegetation amongst the debris. Fish like to hide under this kind of flotsam so our fishing lure strikes and soon fried mackerel is on the menu.

Six days out, the sea lulling us into a blasé frame of mind, we treat ourselves to cocktails at sunset. The rum is just kicking in as we lounge on the cockpit bed, feeling very relaxed with Mara hoeing into crispy fish pieces. "Here we are, 600 miles out of Panama, it's so nice to be far away from civilisation." We busily toast our blissful situation, swigging fortifying mouthfuls of dark rum and orange juice.

Suddenly our ears prick up to the noise of an engine. Like startled seals we leap up and to our horror see a 20' wooden speedboat with a powerful mounted spot-light, charging straight towards us. "Oh my God! No! No, don't let these be pirates," I whimper as my blood begins to pump in anticipation.

They are upon us so quickly, turning close and fast under our stern. Two wild looking, long haired fellows with pigtails shouting at us in outlandish Spanish, while we stand amazed, instantly sober at this sudden turn of events. "Hey, hey tu dirigiéndose directamente a nuestras redes de pesca !" The taller fellow shouts at us. "Vas a tener que cambiar su curso! ¿Por qué estás tan estúpido?"

"Did he mention 'de pesca'?" I ask Carolyn, eyes wide in amazement. Having just learnt my lesson in Morocco with fishermen mistaken for pirates. The cogs of my mind begin to turn and I quickly try to reign in my panic. "Oh my God, I think they're fishermen from Ecuador!"

They continue to gesticulate, pointing to the north, rambling on in their lingo we can only comprehend snippets of. "Oh gosh, thank our lucky stars, they are fishermen! They seem to want us to head north to avoid their net," I point out, sweat chilling on my skin, infinitely happy to oblige these energetic men. Indeed this unique corner of the Pacific Ocean proves full of life, for as we sail north under the fishermen's orders, we briefly enjoy the company of a Minke whale, our momentary brother of the sea, also fleeing the net.

Still 20 miles out of the anchorage on Isla San Cristobel we sail gaily through two packs of large sea lions. They lie basking on the surface with their fins poking out in the sun, flopping back in a blissfully relaxed attitude, their mad whiskered faces stare at us in amazement. By afternoon we drop anchor in Wreck Bay, full of cruising yachts and seals.

A friendly local comes out to tell us there is a concert on if we wish to attend so we dress up, keen to go ashore. Golden sunset lights up our exotic location as I play with 14 month old Mara in the cockpit. Without warning a big sea lion bursts out of the water beside us, letting out a fearsome deep "HAAAARRRR", which gives us both a terrible fright and Mara bursts out in tears. "Andrew! Why did you scare her like that?" accuses Carolyn rushing out of the cabin to see what's going on.

"Me? It was a seal. Great scary beast!" I cry in my defence "Did you hear that? He just did it again to that boat over there. Listen to that lady squealing in fear. Quite a character that seal!"

Aboard *Yanda*, 27 years ago, on this very same voyage, which had so strongly shaped my destiny, we had been free to explore all the Galapagos islands. Now in the year 2000, we are restricted to only 3 anchorages, unless one is willing to pay vast amounts of money.

Nevertheless the sky is alive with such wonders as the blue-footed and red-footed boobies, Galapagos petrels, swallow-tailed gulls, lava gulls, wandering albatross, the magnificent red throated frigate-bird, in fact the Galapagos is remarkable in that it is yet to lose a bird specie to extinction. Mara and Carolyn still get to experience the thrill of swimming with seals and the unique, somewhat fearsome looking marine iguana, the black volcanic seashore alive with the bright red sally lightfoot crabs.

In the blazing equatorial heat we clamber over black lava flows to see the yellow cactus munching land iguana, the giant tortoise, Darwin's finches and the Galapagos hawk, blown away forever by the remarkable tameness of these creatures. There seems plenty of wildlife to see, even with the restrictions, which are helping to preserve this remarkable archipelago.

Our final anchorage, Port Villamil, is located on the south coast of Isla Isabela, one of the most volcanically active places in the world. For the outstandingly affordable price of $5US we are served breakfast, driven for an hour into the hills, set-up on horseback for a wild ride to the caldera of the Sierra Negra volcano. Occasionally puffs of sulphur laden air are emitted from the stark land, while a flock of pink flamingos, stand out remarkably on the grey crater floor. Carolyn is charged with carrying a delighted Mara on her horse but on the ride back the tired horses smell home and start to canter. My heart skips a beat as I see their horse begin to fall on some uneven ground, yet the animal skilfully falls to his knees then regains his balance and they ride on happily.

Having the responsibility of fatherhood upon my shoulders gives me an entirely new perspective on life, far removed from the gay, carefree time I spent here as a boy. Now our longest passage lies before us, 2900 miles of vast open ocean to the Marquesas Islands in French Polynesia.

*

As our track creeps out across the incredibly endless miles of deep blue ocean, days roll by, fluffy trade wind cumulus float dreamily overhead and birds fly back to land. The planet spins on, faultlessly, exposing us to the sun then shading us, gravity holding the whole show together. With barely any input from the outside world, one's mind ticks away, processing thoughts busily without distractions from the modern maze which normally bombards our brain.

Gently *Longnose* sways its way over an ocean so clear, the sun's rays strike into the sea, penetrating down forever, the freshest, clean smelling sea air feeds our lungs, the virtually unchanging view leaves the mind free to finish off thoughts.

Weeks out on the ocean is akin to a natural, enforced meditation. One's mind seems to almost run out of thoughts leaving it vast and free. Back in the 70s, sailing on *Yanda,* lolling along at a sedate 4/5 knots, I used to sit on deck gazing at the weird shapes the bow wash made as it went by, dragons, yachts, birds.

Now *Longnose* whizzes along too fast to make out these shapes so I spend endless hours examining how the bow slices through the sea and how the wake flows off the transom, dreaming of maybe building a new boat. My dad had to spend his hours pouring over the calculations of his sextant sights in order to determine our position, yet with the advent of the Global Positioning System, I am free to roam in my mind. I just hope to be making something worthwhile of my thoughts.

How this all works for a baby, who's mind is so eager for input is a paradox beyond me, yet she is happy, busy and content as the days slip away. She is beginning to string words together, "fishy jumping!" being one of her popular observations. From the cockpit comes the ringing bell of the fish alarm, so I dash out all excited, only to find Mara tugging away at the line, grinning mischievously. During the long nights, her catch-cry becomes "outside see moon!" dragging Carolyn out to admire the sky for hours on end. Imitating our daily radio skeds, Mara picks out a nice big cowrie shell, "Ahoy Skaffie," she pronounces clearly the chief operator's name, then listens into the opening, wide eyed, expecting him to answer back from the distant roar of the sea that magically emanates from inside seashells.

Reaching Fatu Hiva, most windward of the Marquesas Islands after 15 days 10 hours at sea, averaging 188 miles/day, we anchor in one of the most stunning bays in all the world. Towering monolithic rock formations stand about the head of the bay, draped in greenery, like giant sentinels guarding the lush valley beyond. Marvelling at the beauty we stand on deck watching the sun go down on this island paradise. Even though yachts commonly visit here we still receive a generous welcome as some locals paddle out, handsomely presenting us with paw-paw and pomelos.

Our senses heightened, the deep perfume of forest blossom assails our nostrils, along with the pungent aromas of cooking fires, fresh cut grass and damp earth. Carolyn slices up a pomelo, releasing tiny eruptions of citrus oil, revealing the rich red flesh. Slowly all three of us savour the sweet bursts of tropical flavour as the succulent juice sacks explode over our taste buds, while our greedy eyes marvel at this magic destination. Thick green forest dominates our vision, climbing undeterred up the steep mountains from a shinning black sand beach, an abundance of tall coconut palms reaching above the canopy, bask in the day's final rays of sun.

"Wow, this is surely heaven on earth!" says Carolyn, savouring the still anchorage and the immense satisfaction of completing a long voyage.

*

Clearing in to Hiva Oa, it's a great relief to find the $800 bond from our canal transit back in our account, a temporary reprieve for our finances. Now this money must last us back to Australia.

"Maybe we should just stay and live in the beautiful Pacific islands, like Gauguin did," suggests Carolyn, having just fulfilled a lifelong ambition to dance on Ganguin's grave. Mara feels the excitement of this artist's rite and in the stifling heat, strips off her clothes to dance with Carolyn.

I sit feeling moved in the shade of a frangipanni tree, breathing deeply the delicate perfume of the flowers. The lure of the Pacific is strong, but it seems the desire for one's homeland is stronger.

Back in 1973 when we arrived at Ahe' Lagoon in the Tuamotus, sailors were treated like Gods and thrown lavish feasts by the villagers. Now yachts are hardly given a second glance, even so the atoll remains as enchanting as ever, with still a certain magic in the fresh sea breeze that blows gently through the quiet village.

We meet a beautiful Polynesian woman with supple brown skin and glossy dark hair, playing on the beach with her little girl. She remembers the old feasts from her childhood and takes a fancy to Mara, pulling some fine black pearls from her pocket, giving them to her with the spontaneous generosity of these island people.

The world of sail has changed rapidly over the years. Fifty years ago barely a soul had visited these remote atolls, now they produce black pearls for the Japanese and have more income than us.

Huahine and Raiatea, jewels of the Society Islands, are some of the most beautiful islands on earth. Bountiful forested mountains rise out of this rich ocean, ringed by coral reefed lagoons to die for.

The simple lives of the island children make them wonderful playmates for Mara. They show great maturity for their age and I can think of no better place to bring up a baby. Cruising this heavenly part of the world with my family feels like a dream come true, yet I have this uneasy feeling my luck is running out. After this great effort to escape mainstream society, we seem to be sailing straight back into its clutches, drawn helplessly like moths to a flame.

73

*

"OK, so we've been around the world and had lots adventures," I say to my girls. "But what are we going to do when we get back to Australia?" The question looms as our homecoming begins to look uncomfortably close.

"Yes, I do worry Andrew, how we are going to earn money?" replies Carolyn in her sensible way, making me feel uneasy.

"Well, you know that I want us to build a 50' catamaran with more space to organise our lives in. We'll be able to do a few charters and make money," I reply defensively, realising it is a huge undertaking to consider. Yet every day I compulsively spend time at the chart table drawing up various plans, driven in this difficult direction. The obstacles ahead seem impossible, yet somehow I just keep plodding along this path.

"But how are we going to get the money to build such a big boat?" pursues Carolyn. It's the kind of obvious question I find vexing

"Well I don't know exactly, but I know we'll do it somehow," I answer lamely. Carolyn does not appear reassured of our future. "We've always managed before, so we'll be able to do it again," I reason, pathetically.

It's all very well to think that because we've managed to get through challenges which seemed so immense at the time, we will be able to leap the next hurdle. Of course one would like to think this is the case. Yet always the next challenge seems more difficult, like there is no way around it. If you start to think of all the hours required to build a 50' catamaran the thought almost swallows your brain, let alone affording the materials.

Just when I feel I have conquered the world and my own fears, I have put in my way a massive task. *"Why do we do these things to ourselves? Here I am in paradise on a beautiful yacht with a beautiful lady and a happy baby daughter. Why don't we just stay here?"* I ponder to myself

"The point is we need to work hard to satisfy our bodies, for good health and a reason to live. That is why we move on to our new challenges with as much courage as we can muster," I reason, the wild blue ocean surrounding me in its ultimate refreshing power.

Remembering *Zen and the Art of Motorcycle Maintenance* and its lesson that life is not just about focusing on reaching one's destination; it's about enjoying the adventures along the way, I focus on the moment. With the glorious golden rays of sunset lighting up Bora-Bora's lofty twin peaks we row over to visit our friends on *Amaroo*. Content in their cockpit, the children play happily while we catch up on each other's adventures.

"So I suppose you guys know what you're going to do when you get back to Australia," I ask, wondering if others are so obsessed with this question.

"Yeah, of course. Were going into business big time, Stingray," replies Alan in his gung-ho confident manner. "We're going to build sheds. I've been working on this new steel bending technique all these years."

"How does *'Shady Sheds'* sound for a business name?" jests Jerry with her down to earth sense of humour, a steady balance for Alan's mad enthusiasm. It seems their confidence alone will make them succeed.

"God, I wish I could be as confident as you two," I say to them honestly.

*

The steady south-east trade winds are being muddled up by a series of adverse fronts that sweep regularly across the Pacific. We sail to the Cook Islands and then on to Vavau in the Kingdom of Tonga, constantly tested by these changeable conditions. One minute we're sailing along happily in a light wind with full sail set, then a rain squall will blow in packing extra wind, which means we need to drop our headsail and reef the mainsail. As the squall passes, we're left rolling around in next to no wind and have to re-hoist the sails again. All day and night this pattern is repeated, making for tiring sailing.

Now that we're closer to home our family can once again easily afford to visit us, so Carolyn's dad and my mum fly out to see this grandchild of the sea. My mum has always been the reluctant mariner, a farm girl who married a man dreaming of the sea. This male fancy, saw us embark on the voyage of a lifetime, a young inexperienced family cast out onto the high seas. My innocence and lack of responsibility made it the highlight of my life, the thing which sustained me when we finally returned to "normal" life in Australia. For Mum though, bringing up two little kids in the confines of a 35' yacht was not always that easy.

Carolyn's dad Gordon, a spritely, easy going 73 year old, is also a farm boy who moved to the city. He is new to the sea and enthusiastic about its merits, keen to be involved in everything and enjoy himself, which makes him well suited to sailing. So we have a good crew to cruise the sheltered waters around Vavau. Mara is due to have her immunisation shots so Gordon pays for a taxi and we all troop up to the poorly funded Tongan hospital. It's complicated to get Mara immunised, the services being very basic, so Carolyn decides to do it later. Taking my chance, I very nervously I inquire about a dentist as my front capped tooth has come loose.

"Yes, today we have volunteer aid dentist from the US here, you can see him sir," proudly announces a fine young Tongan woman at the desk. This sounds hopeful so I wait my turn with a small group of islanders. It proves a mistake though, as my wealthy sounding dentist does not seem at all interested in looking after an Australian tourist. He hastily mixes up a batch of adhesive, ramming my tooth on carelessly, at a drunken angle.

"You'll have to get that fixed up first thing when you get home to Australia." He tells me as I look at my crooked, protruding tooth. He knows I'm on a yacht and therefore home is still a long way off. Somehow it seems he is actually envious of my life, which sounds like one long holiday.

"Now I'm off to go scuba diving with my son," he boasts to even the score well in his favour. I slouch out of the hospital feeling downhearted and vain about the appearance of my front tooth.

"This isn't going to be a good way to return to Australia," I sulk as we head back out to the islands for some peace and quiet.

The good ship *Amaroo* joins us for Carolyn's birthday, anchored off a pristine coral fringed islet covered in lush vegetation. Our healthy spread reflects the want of processed food in the Neifau supermarkets. A handsome coral trout speared down at 20m, tops the menu baked with kumala the local sweet potato, manioke or cassava the staple root vegetable of many Pacific Islands, and prize rich purple taro, all deliciously crispy baked. Our greens are the local spinach, taro leaves and a fresh garden salad to top off our island fare, washed down with bottles of Tongan Royal beer.

Our cute toddlers, Mara and Rowen labour to blow out the candles on Carolyn's mouth watering carrot cake. Having managed to puff them out, the candles burst into flames again, amazing everyone, especially the poor thwarted kids. "Re-igniting candles! Only the Shakedowns would have a packet of those handy!" After dinner we are sitting out in the cockpit, enjoying some of Gordon's duty free rum, Jerry picks up on my unsmiling and troubled mouth.

"Buck up, Stingray, we don't even notice there's anything wrong with your tooth," she tries, always positive.

"Yeah, Stingray, the girls will still love you," chimes Alan, always ready to stir people up.

One thing that always cheers me up is catching delicious fish with a speargun. Here my confidence is up, able to free dive down to 20m, which has been enabling me to nab deep fish, beyond the reach of the local Tongans. A few days later, keen for another fish dinner, I dive into the pristine sea, with the visibility a good 25m. Deep down on the sea floor I can make out the slinking, camouflaged movements of a decent coral trout. Taking a deep breath I fin down strongly, equalising my ears as the pressure builds. It sees me coming, begins to gradually move down a bit deeper, so I follow slowly, trying not to startle it.

In this obsession with hunting, my eardrums are forgotten. Suddenly there's an explosion in my ear, a mind swirling loss of my whole sense of direction, 24m below fresh air. On the dark edge of panic, no longer equipped with the simple sense of which way is up, only one thought can form in my reeling brain, "*don't breath in, your buoyancy will take you up.*" Forever I seem to float through the most uncomfortable border-less void, lost in space, desperate to breath some air.

Bursting through, I suck in fresh air. Deeply concerned about drowning I wave frantically to a passing Tongan boat, who pick me up. Everyone is alarmed to see me return so shaken with a burst eardrum. Laying down on my side water drains out of my ear, while I wallow in deep despair, imagining I may lose hearing in this ear.

Luckily Carolyn, being a certified dive instructor, knows that it's quite common to blow an eardrum and that it will just heal itself.

The next day we return to the main town Neiafu, where a pleasant doctor looks into my ear and confirms it will heal up in a week. "You won't be able to dive deeply for two weeks or you might tear it again," he says which seems a small price to pay.

"That's what happens when you get old, Andrew," says my well meaning mother, which does little for my dwindling confidence.

*

Our good friends on *Amaroo* are preparing to depart on their voyage straight back to Australia. They invite us over for farewell drinks at anchorage 13, for in Vavau they are numbered for the charter boats simplicity. Carolyn and Jerry set to chatting about life and the kids play happily. "What're you looking so down for Stingray?" asks Alan as we sit in the cockpit nursing his sturdy mix of rum and coke, staring out at the southern night sky, so vivid out here in the clean ocean air, so far from city lights.

"Do I look down? Yes, well everything's getting me down at the moment," I reply feeling cornered.

"Go on Stingray, let it out!" says Alan pressing the point.

"Well here I am, broken tooth, blown ear drum everything going wrong. And even worse I don't know what I'm going to do when we get back to Australia," I say, letting my heart out.

"Is that all? Get a grip Stingray. I wouldn't have thought a little thing like a tooth would worry a bloke like you. Stuff it! Don't let that sort of little thing get in your way. Just get your arse into gear. Look Stingray, you're going to build that big cat of yours, so just get into it," he says with a rising passion, which frightens me a bit, that mad twinkle in his eyes.

Sitting there feeling a bit stunned, I have a laugh at this solid advice. It seems sometimes one really needs a mate to get right to the point and put one's life in perspective. He's right, my tooth is no big deal, it will get fixed soon enough. My ear is fine and I do have a goal to work for, a dream to pursue. I can build a new boat and a better life, all I need to do is take hold of the situation and make it happen.

CHAPTER 8.

THE CYCLE BEGINS AGAIN

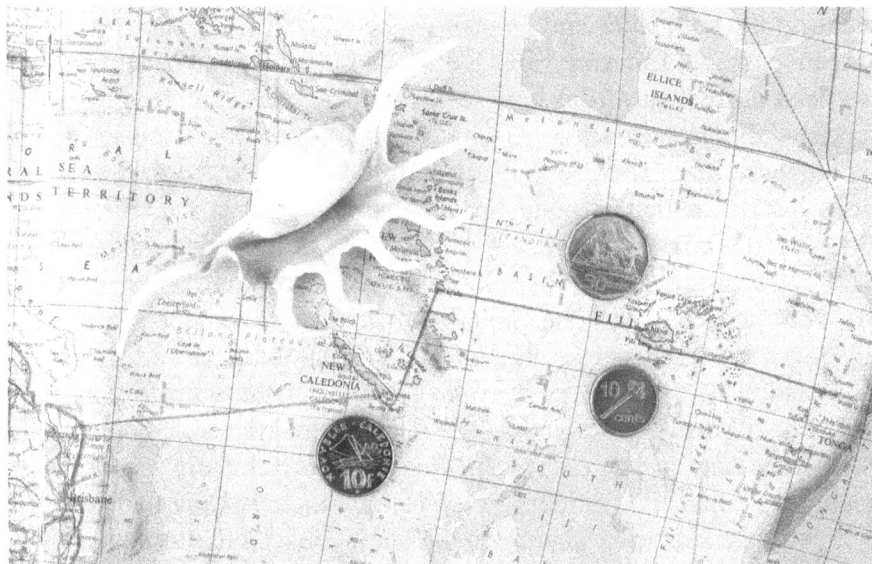

The Musket Cove regatta is soon to start in Fiji and since the Sydney 2000 Olympics are just about to open, my competitive nature is aroused. "Shall we sail to Fiji and go in the races?" I ask Mara, for although she is only 16 months old, she is already my go-to ally for action.

"Yes Papa, let's!" she says in her strong little voice, her vocabulary having evolved well during this Pacific voyage. So we arrange for my uncle Bill to meet us there as crew and set sail for the happy isles. It's the 2nd of September 2000, we have 5 days to sail 525 miles, clear in, stock up, find my uncle Bill then sail out to Musket Cove to enter.

Now that we have a deadline to meet, the trade wind dies right down, leaving us struggling to make miles. As usual we have only just enough diesel for harbour use and running the fridge. On the first day we manage only a disappointing 90 miles.

"We'll miss the whole regatta at this rate!" I fret, yet all we can do is settle into our challenge and work hard at our sail trim. "This is all good training for the races," I add hopefully.

By midnight on the third day, a bit more breeze has filled in, so we drop the spinnaker and change to the reacher, sailing through the Oneata passage. Entering Fiji's Koro Sea marks the halfway point, so we need a great run from here to make it. At least this time I'm not fending off dire seasickness, which was my case back in 95, when this malady threatened to end my sailing days. It was as we entered Fiji's Koro Sea that I found the resolve and motivation to take the helm for 12 hours straight, driving *Longnose* hard and at the same time pushing aside my weakness to the boat's motion.

Feeling cheered at the thought of this improvement in my life, we begin to streak across this enchanted Sea with the old magic of Fiji casting its spell on us once again. During the morning, surfing along at a steady 9/10 knots, we manage to land a 130cm Mahi-Mahi, not easy at such a speed. This catch will ensure we eat well during the Musket cove races, if we can get there in time that is!

"It does seem a shame to be racing past all these beautiful places," says Carolyn as we charge past Suva with Kandavu to the south.

That night we're creaming along with the coast of Vanua Levu visible in the moonlight. By midnight we close with the Navula passage, with still 23 miles to sail across the protected Nadi waters. 'So now if all goes well we'll have the best of tomorrow in Latoka for things to fall into place." Fighting off sleep I navigate *Longnose* across to Toomba Bay. It's 3.30am before we can drop anchor for a much needed but short sleep.

Shrugging off weariness we up anchor early, motor into town in the still morning air, only to discover the marina we've arranged to meet my uncle at no longer exists. This is a setback but the ghost of the jetty still remains and a few ancient boats lie forgotten in the old yard.

"Hope we don't lose your Uncle Bill," says Carolyn as we set off into town on our business. As usual great amounts of walking about have to be done to clear Customs and then we head for the markets.

"Sweet pineapples, lettuce, taro, snake beans, cucumbers, plantains, red bananas, mangoes, eggplants, Indian spices. What a great load of fresh produce," exclaims Carolyn, using Mara's pram to carry this load, while I carry the hefty creature. The sailing life certainly offers plenty of exercise.

Hot and sweaty we trudge back to the abandoned marina, praying my Uncle's taxi driver has managed to navigate his way there. It's a great relief to find the chap impatiently waiting for us, all set with a carton of Fiji Bitter.

"What are we waiting for, lets get out to this island," says my uncle, who owns an Endeavour 24, *Juganew,* and races it enthusiastically on Sydney harbour. Tired and relieved we make sail for Malola Lailai, home of Musket Cove.

The regatta is basically for cruising yachts yet it's the more racy boats that enter. The fleet looks very competitive as we line up for the start of race 1. We hit the line in full trim, making an excellent start to find ourselves commanding an early lead. With the breeze blowing onto our beam, *Longnose* heals over impressively, spilling her wind as she creams along, whereas the big catamarans stand up straight, losing none of the power of the wind. They drive past us rapidly and this sparkling performance of multihull speed adds fuel to my dream of a new catamaran.

Next night, after a welcome, relaxing lay day the crescent moon shines brightly out of a pristine night sky while we merrily drink Fiji Bitter at the beach bar, on Malola Lailai. "So which boat do you think will win this around the island race?" asks my uncle. "It seems to be the premier race of this regatta."

"*Longnose* will win of course!" says I. "Why who do you think?"

"Well that mainsail of yours looks like its off a 18th century pirate ship, it's so patched up. Now that boat *Hijacker,* they have beautiful race sails, or some of those cats are pretty fast!"

"Well I still believe experience and seamanship are worth more than fancy sails!" I reply, feeling a bit stung by my uncle's scathing words, which serve to bolster my drive that we do well.

The strong fleet mills about the start line, cheered on by a boatload of Fijians who thread their way through the jostling fleet calling out the nicest type of blessings to the sailors. The 44' Lidgard design *Hijacker* sailed by a wealthy American family, who have all the best sails and equipment, take the start this time as the yachts work into the wind on the first leg. *Longnose,* in hot pursuit moves into clear 2nd loving the light windward beat.

By the time we round the top of the island *Hijacker i*s leading by half a mile, with the rest of the fleet a quarter of a mile behind us. Now the gentle wind begins to die off as the tropical day warms up. Hoisting our stained and restitched spinnaker, we gybe carefully downwind catching every whisper of wind that drifts lazily over the island. *Longnose* runs away from the island towards the reef edge while *Hijacker* looks for wind closer in. Elated, we see them crawling along, while we catch the firsts puffs of the afternoon breeze, creaming along, steadily closing the gap.

It must be frustrating for them to see us flying down with our spinnaker pulling firmly in the new breeze while they battle with a light headwind. "*Longnose* has now passed *Hijacker*," comes the commentary on VHF and the Australians listening hold great hopes for a win. Suddenly our spinnaker losses its wind, and we realise our breeze was not the new wind at all. With the wind filling in against us, valiantly my crew fights to haul down the back winded spinnaker and set a headsail, while *Hijacker* regains the lead.

Having sorted ourselves out we press on to challenge them, rounding the final cape close on their heels. The breeze has freshened and our old blown out sails can't match *Hijacker's* state of the art Kevlar sails. "With decent sails we could have beat them," moans my uncle Bill, even so we are all very pleased with the race.

The awards night is laid back Fijian style and marks the opening ceremony of the Sydney Olympics. For our second prize we win 80 litres of diesel, a valuable bonus for us. Uncle Bill heads home and we decide to enter the race to Port Vila, caught up in the competitive spirit and the general migration westwards to Australia.

We manage to lead the fleet out through the passage into the ocean but then the breeze falters and most boats take the option of using their engines as this is allowed under the rules. Then a fresh trade wind sets in and we begin to run hard at a hair raising pace. "I can't help you much Andrew! I've got Mara to tend too," says Carolyn. Forced to shorten sail to a more comfortable arrangement we still make excellent speed, but the bigger boats, 50/60' fast cruisers and the big cats forge ahead.

All the next day it's overcast, with light wind so we know the other boats will be motoring. A nimbus rich thundercloud rolls over, bringing a brief squall which rips our mainsail right across a panel high up the sail. We roll along making slow progress under headsail alone as I set to, hand stitching the main. Regular rain squalls send rivulets of water over my needle and thread, wet, cold and tired I begin to concede that our 7 year old main is getting beyond repair. Nevertheless I press on and after 2 ½ hrs it's ready to hoist again.

During the afternoon a rainbow heralds more settled weather and the trade wind favours us once again. Next morning the breeze is quite fresh and the sparkling new day brings us the hope we can make Port Vila by nightfall. With this goal in sight we shake out the reefs and drive *Longnose* hard through the rest of the day.

Throughout the afternoon the sea builds and we begin to surf powerfully under our poled out reacher. Now the windvane can no longer control *Longnose,* so I take over, muscling the tiller to drive my ship down the best waves. "I can make out two yachts on the horizon," announces Carolyn, manning the binoculars up at the mast.

By the time we begin to converge on the entrance to Vila, it's our old rivals *Hijacker* holding only a short lead. To our surprise the other boat, *Barnstormer*, by some miscalculation, sails well past Pango Point and the entrance to Mele Bay. We manage to pass *Hijacker* and round the cape a few boat lengths ahead, set for a thrilling finish.

As we harden up onto the wind for the last beat across Mele Bay we have to make a sail change from our reacher to a jib. It's tense work as we cling to our lead with our little Mara hanging on for dear life, fending for herself as we struggle with sails and the helm, *Longnose* healed over with her gunnels in the sea.

With the finish line in sight our old sails begin to tell against us once again as the powerful *Hijacker* works under our lee to beat us by a boat length. Luckily I'm the type of fellow who prefers a close race to a comfortable win, otherwise I could have been disappointed.

It is a delight to be revisiting Vila with Mara now old enough to be a less demanding Admiral. We enjoy a quiet interlude exploring this busy tropical capital as we begin to realise our voyage is nearly over and this adventure is drawing to an end.

"Jam park, Jam park!" begs Mara in her sweet baby voice, tugging at Carolyn's hand. Her passion for swings and slippery slides is unquenchable. She calls them "Jam parks", from some association with fun, yummy jam and we find our lives evolving around a hunt for "Jam parks." In fact they are quite hard to find in this part of the world and often menacingly dangerous in their state of disrepair. Being an oversized kid I often tear my clothes on rusty spikes, but Mara thinks it's all great fun and never looks in danger.

*

On the trip to New Caledonia our mainsail tears right down the middle and is now beyond hand stitching. Luckily we have a smaller main, the size of our full main with 3 reefs put in, so we hoist this and make good speed in the strong trades anyway. Then our old engine starting battery goes flat and I have to struggle for some time trying to hand-start the engine. *Longnose* is well over due for a refit it seems, but that will have to wait for hopefully more prosperous days back in Australia.

Port Vila had surprised us with the number of cruising yachts anchored in its shelter, but our arrival in Noumea reveals even more remarkable numbers, with hundreds of yachts crowding the city anchorages. The Pacific Arts Festival is opening in Noumea so yachts have flocked here to enjoy the festivities.

We meet up with our old allies on the "Pink boat," *Jovial Tiburon* who we met in the Indian Ocean. Now with a baby of their own they have decided to settle back in New Caledonia, get jobs, sell their boat and build a house. It seems all our friends have solid life plans!

On the big opening day of the festival we walk around to Anse Vata, where groups of dancers from all over the Pacific throng the beach, all in their own unique and colourful costumes. The dancing reaches fever pitch as a group of outrigger canoes bristling with fearsome warriors land on the golden beach, making a wild reenactment of the first human arrival in New Caledonia. Mara clings to me bravely as these muscular islanders play out their heritage with fearsome gusto.

Around 2000 BC the Austronesians from south-east Asia, gradually island hopped down to New Guinea, and then to the Solomons. This would have been relatively easy as throughout this route the next island is always visible on the distant horizon. When they reached the eastern most point of the Solomons, some brave sailors would have had to venture several days from land to discover the Santa Cruz Islands, the remote Eastern Soloman Islands. From here the distances are fairly short and they could have day hopped all the way to the vast Island of New Caledonia.

A crescendo of drums heralds the arrival of a traditional style outrigger multihull, with crab claw sails, having navigated using traditional methods, all the way from Tahiti. "You know, building a new catamaran would be simply following in the footsteps of the Polynesians," I say to my girls as we wander the busy strand.

For as long as possible we cruise about the protected lagoon which surrounds New Caledonia, sailing down to the Isle of Pines to prolong our last Pacific island visit before the trip home. New Caledonia can be an alarming place to visit, even without a baby girl to protect, due to its great population of sea snakes, which are so common on virtually every beach and reef. Even though they show no aggression and it is very hard for them to bite you with their small mouths, it is always unnerving in the company of a snake.

On the 26th of October 2000, we depart Noumea on the last leg back to Australia. For the first four days the wind is quite light and we make slow progress under our small spare main. Then the sky begins to darken and the barometer needle starts dropping. First it begins to rain and then in the afternoon a gale hits from the north-east, which is still a fair wind but we head more to the north hoping to clear the low centre. The next day the wind has swung around to the north-west and we make slow progress in rough seas under the storm tri-sail.

I am not particularly enjoying the storm but Mara seems to think it is great fun and welcome action. She insists on being held outside for hours where she looks in fascination at what she calls the "Jam park waves". That night with the gale at its peak, a big wave slams us beam on, followed instantly by a terrifying shattering sound. For one shocking moment I believe our topsides have been stove in. And then I realise our shell collection from all over the world, has just been thrown out over the fiddles across the cabin, into the galley. The first to break the startled silence is Mara, who had been sleeping with Carolyn in the saloon bunk. "Papa all right?" she calls in her sweet little innocent voice, which sounds so brave in the face of our conditions. Such simple words put hope back into the whole situation.

The next night we are to be impressed by Australian surveillance as they have located us 300 miles out with an aircraft. They make radio contact for our details in a very businesslike fashion. Now that the low has passed the wind drops off again and we struggle to make good time hampered by our small mainsail.

It's a slow and disappointing passage and to make matters worse we arrive in Hervey Bay on Friday evening to be told we will have to pay a huge $270 extra to cover overtime because we have arrived on the weekend. Of course we can't afford this fee so we decide to wait till Monday to clear in. Even worse they will not let us anchor in the Bundaberg river to wait but insist we stay offshore in the bay.

This is a rather inglorious way to arrive home after a 4-year circumnavigation, but we are content to potter about for the weekend. It's great to tune in to the ABC radio stations and hear our local accent and uniquely open minded programs. We know we have a lot of changes to come to terms with and are in a way happy to savour our lingering freedom.

It is all the more exciting to arrive and be cleared in when it does finally happen. Other sailors have overheard our conversations with customs and knowing we are getting very low on supplies, kindly bring us gifts of fresh food. A whole new adventure is unfolding now as Mara begins to discover afresh the country we know so well. She is very excited about seeing "magpie birdies" and very keen on our "real Australian milk," which was not a feature of the places we have just visited.

Our finest cruise has come to an end. We have managed to voyage the world on the most meagre sum of money. Had we waited to depart with a handsome amount in our bank account we may still be awaiting departure. Our family will be happy now that we are back from the perils of the sea, yet it is the dangers of land life that seem to present much more of a threat. What of traffic accidents, killer household electricity, and the mayhem of modern life?

Once again we seem to be cast back to square one. Our escape under sail has drawn to an end and it seems we must now struggle again to plan a new escape.

This time the challenge looms even greater than before. I hope that the lessons we have learnt will help us through the difficulties that lie ahead. "Life must just be one long series of moving from one overwhelming challenge to the next," I reflect as we set off on the next stage of our adventures.

CHAPTER 9.

THE HARD YARDS

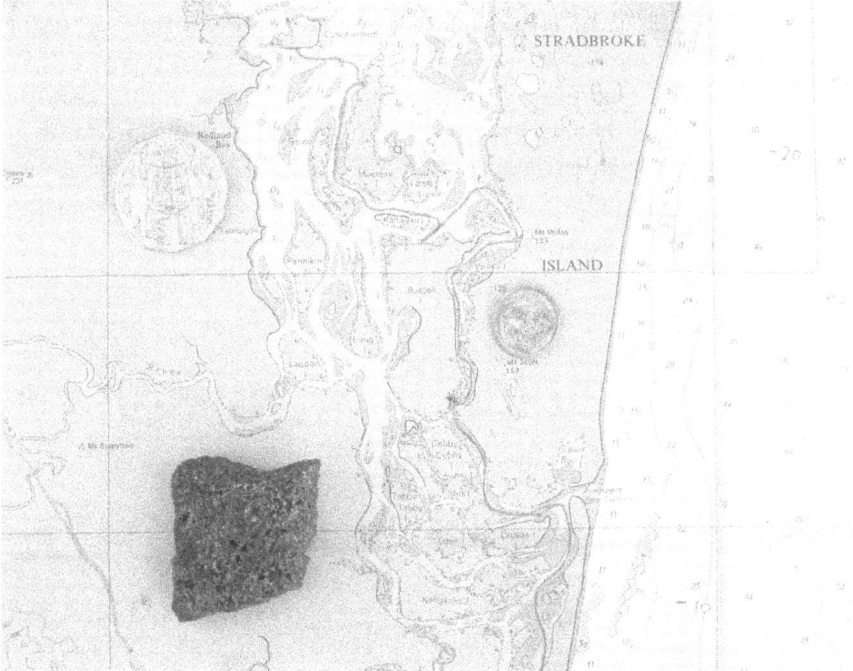

Having conquered the challenge of circumnavigating the world and discovered my new aim for the future, I had hoped that life would be straightforward. Yet it immediately becomes evident I have chosen a lofty plan, that could well prove out of reach.

Where to start is the question? So we cruise *Longnose* south to Ballina, the closest port to my mother's house in Casino. Here the well protected anchorage of Mobs Bay, is beautifully wild, surrounded by mangroves and native trees, with its own white sandy beach. It's only a modest row across the river to the town where I enrol at the local TAFE, planning to obtain a Master V skippers ticket.

Unfortunately the TAFE teachers think very little of my sailing history and it's demoralising to attend classes and be treated like a complete beginner. It seems the teachers want to prove they have more knowledge then me, so do their best to belittle me, even though I had previously covered a great deal of this syllabus in obtaining my Yachtmaster Offshore Certificate.

All the same there are many new things to learn so I try my best to ignore these small minded egoists and get stuck into learning the curriculum. Meanwhile I renovate the garage at my mum's place and begin lofting and building the dinghy I have designed. Here is a chance to practice the techniques used in building a 50' catamaran.

Fortunately I also get a casual job with the famous multihull personality John Hitch, building his new 55' design. It's only for a few days a week, which suits me perfectly, an excellent opportunity to learn his construction methods and design ideas.

Dad is back in Australia working as a locum in Wagga Wagga. I had dreamed that perhaps he would encourage and maybe help me finance this dream, but it seems I am sadly deluded with this idea. He is far from encouraging, suggesting that I lack both the knowledge and money to build such a boat. Saying that catamarans are no good for ocean sailing, and that mine will capsize or break and that I would be better off to build a traditional wooden boat. It's not just my dad though, everybody I meet seems discouraging of my lofty ideas.

"Yeah, so my plan is to build a 50' catamaran of my own design," I announce to any friends or relatives who show interest in my future.

"Well, don't fancy your chances there. It takes years and years of study to learn how to design and then many more years again to develop the skill needed to build such a boat," is the general reply. "And of course you don't seem to have the income to fund such a project."

It's hard to disagree with this common logic and I fail to point out the five years of personal study I've passionately undertaken, not to mention a lifetime of involvement in boats. As a three year old, living aboard my family's 35' steel sloop in Marsamexett Harbour,

Malta, surrounded by the history and power of the crusader fortresses of Valletta, my mind fresh and free, I had dreamed of building a boat. Being a shy and quiet lad, it had greatly surprised Mr Evans, a close family friend, when I begun pouring out plans of how I was going to build a boat when I grew up. As he sat tinkering with the windvane he hoped would steer his family across the Atlantic Ocean, my tiny blond haired self paced about going into great detail and John could not believe his ears. My parents were even more surprised when John relayed the plans I had divulged.

A week later my caring and understanding mother was confronted by her sad little son, visibly depressed. "You know Mum, I'll never be able to build that boat I was talking about!" Perhaps I had been pondering more deeply on the logistics involved and had come to this sad conclusion.

Now, 35 years later I could deeply understand the fears I had harboured as a three year old. Strangely enough, as a slightly more mature eight year old, enjoying the incredible peace and beauty of sailing across the Pacific Ocean, rolling down the trade wind route to the Marquises, these toddler fancies returned to my head.

As much as I loved *Yanda,* our 35' steel sloop with her fine quality varnished red mahogany interior, this didn't stop me thinking of improvements. Out in the cosy cockpit, sheltered by a handsome dodger, I would lie in the warm sun, when my dad insisted on total silence while he did the complex mathematics to work out his sextant sights and deduce our daily position. Here in this dreamlike peace, thousands of miles from any land, my mind set to, designing the boat I would build when I grew up.

They were rambling, weird ideas as I recall, and being faithful to *Yanda,* I pictured it with the same interior, but there would be narrow corridors down both sides. This seemed a very strange concept at the time, which I found intriguing but entirely silly. All these years later it occurred to me that these corridors could well have been a premonition of the narrow corridors that catamaran hulls create.

Of course one has to be determined to achieve anything in this world. The 10' strip cedar dinghy was a tremendous success, carrying 3 adults and 3 children on a delightful picnic upon the Richmond River on its maiden voyage. The strip cedar construction impressing me as incredibly strong. Now the new dinghy is complete, we feel ready to press on with our adventures. With the idea of finding a place to build a boat in mind, we begin looking for cheap properties handy to the sea. Unfortunately this proves a bit like looking for a needle in a haystack.

Along the banks of the Richmond river looks desirable, similar to the fine spot John Hitch has near Wardel but this is way out of our price range. We become keen to sail north, believing that cheap properties might be available on the Bundaberg river. My TAFE course is now holding us up, the teachers would seemingly have me toiling forever, lording it over me with their superior knowledge.

Rowing out to *Longnose* one stormy night, across the river to Mobs Bay, dealing with large waves, it suddenly dawns on me that I am well and truly ready to sit my exam and need only say the word and they should be obliged to let me. The very next day, plucking up my courage and confidence I head into the office.

"Mr Brown sir, I'm ready to take the exam for Master V and then do the practical examination, as soon as possible, sir." The ghost of a thin smile shows across his face, while an uncomfortable silence hangs about the cluttered room. Sweat prickles my palms as I wait, uneasily for his reply.

"Oh, so you think you are ready do you? Well, OK, I'll organise an exam paper for you and if you pass that you can do your practical," he replies reluctantly. "Of course you'll need a vessel to do your practical examination on," he adds smugly as if to corner and defeat me.

"Thank you sir, that's fine. Oh yes and the vessel will be no problem, I have my own, sir," I add as firmly but humbly as possible.

Finally sitting the exam is a breeze, which I whip through with no problems at all. A week later I organise the day for Mr Brown to test my practical skills out on the water. Picking him up at the public wharf, even this haughty character, trained on supertankers, can not fail to be moderately impressed by my confident boat-handling, shipshape vessel and depth of real knowledge on the water.

Having put *Longnose* through her paces and tackled his every test, we anchor and offer him tea and biscuits. He knows he has no choice but to pass me, even though he perhaps would have liked me to remain a slave of the Ballina TAFE, returning year after year until all my confidence had been sapped away.

On the morning of September the 12th 2001, we prepare to depart Ballina on our voyage north. Just as we are about to cast off, Carolyn's brother in law, Terry, arrives to see us off, looking sombre and agitated. "Have you heard the news? Two jumbo jets, full of passengers have collided with the twin towers in New York! Amazingly the buildings have burnt down clean to the ground. They say it's a terrorist attack!" Terry rushes out this grave news of the event that is to change the world.

On this day though, we make very little of such a world event, setting out impatiently on our voyage to the Gold Coast Seaway. The deep blue ocean and pristine coastline quickly soothe away any such global concerns.

Bypassing the glamour and expense of the Gold Coast we navigate the tricky, protected waterways, comprising of 130 islands which stretch north from this busy metropolis. These are wild, unpopulated waters, something like Florida's Everglades, the centre a maze of sandy/muddy mangrove islands, bordered by the glorious white sand regions of Stradbroke Island and the flat sugar cane growing areas on the mainland. The wild low mangrove islands finally give way to gentle hills of sandstone, volcanic rock and sand which form the Bay Islands, four of which carry modest suburban populations.

We anchor off the northern end of Russell Island, infamous for its part in the 1970's land scandals. Back in the days of rampant urbanisation, the developers grabbed the island and sub-divided the entire place into neat little blocks and began selling them off cheap. Unfortunately they subdivided all the southern section which has big stretches of low ground and tidal mangrove areas. Those who bought these cheap blocks, site unseen, lured by the prospect of easy monetary gains from the cold capitals like Melbourne, got quite a shock when they later discovered their land went under at high tide. Thus the island was plastered with a stigma and now many people imagine it as being basically all mangroves and underwater most of the time.

During our very first cruise north on *Longnose,* we had stopped here to make a phone call and found it very pleasant. Now we tie up our dinghy in the park and stroll up the main street to check out the real estate. A pleasant sense of peace pervades the island, with native gums, tallowwoods and pines gracing the rambling hills, plentiful with sulphur crested cockatoos shouting out the virtues of native forest. Visiting two handy real estate agents, they drive us around to a few nearby properties, none of which are spacious enough to contemplate building a 15m catamaran on. In the window of Ray White's, we spy a promising advertisement for an impressive looking place on 3 blocks of land for $110,00.

"What about this one?" we suggest eagerly.

"Oh that one, you wouldn't be interested. Way down the south end of the island, too far from the shops. Anyway I haven't got enough petrol to drive you down there and the station's closed for the weekend. They say a 'stones throw from the water', but it would be one hell of a throw! Haha, nah, forget that one."

No amount of badgering can persuade our chap to take us to see this promising place so we set off down the main street, determined to check it out. Walking along the quiet road feels nice, with scattered houses, the occasional horse, a tethered goat and none of the busy suburban vibe. The first passing car picks us up, adding to the good feel. Carol Wickstead sounds like she has a busy family to care for, yet even though she lives only half way down the island she insists on driving us down to the Lions Park, on the far south-east end of Russell.

"This is what we call Sandy Beach, it's not much of a beach though. Good luck with your house hunting," says Carol, leaving us in the quiet park. A short way down a dusty dirt road we find the house, built up on a slope, with views of the water through the trees, its front veranda overgrown by a rampant purple bougainvillea. A row of golden cane palms line the front of the 3 blocks, which back onto a steep hill, healthy with iron barks and gums. There's an old tin shed down on the street level and trudging up the steep hill the main house has a large empty studio as its lower level. Walking up the wooden steps to the main upper level we peer in through the windows and find the interior modern and neat.

"Look, it's called the '*Butterfly Lodge*', how sweet," says Carolyn.

"Wow, there's heaps of room here to build a big cat!" I enthuse, beginning to think this house hunting gig is easy, with places like this going cheap. We hitch back to the north end of the island, buy some expensive goods in the little local store and walk back down to the park. Mara is keen for a play in the "Jam park" where the local kids seem friendly.

"You'll like it on Russell. There's no hustle or bustle on Russell!" says one cute little girl, rocking happily on a swing, which quite charms me.

Feeling encouraged, the next day we head on to check out the other islands, including the more well-to-do, Macleay Island. Anchoring off its sandy beach on the north-west side we find that a single empty block is as much as the "Butterfly Lodge." It's much busier on Macleay, almost suburban and the lure of Russell's quiet south-east corner begins to take hold of our hearts. Coochiemudlo Island, quite close to the mainland, boasts glorious sandy beaches on virtually every shore, but its prices are well out of our reach.

After a few days of looking about we motor down to the south-east corner of Russell Island for a closer look. There is a handy anchorage for *Longnose* out of the main channel, protected by a sandy bank so we drop the pick and take in the area. From here we can see the prominent white lattice veranda of the *Butterfly Lodge* and quite a few other decent houses slotted in along the ridge above. On Russell, classic Australian bush stretches as far as the eye can see, dotted with patches of red earth and white sand. We row over to the appealing white sandy beach close by on Stradboke Island, cook sausages on a fire and eat our picnic, taking everything in.

"So do you think it would be nice to live in this area?" I ask Carolyn and Mara, who simply adore a wild camp.

"Well, it seems to have everything we need. It's a nice and wild area, the house and garden are spacious and there's a good anchorage for *Longnose*. It seems perfect," replies a thoughtful Carolyn.

"I love it, it's a magic place!" calls Mara running down a steep sand hill, tumbling on the way, emerging covered in sand and black rutile.

After another visit to the house, carefully checking its hardwood verandas, hardiplank walls, steel uprights and aluminium doors, we can see it needs lots of work, which is exactly what we want. In many ways it all seems too good to be true and we figure there's bound to be some catch. First thing the next day we put in an offer for $100,000 and hope for the best.

All day long we ponder our decision. My mind ticks over trying to confirm we are doing the right thing. "Bundaberg seems less appealing as anywhere on a river has the chance of flooding, which would be a disaster for a half built boat. We need to be near the water so that if we reach the point of launching this boat we won't be faced with a 10/15k expense for cranes, trucks and police escorts. Agnes Waters or 1770 might be worth looking at, but then what if we travel all that way and it proves too expensive or remote and in the meantime what if someone else comes along and buys the *Butterfly Lodge*"?

By evening we are beginning to feel pretty nervous. What if they decide not to sell? Suddenly this wild, remote spot on the very far edge of suburbia seems exactly the right place and we begin to desire it with all our hearts. Next morning we receive a call from the estate agent.

"They won't go as low as $100,000, but they will accept $105,000. How does that sound to you?" We're over the moon with excitement. Carolyn has $50,000 tucked away from the sale of our previous boat, *Esychia* a Lock Crowther design, Harrier catamaran, which she refused to spend any of during our frugal world voyage. Demonstrating the wonder of having a child, both our parents chip in $20,000. Also we can claim the first home buyers grant of $10,000, so all we need to do is scrape together the final $5,000. It seems we can afford the place without taking out a loan. Woohoo, the whole house buying saga done and dusted!

Within the week all the legal business is sorted and the owners make the trip out to the island and officially hand the place over to us. They prove to be the most delightful family, who make their money processing salt. They are sad to be selling their holiday house but genuinely pleased to see a young family like ours buying it, full of hope and big plans.

"Here you are Andrew," says Mr Olssen, handing me the keys, "You wanted a place to build a catamaran, but you didn't think you'd find a place to build a whole fleet of them!" he says in a most magnanimous and generous fashion.

Everything had gone so smoothly, it certainly feels as if we were guided to find the *Butterfly Lodge*. "Gosh, there must be some catch to this place! It seems almost too good to be true!" I exclaim as we cast fresh eyes on our new property. A month later we are to find out what the catch is.

CHAPTER 10

WHERE WILL WE GET THE MONEY FROM?

We fly into the *Butterfly Lodge* renovations with great gusto and excitement. "House work is fun really! You get such a big amount done so quickly. Unlike boatbuilding tasks which are so fiddly and slow!" I enthuse, slapping on a fresh coat of paint to the exterior weatherboards, while Carolyn attacks an overgrown section of the garden with secateurs. Luckily the upstairs part of the house is already remarkably smart with a new lino floored kitchen, while the rest of the house has been recently laid with new carpet. The fittings are all in good order, gas and electric hot water, fine shower and bath, fans, fully screened, all this with amazing water views looking over to wild Stradbroke Island. We simply can not believe our good fortune.

"This house was built by our friends the Cusaks in 1985, I think," says Shelagh, our next door neighbour. "Your shed was the old fishing shack, where they used to come for holidays. It'd date back to the early 60s I'd say. And you must be so impressed with all this amazing stonework. My husband helped build all these retaining walls. Isn't the local volcanic rock beautiful, look at those purple and red hues!"

My mother proves to be a great ally, regularly driving up from Casino to help us. She toils from dawn to dusk lending a hand in every aspect of the work. Of course we'll need a car so she spends the day driving me around the mainland car yards. You can tell a lot about a person from the cars they buy. Having test driven a few Japanese and Korean machines, whose motors seemed a little suspect, I come across a 1985 Mercedes Benz 230E, with spotless green-gold duco, leather seats and custom-made sheepskin covers fitted to the front seats. Driving it feels so grand, amazingly solid and nothing seems wrong with it at all, so I nervously buy it for $4000.

Carolyn and Mara marvel at our new car as we clean it out on the grassy lawn, feeling that everything is coming together. Excited by the fancy spares kit, spacious boot and functioning stereo, we all suddenly begin to feel rather painfully itchy. Flitting about our eyes we notice tiny insects floating all around us. Soon this itch becomes a very uncomfortable burning pain on all our exposed skin. "These are midges, aren't they?" suggests Carolyn. The itch is so painfully annoying it becomes almost impossible to think and we are forced to retreat inside.

"Gosh, having those nasty, invisible insects savaging us is going to make building a boat very hard work!" I lament, losing a bit of confidence in my grand plan. Over the next few days it slowly dawns on us what the catch with the *Butterfly Lodge* is! The end of spring is a rare period when the midges vanish altogether. Now things are getting back to normal with sandflies hatching out of the sandy grass and ground.

"Oh my God! Look at how many mosquitoes are buzzing about outside our screen!" says Carolyn, a bit horrified by a further influx of stinging insects. Yet another setback flies in. Mosquitoes prove to be almost unbearable some evenings, swarming about in vast numbers and locking us inside, like prisoners of the savage world outside. Things begin to feel grim as our skin is always itching. At times it's hard to sleep at night with the whining of mosquitoes, outside our screen mesh lusting for our blood. Tiger brand mosquito coil smoke pervades the house.

*

"Look at you with your posh imported Mercedes and dreams of building a maxi catamaran! Delusions of grandeur if ever I've seen them, especially on your income!" jests my good friend Darren a few days later.

"Well us Stransky's were barons back in Czechoslovakia. I suppose that's where I've inherited these mad ideas from," I reply, not feeling that confident about my big plans.

The hot afternoon sun has gone behind the ridge, a welcome relief, while a cool easterly breeze fans us with natures air conditioning. We're sitting on the veranda, contemplating our work while enjoying tea and biscuits. "It does have a lovely feel here," says Carolyn. "Midges really only seem to come in the garden not high up here in the house. Also if there's a breeze on it blows the wretched insects away! So do you think there's much more rotten lattice to repair here?"

"Well hopefully just a few more sections," says I munching on a Monte Carlo. "I suppose we'll be able to cope with all these insects, if we do get this boat building project off the ground! After all, our house is situated in a remarkably wild area and this is the price we must pay."

"One step at a time Andrew. For now I'm really looking forward to renovating the old shed!" Delight sparkles in her eyes at the thought. It turns out to be a singular treasure trove of discoveries. Old paintings and photographs of the place way back in its formation, hand made fishing lures, enough sinkers to last me a lifetime, jars of nails and screws, a fine antique cupboard full of all manner of household fittings, a 10m wooden extension ladder, a lovely long plank, plenty of decent lengths of hardwood, two excellent saw horses and even a wall mounted can opener, which we fit in the upstairs kitchen. It's tremendous fun sorting through this piece of history, a journey back in time to the pioneering days, through all the remnants of the Cusak's old equipment.

From ply and hardwood I build work benches all around the shed walls, knowing just how much space one needs to create a boat. Now I have a perfectly acceptable place to build, if we can stand the midges, yet there is just one fairly big hurdle to overcome. What with buying an endless stream of paint and building materials and purchasing a car, our bank balance is once again scraping the very bottom. Carolyn has work a few days a week and is earning enough for us to get by but we need substantial capital to kick start this monster project.

Every night, sleeping in the strangely still and quiet *Butterfly Lodge*, my mind ventures out to *Longnose*, keeping a sort of ethereal watch and in the morning I dash out, peer through a gap in the trees to make sure our faithful ship is still there. All summer we work on the house, occasionally taking a trip down to the delightful anchorage of Jumpinpin lagoon a mere 4 miles to the south. Here we can refresh ourselves with a taste of the open ocean and the golden sands of South Stradbroke.

Late summer finds us motoring up to Macleay Island to meet up with our cruising companions the Shakedowns, who have been doing tremendously well with their shed business. Suddenly there is a strange noise coming from the engine and it losses much of its power. Thus we meet up with our friends at a bit of a low ebb.

"Shady Sheds is going gang-busters!" exclaims Alan excitedly, eating sausages and salad in the park. "We're building industrial chemical sheds now and I'm planning to build a oil refining vessel that we can go cruising on!" His enthusiasm is inspiring but I can't help being concerned by our problems at hand.

"What's wrong Stingray? You don't seem too excited about your life! What's the problem? Your house sounds awesome and you're all set to build this big cat, you should be dancing for joy!" says my mate Alan, who always manages to cut to the chase quicker than anyone I know.

"Well, we've just blown the head gasket on our motor, which is bound to cost heaps and we have no money even to tackle that, let alone build a mega cat!" I groan despairingly.

"Come on, what's the big deal! Rebuilding your motor won't cost much. Just pull the head off, regrind the valve seats, hone the cylinders and whack a new gasket in. That'll cost you $300 tops. I'll lend you a honing tool, it's easy. Then pull your finger out and get a job. It's simple!" sums up Alan in his usual sweeping fashion.

"Hah! Well, put like that, without even drawing a breath it sounds all pretty easy, but I've got the feeling it will be pretty challenging."

*

With a nice shed all sorted, at least there's a good place to work. Piece by piece I pull the Volvo Penta 13hp diesel apart. It weighs as much as a modern engine of twice its horsepower, yet the individual pieces can be handled easily enough. Having endured 22 years of raw seawater cooling, its internal waterways are solidly clogged up with hard scale. The channels around the pistons would have offered very little water flow over the last few years but can be cleaned out laboriously with drilling and a piece of wire

The waterways in the head are totally none existent, set hard as stone and must be carefully drilled out. No water can have been flowing through here for years and years. No wonder the engine was overheating in the Suez and Panama canals, when it was asked to run full pelt hour upon hour. Apart from the exhaust channels being clogged thick with heavy soot, the machine is in remarkably good condition, with the bearings and cylinders only worn to half their specified limits. It's quite pleasurable to use cutting paste and grind the valve seats. Honing the cylinder bores with Alan's tool, rips off the polished walls, scouring them with an X pattern. New rings, head gasket and a few tins of Volvo Penta green spray paint cost $340, and the old faithful motor goes back together like new, torqued up carefully with not one bolt failing.

"Woohoo, it started first go and runs way better than ever!" I cry out to Carolyn and Mara. "You know, I've been thinking. What if we sail up to Airlie Beach and I get work skippering boats there?" I suggest feeling a burst of self confidence that this would be possible.

"Well, yes, I suppose we could do that," replies Carolyn, always keen for a voyage.

"Yay, let's go sailing on the cosy boat!" pipes up Mara, all of 3 years old.

For us it's a fine chance to show Mara the wonders of our favourite coast in all the world, bordered by the Great Barrier Reef, stretching over 1250 miles. Under the vast aquamarine sky, flecked by fluffy clouds, *Longnose* voyages north-west. Luring us fresh ocean fish, sheltering in golden sandy bays, rolling gently along towards our destiny. Mara thrives on this sea life, always full of energy to get ashore in a new anchorage.

"Come on Puppi, let's go ashore. Mama, please can we go exploring on Shaw island?" So even though we would perhaps prefer to laze aboard and take in the sights from the comfort of the cockpit we row ashore and land on the shell strewn rough sand, the clear water gently smoothing the beach rim. Mara dashes off, delighting in the wild and free feeling of a deserted island. Her body is strong and firm as she hunts about the rocky outcrops searching for treasures the sea may have thrown up.

"Here Puppi, look what I have found!" says Mara in her clear innocent voice. She has bounded over to me, putting a shiny old pearl shell delicately into my hand. "Is it a good one, Pup?" she asks, her eyes full of wonder. Being a passionate connoisseur of sea shells right from Mara's age, I would not have taken a second glance at it on the beach. Yet her enthusiasm prompts me to look at it afresh, feeling that perhaps too much experience makes one jaded to the simple beauty of things.

"Yes, it's a beauty my chick!" I pronounce proudly, grasping the shell lovingly in my hand and fingering it afresh, taking in its wild glow and worn beauty, while Mara dashes off to marvel at nature in the way youth knows so instinctively.

It's wonderful to see her clambering over the old dead coral thrown high on the beach as she sets off to explore the shady forest edge. Her blond hair and pale body dodge effortlessly past pandanus palms, fending off casuarina trees and lantana bushes all planting their roots in the dry sand. There is a certain balmy stillness, the pungent, interesting aroma of wild goats mixes with subtle, sweet bush scents. Cicadas hum in our ears as we follow along, pushing past wattle trees and spiky prickly pear cactus. Midges are roused up by our human stirrings, attacking us, yet Mara is as hardy as us, virtually oblivious to their stings now. A little way along we come across a saltwater inlet, where mangrove trees grow.

"Mama, Puppi, look what's hanging in that tree!" exclaims Mara, bursting with excitement as she unhooks a Rapala fishing lure, snagged in some roots. How is it that children make such simple events feel like one has stumbled across a casket of pirate treasure?

All too soon we sail across Funnel Bay arriving in the commodious and generally well protected Airlie Beach. Sadly for me, Carolyn and Mara decide to return to Russell Island while I look for work on the numerous charter boats. Feeling suddenly a bit alone and concerned about my prospects here, I set too with a will, fronting up at the various charter headquarters, offering my services.

During my first weeks of hanging about Airlie, the phone lies dormant and I begin to lose hope. Getting to know a few of the local characters around the waterfront, a mate gives me the phone number of the Ozsail boss. Plucking up courage I ring him and he bids me to meet at their office around at Abel Point.

He's a young, weather beaten, down to earth fellow, smartly dressed in white, who promptly sends me off on the maxi trimaran *Avatar* so I can learn the route of the typical 3 days 2 nights trip. Here I pick up all the important things, such as how to punish guests who break the ships rules, by making them eat a spoon full of Vegemite, so I'm all set.

Back in Airlie, while waiting around for Ozsail to offer me my first commission, I meet up with the boss of Tallarook charters. He's a swarthy, wild looking chap, as close to a pirate as one could expect to find in the office, desperate to find a skipper for their 38' catamaran sailing tomorrow midday. Later some mates have a good laugh at my expense,

"Your going to work for Tallarook? Good luck to you, they haven't got the best reputation around town!" After a fitful night's sleep, nervous of the task ahead, I rock up early to make myself familiar with my charge. Sounding dreamy and hung over my laid-back boss, shows me how to start the motor and promptly heads off to the café. I set to work, checking over my ship, an aging motor-sailing catamaran. The required safety gear is mostly outdated and worn out, yet it seems that around here it's take the job as is or click one's heels on shore.

All too soon 15 excited backpackers, smelling of suntan lotion and sweat, with cases of beer in hand crowd aboard. At the last minute my hostess rocks up nursing a terrible hangover and it's time to get under way. Hiding my nervousness, I take the helm, carefully motoring out of the marina. It's a challenge to see properly through the horde of bikini clad girls and guys stripping down to their board-shorts up on the foredeck.

Getting the passengers involved in hoisting the main and unrolling the jib puts them nicely into the spirit of the adventure. It's early afternoon and they're cracking open beers at a steady rate, the sea is calm and we're sailing along nicely, across the Whitsunday Passage with music pumping out from the old cassette player. The guests are young and inquiring, eager to chat with me about my life, so I can sit back feeling relaxed as a festive atmosphere envelopes the boat. My deckhand has recovered sufficiently to produce a plate of snacks which are hungrily devoured.

Taking a mooring off the Hook Passage resort, most of us head for a snorkel along the fringing reef to freshen up before dinner. While it's a fair responsibility keeping an eye on this inexperienced crowd, I'm a powerful swimmer and feel confident of everyone's safety, enjoying a nice swim with them.

Back aboard my laid back deckhand, blond, beautiful and carefree is proving very easy to get along with. She cheerily sets to preparing dinner, while the guests happily lounge on deck taking in the last of the suns warmth and laying into the ales. The skipper of course is in charge of barbecuing the steaks, so a task I'm not that familiar with hangs over my head uncomfortably.

"When shall I start cooking the steaks?" I ask Angela, who seems enviably without a care in the world.

"Oh, not just yet. I've only just put the broccoli on to boil." This is enough to set my hair on edge, for even I know that broccoli should not be boiled for long at all, otherwise its turns soft and falls apart at the touch. Dashing out I fire up the BBQ and set to with the steaks. Hungry fellows, sated with beer begin to smell the grounding aroma of searing beef and crowd around to give me welcome advice.

"Oh yum, I like mine well done," announces a sunburnt Englishman.

"Medium rare for me please," from a burly German.

"The blood is rising, that's almost done enough for me," specifies a particular Frenchman. And so it goes, the enthusiastic fellows nurse me through this dreaded task without even their knowing. The broccoli is too far gone for some but in general it's a happy meal. A guests hands me a 4x beer, and I savour it happily with my meal, feeling satisfied with my efforts so far, as the good vibrations are humming and everyone is in fine spirits.

It proves to be a busy job, partying on into the night, then chaperoning those who want to party even more, ashore to the resort bar and pool table. Lucky we're all so tired as sleeping 17 people on such a small boat is fairly crowded. Up early, help prepare breakfast, take everyone ashore for the aboriginal cultural show, sail down to Tongue Bay for the night, more parties and taking guests over to other boats to party more. Next it's the big day walking over to the magnificent Whitehaven Beach, getting my lethargic crowd into a vigorous game of volleyball, then sailing up to the north coast of Hook to take in the superb snorkelling there.

Three days of non-stop action, and as we dock up back at Abel Point Marina everyone gives me three hearty cheers. My piratical boss is on hand looking fairly amazed. "That's the first time I've heard that. They must have had a good time!" he exclaims with the gleam of money in his eyes. The jobs not over yet for I must head out for dinner with all the gang and then join them for a night club crawl, with the skipper being shouted free drinks for bringing his crowd in. When I finally return to my beloved and cosy *Longnose* in the early morning hours, bleary with drink, I'm totally worn out, drifting slowly into a warm and contented sleep.

Things continue in this positive mode for several weeks although not without trials and tribulations. Awaking the next day, I am only just enjoying my morning coffee, admittedly it's 10.30, when the Ozsail boss rings up keen for me to skipper *Carefree* tomorrow. All the next morning is spent scrubbing months worth of guano off her decks. While filling the water tanks in the marina, making ready for the imminent arrival of the guests, one of the tanks blows, sending water everywhere. Shoddily built ply glass affairs installed to handle the high demand of a horde of backpackers all wanting regular showers. No such luxury on this voyage it seems.

This 2nd trip is marred slightly by a trying hostess/deckhand who has her heart set on becoming a skipper and can't wait. She spends most of the trip belittling me to show that she would be a better skipper and has none of the easy going fun charm of Angela. Nevertheless we enjoy a good trip, and the work keeps rolling in. Unfortunately the pay is fairly average, less than $100/day as one is living the high life, sailing on a boat and partying every day with meals laid on, which is the real reward, supposedly. This is all very well, yet my true purpose is to earn money.

Generally all the different boats I take out prove not up to the standard I imagined they would have to be, having just completed my studies, lectured continually on the high level that yachts under survey must meet. It seems that what happens in practice is another matter entirely. In the back of my mind I begin to think that perhaps it is not an impossible dream to consider getting *Longnose* up to survey,

With half a dozen trips under my belt, the blow suddenly falls, just when I am really getting used to the party pace of the job and in constant demand by my employers. While enjoying a rare day off I am chatting with one of my mates at the Whitsunday Sailing Club.

"Yeah so where did you get your Master V ticket Andy?" asks my bushy bearded old seadog, a barnacle on the Airlie waterfront.

"Oh gosh, it was a drawn out drama that. Studied for it at the Ballina TAFE Jimmy."

"Oh, NSW ticket then! Your not going to like this mate! Pissed off in fact, to know that a NSW ticket ain't valid up here in Queensland. It's plain crazy stupid, a sane person would think it valid Australia wide, but foolishly it's not!" There's pity in my old mates eyes as he lays this piece of bureaucracy at my door.

"What, you've got to be joking? You're not are you! Hells bells!" Making my way back to the sanctuary of *Longnose,* torment takes hold of my heart. The next day I set off on a trip knowing that if something goes wrong, I'll be in deep trouble. While I'm still able to hide my concern from the guests and have a great time, I realise this must be sorted out pronto.

Back in town I contact the maritime office of Queensland Transport, outlining the situation but of course not exposing that I am currently employed as a skipper.

"Naw mate, it's not that easy. NSW operates quite differently to us." A nonchalant clerk drawls in a disinterested manner. "We won't accredit your sea time, so the only way you can get a Queensland ticket is to log your hours up as a deckhand."

Feeling the blood rising to my head, I feel angry and disgusted. "Yeah, I've seen what goes on here in your great Queensland system! You can get your skippers ticket by just logging time doing maintenance on the dock and you've got green teenagers doing 6 months as a deckhand then becoming skippers with barely any experience. Here's me with a lifetime of genuine yachting experience and your brilliant system 'won't accredit me!' I've gone through all the drama of getting accredited in NSW, thinking like a sensible person would, that I'd be able to skipper boats all over Australia. Now I have to stomach the thought of starting again and being a deckhand under someone with none of my skills?"

"Yep, that's about it mate. Can't do anything for ya! Anything else I can help you with?"

I'm tempted to tell him to get a brain but just hang up and storm off. Angry and in a daze I row back out to *Longnose* sweating under the hot tropical sun. No breeze has sprung up yet and the heat feels cruel and unjust, the world an unfair place. Brewing some tea I gather my thoughts in the cool cabin. It doesn't seem that my destiny lies here, away from my family, making poor wages. Sure it's a wonderful life, yet such crazy officialdom has put paid to my prospects.

One thing I am allowed to do is work as a yachting instructor in a sailing school. Already my mind is ticking away at the possibilities of setting up *Longnose* as a sailing school, thus having the freedom of my own business. For now though I must complete two trips which I have already agreed to do, looking out the whole time for the appearance of an official looking boat, come to check skippers tickets.

Carolyn is understanding when I explain the situation and happy that I will be returning. I post an add on the noticeboards around town, advertising for crew to share costs on a voyage south. Three Irish backpackers excitedly join me at $50/day each, so I'm making more doing this anyway, perhaps this would be the way to go, pirate charters, beyond the law. Yet I have this sense of doing things properly and the sailing school dream grows.

Back in Moreton Bay, Carolyn and Mara have been missing me fiercely but doing their best to keep sorting the *Butterfly Lodge* out. The idea of creating a sailing school soon takes hold of us all and we devote our energy to the myriad of details such a plan entails. The *Escape Sailing School* begins to take shape.

We make banners and flags for advertising, the *Butterfly Lodge* studio is converted into a classroom, complete with a big part of one wall painted into a chalkboard. Classes are planned out and *Longnose's* safety gear is meticulously upgraded. It seems the perfect path for us. Get the sailing school up and running, get some cash flow happening, then start building the new boat in our spare time and eventually it will become the new sailing school vessel.

Unfortunately these are the easy aspects of the sailing school dream, the complex part is figuring out one's obligations under survey, none of which seem to be outlined anywhere. We only have dail-up internet so the information revolution hasn't broken on us yet. Somehow me and bureaucracy don't seem to get on that well, perhaps it's the pirate in me, refusing to keep banging my head against their wall, pleading to be let in. All the same I realise we need to embrace our society so I reluctantly push on.

Slowly we sort through issues like our mooring permit and getting a permit to operate a commercial boat on Moreton Bay. Meanwhile I can't help myself and buy a few sheets of ply to start building the chart table and seat module, the control station of our dream catamaran. Now my heart seems content, absorbed in this hard core wooden creation. It's 1.5m wide, built with the idea of being big enough to draw a 10:1 scale drawing. A boat designed on its own chart table, now that'd be tricky!

Soon the studio/classroom has its own chart table, which is quickly nabbed by Mara and her friends as the perfect cubby house. Life is good on Russell, Mara is doing a few days a week at pre-school, Carolyn has some work looking after a disabled boy and our sailing school is slowly getting sorted. Yet an email is about to arrive which will change everything.

It's late March, summer drawing to a slow end, the way it does in southern Queensland, where the winters have been barely warranting a jumper. I power up the trusty old Toshiba laptop, waiting patiently while Windows fires up and dial-up internet loads my emails.

"Woah, this is kind of interesting! Hey Carolyn there's an email here you might like to read!"

"You read it to me," she calls, busy painting the bedroom door a rather impressive earthy orange.

"Ok, here goes. 'Hello Andrew, Carolyn and Mara. You guys were recommended to us by your friends Bruce and Jean, who are our marina neighbours here in Toulon France. We have a beautiful Lagoon 55 and are looking for a skipper and crew to take us around the world. We also have a 4 year old daughter, so we kinda figure our kids could keep each other company along the way. We have our business back in the States so we can't be on the boat that much. So if you're interested, how much would you like to be paid to make it worth your while? Regards Paul.' My God, what about that for an offer?" I finish, my whole world going into a spin.

"Wow, that does sound amazing!" says Carolyn, who has put down her brush to join me by the computer. "As much as I like living here, it would be great to be out cruising the world again. Why don't you ask them for some more details. How much do you think we should be asking them?"

Carolyn doesn't seem too concerned about abandoning our sailing school plan, although for that matter nor am I. There seems a huge amount of paperwork and grey areas involved in the set-up and then there is the question as to whether we would be able to attract clients. On the other hand here is a chance to earn, say $5000 US a month. After 2 years we'd have $120000, which in my mind would go a long way to building our dream machine.

The whole idea is looking pretty attractive, so we send off an email expressing our interest. In reply, Paul is fairly excited that we seem eager to join them. "Yes, $5000US/month will be fine. You guys are going to love *Good Vibes!* 90' mast, all carbon construction, HUGE lounge area in the main saloon. She's loaded with fun toys, two windsurfers, two kayaks, two fold up motorbikes. All beautiful varnished wood interior, tv and video, a toilet and shower in every cabin, a HUGE table in the cockpit for relaxing at and enjoying snacks and drinks at sundown. This is to be a celebration of the success of our business and we want you to share it with us as our soulmates. Could we come out to Australia and visit you guys to, you know, make sure we get on OK?"

It all sounded amazing. Seemingly we had a benevolent, rich American couple, wanting to pay us for doing what we loved most. We did sort of feel we'd been a bit hasty in only asking for 5k a month, but to us it seemed a great deal of money. Two weeks later we nervously await their arrival at the Botanical Gardens in the heart of Brisbane, where *Longnose* lies anchored.

They arrive at the jetty looking fairly worn out as one would expect. After a cup of tea and biscuits we set off down river to escape the annoying wash from the city cats. Paul is keen to help, displaying that American inquiring mind and thirst for knowledge. When we hoist the main he bounds up the deck full of enthusiasm, his rather scrappy khaki shorts and shirt at odds with the huge wealth he hints at. He is a good fifteen years my senior, his suntanned features care worn, his brown hair thinning, grey flecks invading his youth, yet he works manfully hauling on halyards and sheets, so he probably works out at the gym.

"It's a nice boat you've got here Andrew and you sure know how to sail it," he says as we reach across Moreton Bay. Meanwhile Carolyn seems to be getting along fairly well with Catrina, who looks less comfortable aboard, sitting stiffly in the shelter of the dodger, but talking happily in her oriental way. Her neat dark hair and pale brown skin look to have had little exposure to the elements, yet she seems enthusiastic.

"Oh isn't this beautiful!" she proclaims, the sky a stunning blue and the sea barely ruffled by a gentle breeze. "When we finish this trip around the world, Paul is going to buy me a nice big home in Hong Kong, where I was born, and Candice can go to a good school there," she pronounces happily, squinting at the bright sun, creasing the corners of her eyes.

Young Candice has taken all her mother's looks and seems a bit of a handful. She is proving a bit needy and hard to satisfy, yet Mara is playing happily in the cabin with her. We feel sure they would get along famously given time.

Anchoring in our favourite spot inside the Tangalooma wrecks, the rusting dredges break the swell. Here the sea is remarkably clear, with coral and fish abundant about these interesting vessels, which once proudly dredged the Brisbane River. We snorkel, beach-comb, laze in the sun, watch the dolphin feeding off the resort at night and generally have a wonderful few days. They are helpful with the chores, understanding and interesting, yet there is only one incident, which we perhaps should have taken more note of.

Mara and Candice are playing on the back of the boat, geared up in their floaties, while we enjoy morning tea in the cockpit. There seems to be a bit of squabbling going on but we are doing our best to ignore it, when suddenly Candice shoots into the water. Paul rushes over and plucks her out, crying and spluttering.

"Mara pushed me in. Mara pushed me in!" she cries angrily.

"Did you Mara?" we ask her gently as she sits brooding in the corner.

"Yes I did! She was being horrible to me!"

We let the incident blow over and think nothing of it. Within two weeks we have packed up the house, sailed to Tin Can Bay and winterised *Longnose* very thoroughly. Before we know it we have two years worth of equipment, clothes and schoolbooks packed into quite a number of bags and we are boarding a Korean Airways flight with one-way tickets to Paris. Later we are to regret not thinking more deeply about Mara's little tantrum.

CHAPTER 11

THE NIGHTMARE

The fact there is no one to welcome us as we stagger off the train at Toulon Station does not bode well. The crowd thins out, leaving us all alone on the platform. We wait half an hour, sitting in the shabby foyer, beginning to feel rather dejected and confused as to what our next move should be. It's after 10pm, tired and hungry after our long trip half way around the world, we feel certain our affable American employers will soon bustle up with a most suitable excuse.

At last Paul rocks up, with barely a "welcome" uttered and hurriedly ushers us into a ratty old car. He seems more put out that he has had to leave his dinner to collect us, than pleased at our arrival.

He bombards me with all the problems he has aboard *Good Vibes,* by way of "hope you had a nice flight" type of normal niceties.

We trudge down the concrete jetty somewhat eager to catch the first sight of our new charge, which our employers have touted as "55' of luxury, the carbon fibre version with a huge rig that will frighten you!" From a distance the older Lagoon shape, with the steeply sloped cabin looks powerful, almost racy and a tinge of excitement rises.

As we troop aboard, the cockpit presents an alarming sight, every surface piled chaotically high with tools and equipment. Entering the saloon, Catrina's welcome seems flat and cold, "So you finally got here! Brought so much luggage!"

Candice pretty much ignores us and her greeting is equally disinterested. "You guys are here! Huh?"

Paul impatiently urges us to bring the luggage into our cabin, where things get off to a bad start. "Did you put this suitcase on the floor?" He demands in a harsh tone that surprises me. In fact our friend Bruce, who greeted us on the jetty, had put it there, but he gives me no time to point this out. "Look!" he hisses "Can't you see these metal feet will scratch the varnish?" I look down at the finish on the sole, which is remarkably scratched and blotchy already, feeling stunned.

"Sorry," I manage. "We do plan to throw that case away."

He continues now to ramble on with a stream of information, as one would lecture a child."Now don't go splashing water on these bathroom lights, and don't flush the toilet for more than 8 seconds........." on he goes as we listen in astonishment to this unfriendly welcome. Reluctantly he finishes his lecture as though we will never understand and herds us back up into the saloon. Catrina motions to a few soggy bits of pizza lying on the table in their box. We hungrily devour our single slice of old take-away and try to take in our new vessel, ignoring the dismal welcome. They offer Mara a cabin of her own, but it's piled high with boat parts and other junk, the offer seems only half-hearted.

"Thanks guys, but we'll be ok all in the one cabin, and Mara is a bit young to be on her own," I suggest trying to be diplomatic.

"Our Muzzy has her own cabin!" shoots out Catrina in a superior tone, thus introducing us to Candice's pet name.

I stay up well past midnight, looking over the boat with Paul, hoping to show him my knowledge and familiarity with the systems and equipment, which are in a state of disorder and confusion. For all my efforts, Paul is certainly behaving far more like a tyrannical boss than a soul mate. As the new captain of the ship I had thought my boss would show a little respect for my opinions, but on the contrary he treats me like someone who has never been on a boat before. This is very discouraging and when I finally sink into our bunk my spirits have sunk very low indeed. What kind of crazy adventure have we got ourselves into? How welcome it feels to fall into the oblivion of sleep, too tired to dream.

Shrugging off jet-lag and lack of sleep I awake early, determined to sort things out. We have given up so much for this and I really want to make it work out. I power up the HF radio and try to tune into the morning weather sked, but it seems unable to tune into any station at all, picking up only static and crackle. I pick my way out through the cluttered cockpit, into the cool morning air to take in my surrounds. Toulon is certainly not the most beautiful French seaside town and the ugly grey buildings that circle the marina are not very uplifting.

Relieving myself in our toilet, careful not to use the noisy electric flush for more than 8 seconds, to my alarm the most foul stench fills the head and follows me out into the saloon. Feeling embarrassed, I realise something is seriously wrong with the toilet system. Carolyn is up industriously working away in the galley making coffee, yet it seems even life's simple pleasures such as coffee are to prove complicated. There is a large supply in the pantry of vanilla flavoured coffee from California, which to our taste, destroys the real flavour of coffee and leaves us feeling most unsatisfied.

When the Boss finally arises at about 9.30am, his long sleep has done little to improve his temper. "Morning," he mutters in a curt fashion. "What the hell were you doing up so early playing around with the radio?" he snaps at me.

"Oh..., I was trying to tune the HF into the morning sked to get us a weather report," I reply, as this is surely the captain's duty.

"Well don't ever do it again, understand?" he demands in a tone of finality. "Here's the list of jobs you need to finish today!" He thrusts me a couple of crumpled foolscap pages, filled with an untidy, barely decipherable scrawl. "Look, start here. Screw these saddles back on. Use these type of screws here, the ones with the v-heads."

"OK, the ½ inch countersunk, phillips heads. No problem I'll get straight too it," I say polity, keen to get to work and show my long experience in boatbuilding.

"Hang on now. You'll need the 3-M stuff, it's on the table, somewhere. The drill and drills, are somewhere there too. You'll need to drill a small hole first, and be careful not to go right through. Then get your screws, put some stuff on them, and carefully fit them in your holes. Now turn your screwdriver clockwise, until they're tight, but don't over-tighten them. Next clean up the excess, with a rag and turps, you'll find that over by the table too. When you've done there, report to me, and I'll explain the next job."

"I'll be OK to work through this list Paul. I have built entire yachts before," I say, stung at being treated like a 6 year old.

"We'll see. Make sure you put each tool away as you go," he demands. I can't help but cast my eyes around the piles of tools and equipment that litter every surface. "These jobs are pretty complex, we've been here for 6 months already and only managed half the jobs. That's with real professionals helping me," he blurts out a derogatory laugh and lumbers off to drink his coffee.

Carolyn is busy tidying up the galley when Catrina emerges from her cabin at 10am. Fresh coffee and a fine breakfast is all ready for her. "Here is your list of chores! You are to awake first, sweep and wash all the floors, while he is to towel down all the decks. After frying anything, all the contents of any nearby cupboard must be washed and wiped over and the floors swept on the hour. I'll be drawing up an extensive list of rules for you today," she announces, rudely pouring her coffee down the sink. "Only fresh coffee!"

As I wade through my tasks, I'm amazed and taken aback by how overloaded this Lagoon 55 is. Every storage space, nook and cranny is packed to the absolute brim with spares and equipment, even the old broken parts have been kept. Carolyn reports the galley overloaded with electric cooking aids. They have an incredible 15 toasters for instance and 5 rice cookers. None of which can be used beyond a marina, because there is not enough onboard power. Even under the fancy cockpit table, there is no room for one's legs because two folding motorbikes are stored there.

Meanwhile, out of the corner of my eyes I have to watch Mara sadly attempt to play with the ferocious Muzzy, who has been brought up with rough little boys "Nyyaarrr! You're not my friend! You cant play with those!" she shouts, wheeling her head like a club and thumping poor Mara. At the end of our first day's work, well after midnight, Carolyn and Mara are feeling pretty low.

"Catrina is impossible to work for! Nothing I do is right! This is so hard! What have we let ourselves in for?" We crash into our bunks exhausted, with no energy left to ponder this dismal turn of events in our lives.

Powering through my list of tasks, in the hope of impressing Paul just means he piles more jobs onto my plate until I am overwhelmed and feeling stressed. Catrina herself shows no ability to cook or clean, but sits about copying out recipes that Carolyn will be allowed to prepare. Her greeting each morning is to bend down and wipe her hand over the saloon floor then scowl at Carolyn as though it is not clean enough, even though Carolyn has it spotless.

The one thing she does do, is make Muzzy the only food she will eat, macaroni and some strange, highly processed, orange cheese powder or bread with ham and butter. "Ham and Butter! I want only ham and butter!" seems to be Muzzy's mealtime chant as she refuses to even try any of the fine meals Carolyn prepares and we worry how this difficult behaviour will affect Mara.

Working from dawn till late at night, there is never any suggestion of some hours off to see a little of Toulon. They do not like foreign foods, so we are not allowed to buy any fine French breads or cheeses, but have to get the processed sliced bread in a packet and processed Kraft cheese. After a few mornings of suffering the Boss's vanilla flavoured Californian coffee I decide to take the risk and head off to town early before he awakes and buy some proper fresh ground French coffee. It's my first taste of freedom to be wandering around the town alone savouring a quiet walk. Back aboard the Boss notices the coffee is different.

"What's wrong with the coffee this morning?" he demands after his first few mouthfuls.

"Well, we prefer just plain coffee so I bought some in town. With our own money of course," I explain. "We'll make some of your coffee for you if you're not fond of it." I add reading the expressions on their faces.

"What's wrong with our coffee?" demands Catrina. "It always tastes good when I make it," she spits out angrily. She is never to make coffee the whole time we are aboard. Anyway, having suffered their anger, we can at least enjoy decent coffee for breakfast!

"We simply have to make this work!" I whisper to Carolyn, who is washing all the galley cupboards and has literally hundreds of pots and pans neatly washed and dried, covering every workspace as she spring cleans the galley. "If only we'd bought return tickets, we'd be out of here in a jiffy, but as it is we'll need to stay on for at least a month to pay our way home." I plough through my work desperate to get us out cruising where I hope things will improve, yet beginning to wonder about my position as captain.

The Boss certainly does not treat me as anything of a captain and constantly refers to his French friend, the "highly experienced" Jacques who he hopes will be able to join us for the Atlantic crossing. Another thing that gives me doubts, is the condition of the safety equipment. The life raft is 2 years out of service, the flares way out of date, the HF radio doesn't work, even the VHF performance is fairly poor, and in general much of the equipment is a bit dodgy.

When I try to tell Paul the life raft and flares need renewing and some of the equipment doesn't work, he lashes out at me, "What would you know! They look alright to me and we paid a huge amount of money for this boat and the equipment is all first class!"

What can one do when faced with such adamant logic? It may have once been an expensive, fancy boat 15 years ago but the fact is, she has been neglected in a marina for many years and much of the equipment is well past its prime. As the captain I will be liable for any accidents, so I begin to wonder whether I would want to be in charge of this ship anyway.

One day the Boss and I are down in the toilet, dealing with an exploded holding tank and a bilge containing the last two weeks or more of its foul contents. The Boss is kneeling on the floor making difficult suggestions about how I can deal with it, when suddenly Muzzy, dreaming her way along the deck above, steps though the hatch and lands fairly neatly on the Boss's shoulders, giving them both a dreadful fright.

Another day Muzzy is strutting about on the wharf, eating her "ham and butter" sandwich and the next thing we know she has strolled right off into the water. Having been rescued all she is concerned about is the loss of her "ham and butter, ham and butter!" She will not let up until she gets a replacement, which means Carolyn has to drop the dozen things she is busy with and ask around the other boats for some more bread as we are all out.

Our Bosses own two companies so we had imagined them living a grand, rich life. In actual fact they seem to live very poorly. Paul's work clothes are two pairs of Speedo swimmers, one pair to cover up the holes in the other. During our time in Toulon, we dine out only once in a rather cheap pizza place, to celebrate Paul's 50th birthday. Fortunately Paul is a wine snob, so each night we drink expensive wine with Carolyn's fine cuisine, which is heavily limited by Catrina, who will only allow her to cook the most unadventurous recipes.

"So Paul, things are looking pretty shipshape aboard now. We could easily leave the marina and set off," I suggest carefully. It's been two weeks and we've achieved wonders in making order on *Good Vibes*.

"We'll probably go tomorrow," he replies gruffly, his stock standard reply every day for another week. I persist with my suggestion that we are ready to leave the marina and finally he reluctantly concedes.

Paul is a bundle of nerves as we sail out to the beautiful Porquerolle Islands, which is a breath of fresh air after 24 days in a crowded, stuffy marina. Finally a ray of hope creeps into our hearts, with the magic of the clear blue Mediterranean seeping aboard. Yet our dreams are soon to be shattered.

That night the Boss announces we now have a deadline organised. *Good Vibes* needs to be in Cephalonia, Greece within 12 days, as they have booked tickets to fly home to sort out business troubles. This means no pleasant lingering in beautiful places, enjoying the delights of France and Italy. Now we are faced with a testing 850 nautical mile dash across the Med to an airport.

Departing at 5am, hoping to make the 115 mile run to the Port of Calvi, on the north-west coast of Corsica, we must leave the joys of the Porquerolles to the imagination. Luckily we have a fair breeze and a bright sunny day, the sea a deep blue so our trip begins well. Just before noon we catch a nice small tuna.

"Look, Chow Mein, your favourite! We can have Ahe seared tuna for dinner," Paul calls out in a rare moment of happiness, using his cringe-worthy, affectionate name for Catrina.

The breeze is modest and steady so I talk the Boss into allowing me to hoist the kite in a effort to reach Calvi in reasonable time. He's very reluctant, having never flown it before, yet when the sock releases the green and white mass of nylon cloth, it snaps open in that majestic way and begins to pull us along nicely at 9 knots. Paul seems very nervous, yet pleased at the same time. Now we stand a chance of arriving before dark. After a fine lunch that Carolyn prepares, both the Boss and Chow Mein become sleepy. With full bellies and the relaxing motion of the sea, they disappear into their cabin to nap. This leaves me hand steering alone on deck which is a rare chance to enjoy some peace.

For over two hours it's glorious sailing as old *Good Vibes* surges along, the world beginning to seem bright and hopeful again. Eventually I feel it prudent to check the navigation and trim the spinnaker. Carolyn is down in our cabin taking a well earned break with Mara so I nip in to engage the autopilot. Unfortunately in the time it takes me to engage the pilot, we luff up enough for the kite to collapse and this brings the Boss dashing out of his cabin.

"What the hell are you doing?" he shouts as I work to get us back on course. To my horror I notice a piece of the leech has caught in a spreader end. There is a small rip already and I fear that any action, either easing sheets or lowering the kite will make this rip worse. "I knew this would happen if I left you alone!" growls the Boss as I consider my bleak options.

Now everyone is on deck, Chow Mein scowling and Carolyn and Mara looking worried. Taking the only obvious option, I hurriedly begin to free climb the huge spar. It takes a super human effort to reach the second spreader and pull the kite off the protruding strut. Returning to the safety of the deck we drop the kite, which thanks to my efforts only has a small insignificant rip. Yet this does not spare me a harsh reprimand, the Boss now treating me with zero respect. Nevertheless I still must work hard on sail trim and navigation, if we are to reach Calvi before dark.

The breeze freshens and I harbour hopes we will not have to make a night entry into this foreign port on a boat, whose systems are proving distressingly faulty. It looks like being a close thing before we hook up another tuna, a big one this time, which entails stopping the boat so the Boss can valiantly play the fish on his rod. After a prolonged battle we land the beast and can once again be on our way, losing a vital half hour. Now I have to fillet this big bluefin tuna out on the boarding steps for another half hour, covered with blood and unable to trim the boat or check our navigation. It is certainly a fine fish, on that score I cannot complain.

Entering port in the dark proves quite stressful with the Boss constantly looking over my shoulder and belittling my efforts, rather than trying to help. Later that night, safely anchored, eating Carolyn's fine beef bourguignon and drinking a Bordeaux cabernet franc, we should have felt elated, having successfully completed our maiden passage together, arriving in exotic Corsica with two good fish chilling in the fridge. Unfortunately it seems our employers just want to grind us down and make us feel low, for a single small mistake which I had sorted out so quickly.

Having given up such a nice life, to travel here and find ourselves disrespected and poorly treated feels like a physical shock. Knocking off around midnight after yet another disappointing day, we discuss our dilemma. As things stand, we are that cast down, we would happily pack our bags and leave tomorrow. Having paid two years storage for *Longnose,* we are deeply committed to this enterprise and conclude that it is necessary to knuckle down and endure this work for as long as we can stand. There is the promise of our bosses leaving for a month in Greece, which gives us an element of hope to live for.

After a day anchored off the magnificent town of Calvi, where I spend most of the time working in the engine room and Carolyn endlessly cleaning things that are already spotless, we sail on to Elba. Once again we barely glimpse the wonders of this historic town as the bosses seem disinterested in the charms of European history and culture. Carolyn wants to buy some fine Italian bread from a proper bakery and some real sliced ham for Muzzy's "ham and butter" sandwiches, but Chow Mein rudely turns up her nose at such an idea and insists on buying sliced white bread and pre-packaged ham from her shiny supermarket.

Thinking the children could do with some good quality eggs, she purchases a box of free range eggs. Unpacking her purchases back aboard *Good Vibes,* Chow Mein flies into a fury. "Who told you to buy free-range eggs? These are too expensive! Take them back and get the no name ones," she demands. So at great expense in outboard fuel and time I drive Carolyn back into the harbour, while she takes back her free range eggs and exchanges them for the caged, no name brand, at a saving of less than one euro. For such rich people they certainly do not lead wealthy lives!

Good Vibes, being an extremely overloaded cruising catamaran, with none of the promised sail area, does not sail well in light breezes. We are forced to motor most of the way to Isla Giglio. Being on a tight deadline, we stay only for the night and head off again early, on a 120 mile voyage to the island of Ponza, motoring yet again. Of course the Boss cannot simply relax and read a book, as we cruise over the unruffled Tyrrhenian Sea, he frantically insists we spend our time polishing all the stainless. Even when we have every item on deck shining, he is not content. No! He goes and pulls out the spares box and sets me to polishing the spare shackles and fittings.

Slow progress sees us sailing overnight, but arriving in the amazing bay of Cala Chiaia di Luna is a just reward. The sheltered crescent moon bay is backed by sheer, towering white cliffs, with striking rock formations jutting out of the clear azure sea. Our bosses are worn out from the night sailing, and although they slept most of the night, return to their bunks for more rest.

We grab the opportunity to explore, unlashing the two plastic kayaks from the lifelines and setting off. Muzzy has been forbidden to watch noisy videos so she reluctantly joins us. The beach feels magic, with a few lazy tourists enjoying its peaceful charm. The sand is coarse and reflects the long history of the Mediterranean, with many of the grains being pieces of coloured glass worn smooth by centuries of wave motion.

"I don't like it here! I wanna go back to the boat," complains Muzzy, while we drink in the otherwise charming holiday feel. We paddle around the expansive cove and find an exciting sea cave to explore. As we row in through a narrow entrance, the cave opens out into a deep chamber, the clear aqua sea refracting light into the darkness. Mara and Carolyn are enthralled but Muzzy is totally out of her comfort zone. "I don't like it! It's horrible in here, take me back to the boat at once!" she shouts before bursting into tears. We linger for a short while, but soon have to bend to the vocal Muzzy's demands.

For the rest of the day we are set to work on *Good Vibes*, it seems we are to be on call 24/7, not even having an allocated day of rest. The following day I plead that we all go ashore to visit the main town of Ponza, yet the Bosses are not interested. Eventually they concede I can take Mara and Candice into town but Carolyn must stay aboard to prepare lunch. Behind the beach we set off to discover the town, walking through the ancient Roman tunnel, which is cut right through the cliff, leading out onto a tree lined road, which winds down to the town.

Ponza is a gem of Italy, it curls around a busy fishing harbour, where ferries arrive from the mainland. Moorish-style, cubed houses in faded raspberry pink and lemon yellow, rise steeply from the water, forming an amphitheatre around the bay. A myriad of stone staircases lead off in every direction from the bustling waterfront, lined with cafes, bakeries, restaurants and open air stalls. The air is filled with the exciting scent of fried fish, fresh coffee and baking bread.

Mara is enthralled by this uniquely Italian scene, with barely a tourist to be seen, while Candice seems not in the least interested. We stop for a gelato, where she will have only "plain vanilla" but I encourage Mara to get something more exciting. She chooses a raspberry pomegranate sorbet and we stroll along, enjoying our freedom. "It smells bad here! I want to go back to the boat now!" insists Muzzy, dragging our thoughts back to a place we had briefly forgotten.

One of the biggest conundrums of our work occurs every morning just after dawn. Paul, in his wisdom, ripped out the original engine powered eutectic refrigeration system and simply dumped in a huge, inefficient, 115v house fridge. Having very poor insulation and being front opening, this system is extremely power hungry. Catrina, regularly stands with the door open for 5 minutes, whilst trying to remember what she is looking for, which doesn't help the situation, cold air pouring out. Compounding this inefficiency is the fact that the inverter, which converts the boat's 12 volt supply to 115 volts is only about 85% efficient. So with no solar system and only high output alternators on the engines, *Good Vibes* electricity production is greatly lacking.

By early morning the batteries drop below 11.5 volts, which is extremely low and not good for battery life. At this voltage the inverter starts to sound an alarm, promptly waking us all up. When this first happened I got up and fired up the engine under our bunk, rather than the one in the owner's cabin, hoping not to wake them, but knowing the batteries desperately needed charging.

When Paul awoke he did not see things my way. "Jesus! What the hell were you doing starting an engine so early in the morning? You woke us all up, you know!" he growls.

"But Paul, the inverter alarm was going off, the batteries urgently needed charging."

"Don't ever start an engine before I get up - is that understood?" he demands. I try running the engine for an hour before we go to bed, but it seems the batteries simply can't handle a full night of running the power hungry fridge. Every morning we are faced with this catch-22. Either we turn off the inverter and get in trouble for letting

123

the fridge get warm or start the engine, either way we cop Paul's wrath.

Making the most of an early start to charge the ailing batteries, we set off motor-sailing, passing the Gulf of Naples to reach the famous island of Capri, shortly before sunset. A fresh west-south-westerly is blowing from which the island's anchorages offer little protection. Our Boss, owner of two major companies listed on the public stock market, is too mean to spring for a night in the comfortable marina, insisting we anchor off, open to the substantial sea and swell. We spend an uncomfortable evening, *Good Vibes* lurching and swaying in the disturbed sea. Chow Mein and Muzzy soon become seasick and everyone retires early to avoid being joggled about.

By morning the breeze has died off and the sea has fallen, so we enjoy our early morning coffee, as the Bosses sleep in. By 9am, with our chores done and still no stirring below, we decide to swim ashore with Mara riding on my back. The day is warm and the sea so refreshing. With no fear of sharks lurking in the crystal clear Mediterranean, we let the sea refresh our souls. Savouring the sun's warmth we walk up a quiet road and look down on the fancy yachts moored in the marina. Capri is an island that promises much, but not for us, as we soon spy Paul on the deck of *Good Vibes*, binoculars in hand, searching the shore for us. We hurriedly swim back to prepare their coffee, as of course Carolyn already has breakfast laid out in the saloon.

This is to be our last taste of Italy on this voyage. After a hurried breakfast we set sail, bound for the Straits of Messina, 150 miles across the Tyrrhenian Sea. Favourable but light breeze sets us on our way, while a balmy blue sea slips gently by, bathed in warm sunshine beaming down from a cloudless sky, life should have been full of joy. Yet one of the most disturbing times of the day is when Catrina gives Candice her school lessons, a time we begin to dread more each day.

Mara and Candice are only 4 years old, too early even for kindergarten. For Mara we are content to be showing her more of the world, hoping to experience new cultures and ideas, although the *Good Vibes* experience is proving way less of a cultural learning than we had hoped. Catrina on the other hand, seems bent on training Candice to be a childhood genius. Each day after lunch, she ushers her into their cabin for several hours of lessons. As much as we try not to listen, it is unavoidable, with Catrina getting more and more angry at her unfortunate student.

"That's not right, that's not right. You don't do it that way you stupid girl!" she can be heard shouting at the hapless Muzzy. Then the alarming striking of a ruler and sobbing, as Catrina frustratingly strives to raise Candice to the heights of her destiny in a private school in Hong Kong. It seems Catrina's only aspiration in life is to have a nice big home in a wealthy suburb of Hong Kong with servants to once again look after the bothersome Candice.

Meanwhile Paul, in search of his dream to sail the world, is doing little to lure his two girls into the ideal, with this Mediterranean cruise, which has become just a mad dash to meet a flight back home. Now he stubbornly refuses to use his valuable diesel, so we make a slow passage of 36 hrs at an average of 4.2 knots, to the Straits of Messina.

In the approaches to the straits, Paul's foolishness presents me with another insurmountable conundrum. A march of ships are bearing down on Cape Peloro, the north-east corner of Sicily, which seems to be making him increasingly nervous. "Now I don't want you to let us come closer than 2 miles to any ship! Is that understood?" he demands, looking flustered.

"Well, considering the straits are less than 1 ½ miles wide I don't see how we can manage that!" I reply, feeling forced to state the obvious, knowing such logic will not help to calm his rampant worries. He continues to pace about the wheel house, looking haggard and sending me dirty looks as we skirt along the edge of the shipping channel, with the ships unavoidably still ½ mile away, but looking monstrous in the moonlight and dull glow from the many lights along the shore.

It is here in the straits, rich with myths of sea monsters, amid the busy European sea traffic and cross channel ferries, we experience the strongest wind of the *Good Vibes* adventure. When we first met Paul he had painted a picture of this magnificent performance catamaran with a 90ft mast, questioning our ability to handle such a powerful boat. When we arrived and found the mast barely reached above 60ft I was a dumbstruck with disappointment. Now with the wind picking up to a decent 20 knots, *Good Vibes* hits her top speed of 10.5 knots, her moderate sail area finally managing to push the overladen cat up to hull speed. The breeze is simply funnelling down the channel, but Paul begins to act like a major storm is upon us.

"This is dangerous! We have to drop the main now!" he cries out on the edge of hysteria.

"But Paul, this breeze is just funnelling through the narrow straits. When it opens up in a mile or so it will die off and *Good Vibes* is loving a bit of breeze," I reply as rationally as I can, but no, he will not be placated. Only after we perform a nasty rounding up into the full force of the wind to drop the mainsail, all in the rather dangerous close confines of the narrow straits, will he quieten down. Now we are forced to motor along wasting our best wind. Sure enough, 10 minutes later the breeze dies right out and we are allowed to hoist the heavy main again.

After the stress of the straits Paul retires to his bunk for the rest of the night, but not before insisting whoever is on watch does a round of the deck every 10 minutes and refusing my gentle suggestion to start motor-sailing. We make only slow progress of 2 to 3 knots, with any sense of peace removed by the rapidly looming deadline. Morning sees us only 20 miles into our voyage across the Ionian Sea, still with 210 miles to sail before we make our destination of Cephalonia, largest of the Ionian Islands. Now we have a mere 2 ½ days to reach the island capital of Argostoli, find a secure anchorage and get them packed off to the airport. With only light zephyrs wafting across a lazy sea, our speed is down below 2 knots.

"Paul, you do know we have to average 4.3 knots to make Argostoli by the morning of your flight?" I suggest delicately, for he has awoken in a vindictive mood.

"Well what do you think you're doing? Why haven't you got the motors running?" he demands unreasonably. I shrug off the rebuff and fire up an engine. Normally I too like to use engines as little as possible, but one needs a higher performance boat for such ideals.

Now there is just one mission on my mind, getting them to the airport in time for their flight.

During this long sea passage, Mara is having a hard time playing with the beastly, bossy, insensitive Candice. Mara is not a great fan of watching movies, but Catrina constantly orders the two of them to "be quiet and watch dvd's." Even in this simple pleasure Candice is cruel.

"This time you can choose what dvd we watch Mara. So long as it's not *Lady and the Tramp* or *The Aristocats!"* which are the two gentle videos in her collection of rather violent movies. She knows Mara would really like to see them, so makes a point of not letting her.

At other times they are allowed to play hide and seek, "I know, why don't you hide under the chart table," she bullies. Mara reluctantly squeezes in, just wanting to try and keep her happy and win her friendship. Next Candice proceeds to pile up all the folding chairs so Mara can't get out and sneaks off to her cabin to watch a dvd. Now Mara is trapped, afraid to push the chairs out of the way and risk getting in trouble for scraping the floor and fearful of calling out and getting Candice in trouble. Eventually we find her there, looking sad and forlorn. Lifting the chairs away we give her a big hug and whisper to her that she will be free of Candice before too long, if all goes to plan.

The breeze remains light for the next 48hrs, glassing right out on the morning we motor into the deep bay on the south of Cephalonia, that leads to Argostoli. Paul is marching around grumbling about how I have used all his diesel, while Catrina is fussing about importantly, busily packing her bags, excited only that she will be leaving *Good Vibes* behind for a month. Candice is generally getting in the way, hoping for some attention but generally being ignored.

Of course Paul will not consider berthing up at the marina, which is fine by us, but we desperately need to find a suitable anchorage, where he will agree to leave us. It's looking very much like they could miss their 5pm flight to Los Angeles. Just over a mile north of the town we find a lovely cove, where a few local fishing boats are moored and some half finished houses adorn the hill behind. The anchorage seems perfect and even Paul concedes that his boat may be safe here. We drop anchor and then the rush begins.

Catrina launches straight into a mad panic when she realises they have only 4 hours to get ashore, arrange clearance for *Good Vibes* into Greece, then find a taxi to the airport, all on the first visit to a strange foreign town. Paul hands me a list of jobs to do while they are away. It is more than four pages long, his untidy scrawl less decipherable than usual.

"I want this boat looking like a show-boat by the time we get back, so don't go thinking you guys are going to have a nice holiday here," he says, giving me an evil grin, then launches into a half hour lecture. The gist of his rant is that we are under no circumstance to move *Good Vibes* from this anchorage and at least half a dozen reminders not to forget to close the hatches when washing the decks. Time is running short and I am eager that he gets on with their departure, so I nod my head regularly and agree with his every word. Finally Catrina begins to tug at his shirt, virtually dragging him down to their cabin to finish packing.

We quickly get dressed in our best shore going clothes, and grab our passports. I launch the huge RIB, with its 100hp outboard and centre console steering, that weighs down the stern of *Good Vibes*. The motor has been playing up and I want to ensure it's running and warmed up so no time is lost. To my relief it starts up nicely and I leave it idling while loading aboard their luggage. Catrina and Candice are keen to board the RIB, but Paul seems reluctant to leave *Good Vibes* in our hands.

"Now you won't forget to close the hatches when you wash down the decks will you? And under no circumstance move *Good Vibes* from this anchorage!" he commands, shoving the gear lever forward too quickly, stalling the engine. Somehow he doesn't have the knack of this motor, mercilessly turning over the starter motor in vain effort. He is looking sweaty now in his shore going clothes, which seem surprisingly scruffy, considering he is about to visit customs and take an international flight.

It only makes him more surly as I throttle back the accelerator and gently fire the engine into life. We roar across the bay towards Argostoli and moor up at the town quay. The waterfront looks exciting, but we have no time for sightseeing as we must find customs and immigration fast. Leaving the girls to arrange a taxi to the airport, we set off in search of the relevant offices. A disinterested Greek, points us towards the commercial shipping wharf, where the offices are apparently located.

"Jesus, is that the time? We've only got 2 hours to get this clearance sorted and get to the airport! You better get a move on!" growls Paul, now dripping perspiration in the Mediterranean warmth. The Greek Customs men look grand in their neat blue uniforms, while Paul has failed to heed my recommendations to wear long pants, the customary dress to show respect when gaining clearance. He treats the officers like his minions, putting on a commanding CEO voice, which undoubtedly slows down our progress.

Paul begins to get frustrated and even a bit rude, so all I can do is busily fill out the forms and smile understandingly at the bemused and angered Greeks. We must repeat this process again with the Port Captain and Immigration so our clearance is a long drawn out affair. Paul gets positively frantic and demanding as the minutes tick rapidly away in these offices of Greek bureaucracy, his behaviour simply bogging the process down.

Eventually our paperwork is done and we dash back to find the girls waiting anxiously, a taxi already loaded with their luggage. "What took you so long!" screeches Catrina, bustling Candice into the taxi.

Shaking Paul's hand as warmly as I dare, assuring him *Good Vibes* will be safe in our charge, does little to calm him. Even after the beastly time he has dealt us, my heart goes out to the man at this point, standing there, hair dishevelled, sweat rings under his arms, hardly the image of a successful company boss. We have at least got *Good Vibes* under way and managed to cross half the Mediterranean, but it does not seem Paul has made much progress, wooing his family into the joys of the cruising life. As the taxi drives them off towards their rapidly approaching flight, I feel almost sorry for them. For all their money they seem to live a fairly poor life.

Their departure leaves us a bit stunned, as if we have just woken from a bad dream. We gaze around in the remarkable clear Mediterranean air, the sea a glorious blue, ruffled by a gentle breeze, the town alive and bustling with people going about their day's business. Slowly, beautifully, the realisation spreads over us, we are suddenly free from the tyranny of the last 35 days. A month of blissful peace without Paul, Catrina and Candice making our every moment a misery, lies before us.

We set off into town, excited by the first real 'holiday feeling' we have experienced since landing in Europe. Here is a chance to re-charge our confidence for what will undoubtedly be another gruelling experience when they return.

CHAPTER 12

THE HOLIDAY

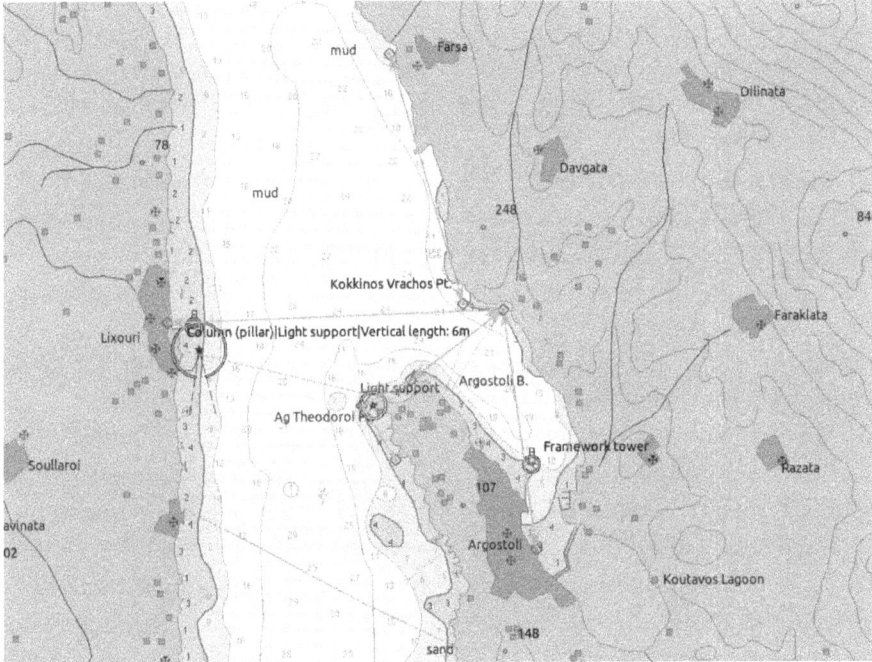

"Yeehaa! Look at this beautiful, exotic town we're in! Let's explore some of these amazing looking shops!" I call out joyously to my girls as we dance about happily on the cobblestone street, attracting some bemused looks from the locals. "Let's find you some treats my little chick! You've certainly earned some!"

The morning bustle of townspeople is slowing down as the oppressive afternoon heat floods the streets. We breeze into an authentic Greek deli, alive with the aromas of foreign food. From large wooden barrels we purchase tubs of olives, taramasalata (pinkish fish roe dip), tzatziki (yoghurt, cucumber and garlic dip), slices of a Greek-style pork sausage flavoured with oregano, fresh

131

butter, thick Greek yoghurt and a two litre bottle of local red wine. From the open air market we find crispy cucumbers, sun ripened tomatoes, baby cos lettuce, fresh black cherries and lastly from the bakery, we indulge with oven fresh Greek bread and rich sweet Baklava. Out in the open, the sun is fearsomely testing so we take our treasures and retreat back to the cool of *Good Vibes,* which can finally live up to its name.

Now, the Lagoon 55' feels welcoming, luxurious and spacious, which it never did with our employers on board. We unpack our shopping and lay out a feast on the cockpit table. Sipping wine and savouring the type of exotic food we have been forbidden, is pure bliss. A great sense of tiredness and relief floods over us as we sit quietly gazing at our new-found location. Our small cove is rimmed by a white pebble beach and a scattering of houses, a road snakes up through steep rocky hills, sparsely vegetated with the occasional clump of trees, inhabited only by a few goats. In our haste we have stumbled upon what seems the perfect place to spend a month.

Inside *Good Vibes* bridgedeck cabin none of this view can be admired. Although it is surrounded by large Perspex windows, they must all be kept covered as they let in too much heat. "I do like the look of the *Good Vibes* bridgedeck cabin, with its gradually sloped front windows, making it look kind of racy. She's certainly no greyhound though, overloaded and built like a tank!" Sipping wine and laying into real Greek fare, I finally have the leisure to assess this Lagoon 55. "It has some good points though, so I'll take lots of measurements while they're away. I'm sure I can build something that will sail better than this!"

*

"Huh, old Paul thinks we'll be battling to work through his mighty long list!" I burst out with a happy laugh. "Luckily he doesn't understand what clever boatbuilders we are. We'll sail through this lot with ease and have plenty of time for leisure." We've been working steadily through the cool of early morning, yet now the fierce Mediterranean sun beams out of a cloudless blue sky. "It's getting too hot for working now! Who's for a swim!"

Diving into the clear azure water of the cove we savour its refreshing power. Swimming towards the shore, Mara riding on my back, up-wellings of icy cold spring water surprise and chill us so we scramble up the rocky beach, our skin smarting from the cold.

Warming up in the hot dry air, we set to building model catamarans from bits of foam and sticks, using plastic bags for sails. Launching them in the cove, we race about watching their progress, as they make epic voyages along the foreshore and sail into miniature harbours to replenish supplies. Eventually they're destroyed on the rocks in terrible storms.

At the back of the beach, branches of an apricot tree hang over a fence. "Yumm, this flavour is so sharp and sweet, so full of real taste! This is the best apricot I've ever had!" Time moves slowly in the manner of a young child to whom every hour is an eternity of new discovery.

"Can we go to town on the Booffer boat?" asks Mara. It's 9pm and the hot Mediterranean afternoon has just begun to cool. Boarding the inflatable, we zoom towards town, booff, booff, boofing as we crash over waves, tying up at the old stone waterfront with the fishermen. In the relative cool of darkness, Mara insists we visit the old playground, with its giant slippery-dip, edges rusty with age. Freed from the tyranny of Candice, she can enjoy the simple pleasures of the merry-go-round and the see-saw.

As these pleasant days slip by, we often make a holiday during the heat of the day setting off in the "booffer boat" to explore the many coves and beaches of this vast surrounding inlet. Refreshing our souls in the cool sea, snorkelling amongst the seaweed and white rocks, urchins and occasional fish. Ashore we roam about picking wild figs and mulberries in the hot, dry, herb-scented bush and marvel at the smooth alabaster stones of the beaches, polished by the eternity of history, which seems so tangible in Mediterranean waters.

Dreamy heat washes over us as we land on Fanari beach, a little way to the north of the town. We splash water up joyously with Greek families, who prance about like comedians, trying to mount their crazy assortment of inflatable toys. Life is good again and we wish it could last forever, yet always the return of our employers hangs over our heads, like a guillotine.

Emailing the Boss with the news all is well on *Good Vibes* and that work is progressing well, is a chance to remind him to deposit our first month's wages into our account, for God knows we have worked hard enough for it. In reply, Paul demands I ring him on *Good Vibes's* Sat-phone, one of the newer pieces of equipment aboard, which actually works. Regardless of the immense cost of making calls via satellite we often had to endure Paul's long conversations to people he was obviously trying to impress.

"Yeah Ralph, we're just sailing past the island of Capri (which we had barely seen from a rough anchorage and the cost of this call would have paid for a comfortable marina berth).....*Good Vibes* is doing an easy 12 knots under sail (when we are motor sailing at 7 knots).....Yeah we're on our 2nd voyage around the world (this after a brief Caribbean trip, where they had the boat shipped to Toulon France, and you know the voyage so far)......Yeah Catrina and Candice love it, they're becoming real sailors (meanwhile Catrina is beating Candice with a ruler down in her cabin, totally disinterested in this voyage)." On he would go, every word a shallow lie, designed to impress.

Rather reluctantly I call him early in the morning, Greek time, to catch him in his office back in California, obviously after a trying day's work. He cuts me down as I begin to report on the good work we have been doing aboard.

"You better not have moved *Good Vibes*! You haven't changed anchorage have you?" he demands.

"No... Of course not, it's a very good spot here...."

"Well you better not move that boat, and for God's sake don't forget to close the hatches when you wash down the decks!" Nothing has changed here and he is very abrupt with me when I ask about our wages. Fortunately, he does not bother to talk to me for long. "And try not to break anything!" is his exasperated farewell. Once he has belittled me sufficiently he hangs up.

Something of the nightmare floods back after this encounter with the Boss. Later, while putting a 2nd coat of paint to the dive tank holders, I notice an older lady rowing out from the shore. Her weather beaten olive skin reflects a hardworking life, her clothes neat and simple. "Kalimera! Please excuse my Inglise. I see you have baby on boat. I think baby must have fresh eggs, so I bring some for you." She lives in one of the houses that overlook the cove and on presenting us with a handful of freshly laid eggs, invites us all for dinner that night.

Carefully we tie up the "booffer boat" in the rocky cove, then climb the steep stone stairs up to the small church and house. Argostoli Bay stretches out before our eyes, the sea sparkling in the diffused light of late afternoon. As we admire the sights a tall, elegant fellow strolls over to us, "Hello, welcome! Welcome to our family home. My name is Vangelis, it was my mother who brought you the eggs." He leads us inside the small whitewashed house and introduces us to the numerous members of his family. Mara, engulfed by a flock of children is given a generous glass of lemonade, while Vangelis's brother in law, Costas hands us icy Mythos beers.

"We are honoured to have you and your family with us Mr Andrew!" With a wide grin this stocky young Greek takes me outside to light the BBQ. Loading up the low metal tray with pieces of hardwood, he tells me of his life driving trucks on the harsh bitumen highways of Greece. The wood blazes cheerily in the growing darkness, Vangelis brings out more Mythos, "So Mr Andrew, tell us of your life aboard this beautiful catamaran,"

"Well we were hired by these rich Americans as skipper and crew. When we first met them they pretended to be very nice, said they wanted soulmates to celebrate their lives with. Yet when we began to work for them they suddenly became the most tyrannical bosses you could imagine!" I begin, launching into stories of our unfair treatment. My two Greek friends listen patiently, sipping their beers and staring at the fire.

"Things have not been easy in our lives lately either," says Vangelis, having heard my story in some detail. "Since they have replaced the Drachma with the Euro, everything has become so much more expensive. Because we are paying for other countries to join this European community it's making life much harder for us." Our own woes begin to seem trivial on hearing how hard my Greek friends must work to make ends meet. Their own dreams of building a big family house in this wonderful spot are now out of reach in the current economical climate, a parallel to my boat-building dream.

Mara troops out, surrounded by her smiling gang of olive skinned children. "Look Puppi, I have all these nice friends!" Her joy is contagious and the men burst into smiles to see all the children so happy. Nina, the elder of this group, is looking after Mara most lovingly, a beautiful girl with shiny black hair, a picture of health, fun and caring without pretence. Bathed in hugs, Mara is in heaven.

The children's joy shifts our thoughts from life's difficulties. By now the wood has turned to glowing coals and the lamb cuts, sausages and fish are laid over a grill. Pungent wafts of wood smoke and sizzling meat drift about the warm night air, the honey sweet Mythos beer has us merry, our appetites sharp. Carolyn is having a splendid time learning Greek recipes with the grandmother and wives, where the children are given big chunks of feta to ward off hunger. "When did you last eat Costas?" By now it is past 11 as the kids munch happily on the feta, leaving me a bit envious.

"Oh, for breakfast I just have coffee on my way to work, maybe a biscuit. Then I work all day with no lunch, just running the whole time on a big dinner." When the food arrives I begin to understand how a man could go all day on just the one meal. Our plates are piled high with the grilled meats and fish, a great hunk of fresh Greek feta cheese, fresh garden salad and baked pasta served with red wine. Next we have the grandmother's stew, a succulent slow cooked dish of tomatoes, onions, potatoes, herbs and an unfortunate rooster. More wine and then baclava and Greek cakes from the bakery where Vangelis's wife works. It's well after 1 am when we make our way back to *Good Vibes* under the canopy of stars, which seem to shine so much brighter after the genuine friendship we have just experienced.

Next afternoon Nina and her younger brother Jimmy paddle out to *Good Vibes* and we all enjoy a swim off the transoms, which for them is a novel experience. A few days later, Nina's father Vangelis, takes me fishing off the rocks in the cove, while the children play about the foreshore. Under an old overhanging tree we bait up our hooks with flour and fish food mixture. The lines are exactly the length of the long rods, so that when the rod is lifted up the hook swings into one's hands for re-baiting. We catch dozens of the local herring that school prolifically in the cove. As we fish a dog pursues a goat along the rocks. So desperate is the goat to escape she jumps into the sea and goat-paddles out of the frustrated dog's reach.

The children help scale the fish then we head up to the house to barbecue them over the coals. Their crispy skin and sweet moist flesh goes down easily with a few bottles of Mythos beer. "I think we should call this island, Nina's Island! Don't you Mama and Pupa?" says Mara, loving her newfound friend. Life feels quite idyllic yet the days are quickly disappearing and the imminent return of our employers begins to weigh us down afresh.

Every job on the list has been completed and *Good Vibes* is genuinely looking like a show boat. All her gelcoat is polished to a gleam, her stainless steel shinning, engine bays fit to eat off, she is spotless. On the eve of the dreaded return of Paul, Catrina and Candice, the watermaker is running, topping up the tanks, when all of a sudden it shuts down. This is a great concern as the ability to make water is of the utmost importance on a boat, especially with the owners aboard. They use water as though by magic *Good Vibes* is connected to the council pipes.

Carefully checking over the watermaker systems, there seems no obvious problem. Hunting out the instruction manual I ponder over the complex circuit diagrams, breaking out in a nervous sweat, as I can clearly see Paul's reaction, if he returns to find the watermaker not working. Even if the fault is none of my doing, I know he will blame me.

Sweating away in the forward locker, open to the burning afternoon sun, I study every connection, undo every possible part of the machine, no matter how complex it looks. Beginning to panic, knowing I must find the cause or face the grim thought of greeting Paul's arrival with the news that the vital watermaker isn't functioning. While considering this unpleasant moment I unscrew one of the relay housings and find a burnt out contact. Eureka!

Short circuiting this relay, the watermaker runs perfectly. I try cleaning the contact, but to no avail. I must try to find a new relay and fast. Carolyn and Mara wish me luck as I roar off to town in the "booffer boat". On foot I visit all the car spare parts shops. They recognise the relay, which gives me some hope, but no, sorry, they have none in stock.

My last chance is a wrecker's yard some distance out of town. Worn out, having given up all hope I dejectedly show the relay to an ancient Greek man, hands blackened by years of oil and grease. Without a word he wanders over to an old truck, pulls a few tools from his deep overall pockets, then precedes to rustle around under the bonnet. Minutes later he nonchalantly hands me a scrappy looking relay.

I try to hide my joy to keep the price down, but my hero only asks for a few euro. I fairly run back to town and gun the old "booffer boat" to its top speed out of sheer delight, but have to settle down when it gets airborne. The girls are waiting for me, looking concerned, but they soon read the hope on my face. By torchlight I replace the rusty cover of my prize with the clean original relay box and fit it back into the machine. Now the big question is, will it work?

Firing up the genset, I flick the watermaker switch, rewarded with the welcome hum of pumps and pressure. Full of triumph, we enjoy our last supper in peace, hoping this next chapter in our lives will be more positive. Mara is sure that Candice will have missed her and will now want to be friends. Even Carolyn believes they can not fail to see *Good Vibes* looking in such good condition and begin to respect us at least a bit. Personally I have my doubts. I'm concerned it will surely be more of the same ill treatment and just pray I will be able to cope. At least we have enjoyed a delightful interlude and feel refreshed again before this next onslaught.

CHAPTER 13.

THE ESCAPE

With *Good Vibes* looking immaculate and a fine lunch laid out on the table to greet our employers back on board, I set off in the "booffer boat", for the dreaded reunion. They emerge from a taxi, clothes disappointingly shabby and skin pale again from their month spent in an office. An uncomfortable sense of foreboding, confusion and ill feeling instantly bombards me, replacing the peace and serenity I had been feeling. They jumble their baggage aboard the dinghy without much pretence of greeting me, even though I make a mighty effort to welcome them back. They treat me quite clearly as a lowly servant.

Paul takes the dinghy controls and renews his uncanny knack of being unable to make the engine run properly, even though it has been fine for the whole month of their absence. It splutters and dies as he seems to apply too many revs too early. Now no amount of cranking the starter motor will fire the engine again.

"What have you done to the motor? It was working fine when we left!" he growls. Everyone is getting hot and short tempered in the blazing sun. Knowing our situation is on a knife edge, I tactfully assist him in coaxing the engine back to life and we make our way out to *Good Vibes*.

Carolyn and Mara's cheery welcome is cast aside rudely as they pile aboard. Soon the boat is in chaos as they unpack and strew stuff everywhere, claiming back their territory obnoxiously.

"Clear this old food away!" Catrina orders Carolyn, who has had no chance to offer it to them as their lunch. I see the old hurt return to Carolyn's eyes. Later in the evening, the frenzy of their return has died down and they are sated by an excellent coq au vin - their favourite, one of the few slightly exotic dishes Catrina will allow Carolyn to prepare.

Having devoured the succulent chicken, pork and vegetables braised in wine, Paul has calmed down a bit. With a glass of excellent French shiraz in his hand, I take him on a tour of the deck explaining all the works we have carried out in their absence. Opening up the foredeck locker, I mention that the watermaker relay had blown.

"WHAT!" he cries out "I knew you'd break something, I knew I couldn't trust you!"

"But Paul, I've fixed it! And in no way was it my fault that relay failed and I paid for the new one!" I manage, stinging from the deep injustice of his words. Their long absence had been a wonderful tonic, soothing our nerves and ironing away the memories of our nightmare first month aboard *Good Vibes*. Now with their return, the whole unpalatable situation is flooding back all too rapidly.

Luckily we have said our goodbyes to Nina and her family. When the children come out to frolic off *Good Vibes* transoms, Paul and Catrina give them a frosty welcome. Although Candice seems keen to join in the fun, her bossy spiteful character rather spoils the usual joy of their visit. She can see that Mara has found a nice friend, so she leaps onto Nina's inflatable dolphin, bursting its seams. Nina takes no offence, but it is hard to ignore Candice's wicked grin. "Off you go! Off you go! Candice must do her school-work now," says Catrina, shooing away our friends.

We suggest a trip in the "booffer boat" to the beautiful Fanari beach, which we had enjoyed so much. Having coaxed them into this little adventure they are aloof and extremely disinterested and will stay for only a few minutes. The next day, Paul and I find a mechanic to overhaul the outboard, while the girls, under Catrina's command, stock up on the plainest food available. As we walk back to the mechanics shop on the outskirts of town, past rambling Greek houses with wild gardens, Paul becomes quite open with me.

"You know, my life is too busy, I never get to smell the roses. You're lucky. You seem to always smell the roses!" Perhaps affected by the brisk exercise, the fresh air and the unique landscape, he rather touches me in this candid moment.

"Well let's see what we can do to allow you to smell some roses too," I reply, yet his mind, as always seems to be elsewhere, while the wonder of the present passes by unnoticed.

We depart Cephalonia and head north through the Ionian Islands, arriving at Ithika's main port Vathy, a deep narrow cove, where Paul renews his pedantic anchoring methods. Admittedly the Mediterranean sea floor is notoriously difficult to set an anchor in, and the ultimate result is fairly seamanlike. It's just that the execution is so frustratingly slow, beginning with a long drawn out period of motoring about deciding where to anchor. Discarding my advice as usual, he picks the most difficult place. After dropping and hauling up the anchor 3 times before he is half satisfied, we can then begin his arduous, time consuming process of swimming out four or five long lines to the shore, tying onto trees and around rocks with lengths of chain and rope, which we swim over on a boogie board. Hours later, with everyone extremely hot and bothered, *Good Vibes* is bound up like a giant spider in her web, blocking up most of the harbour entrance.

Paul seems to have an expectation that yachting should be difficult; this mindset does make life trying. Now we are all thoroughly exasperated and worn to a frazzle. With not much of the day remaining, it is hard to really enjoy our magnificent location.

That evening Carolyn serves up a superb lasagne, with a fresh garden salad, accompanied by one of Paul's expensive wines, the only time we actually enjoy his snobbishness. After dinner he uncorks a second bottle of the Bordeaux rosé and begins to open up about the company troubles they've had to deal with.

"It's just impossible to find good workers to run our company!" he complains. "None of them will do what they're told, they're all lazy and stupid. We had to work like mad people the whole time, sorting out the books, sacking useless staff and finding new ones, who seem as hopeless as the others. The company is losing so much money while we're not there."

This sparks a grain of hope - perhaps they'll decide to spend more time back at work, leaving us with the enjoyable prospect of looking after *Good Vibes* on our own. Unfortunately he also lists off an extensive sailing schedule that must be achieved in the next few months, zooming all over the Mediterranean. While their tongues are loosened by the mellow rosé, we also learn more of their early days on *Good Vibes*.

"We bought *Good Vibes* in Port Lauderdale," begins Paul, slouched in a directors chair at the head of the cockpit table, dressed in his customary two pairs of Speedos and a scrappy T-shirt, quaffing wine. "She was a bargain, already proven by a world voyage. Being the all carbon version she is super light!" he waxes on about *Good Vibes* imagined great qualities, before getting down to the first voyage.

"Our skipper was an idiot! He came with the boat, but we should have sacked him straight away. Our first sail was a rough trip across the Florida Strait to South Bimini Island. When we got there the anchorage was pretty rough so he tells me to head further into the bay where it'll be calmer. So I drove on in and then the next thing we know, BANG, we hit bottom and one of the rudders breaks off!" Well I can imagine that would have been fun! The white sandy beaches and glorious aquamarine sea sparkling in the sunshine would have done little to calm Paul's raging temper.

"We managed to motor back to Fort Lauderdale on a calm day and hauled her out to repair the rudder. While she was out of the water we discovered the hull paint was peeling off. Somehow it hadn't bonded to the carbon, so we had to have the whole boat stripped and then repainted. Eighty thousand dollars later I decided we'd ship her over to France and cruise the Med instead." Somehow I felt he'd left a lot of things unsaid in this wrap up of *Good Vibes* illustrious history in his hands, a disastrous voyage of only 100 miles. It seems we've already achieved a great deal compared to their first trip so it's deeply confusing why they aren't a tad more grateful.

Sailing north, stopping at Levkas and Corfu, the uniquely vibrant Mediterranean sunlight pours magically over the Ionian Islands, whose trees, rocks and buildings emanate the rich history of human endeavour. To be sailing the Ionian sea is the chance of a lifetime, yet here we are on *Good Vibes*, in a situation which could be heaven on earth, feeling more like galley slaves, whipped by cruel words.

When we cleared into Greece, tactfully I played on Paul's ego and had him sign as the skipper. The state of the boat's safety equipment means I really do not want to be the one legally responsible. I bide my time, leaving the decisions to Paul, while keeping a sharp eye on his navigation to ensure we will be safe.

From Corfu we sail up the Adriatic and clear into Croatia, at the remarkable stone fortress of Dubrovnik. Here we take on friends of our employers, in the port of Gruz. Actually, the bosses barely know this family of four, having met them briefly in Toulon, where they grandly invited them to holiday in the Adriatic.

Their presence aboard in many ways improves the vibe, as Paul and Catrina and even Candice, try hard to appear the generous and fair owners. Charles, an amiable Englishman and his Korean wife Soo-jin are very friendly to us, as are their two teenage children, Grace and Harry.

Departing Gruz we sail for the town of Polace, on Mljet Island. Here Paul is disdainful of the town anchorage and insists on another complicated mooring off the point. Once again the eventual result is good but nerves are frayed in the process. Life is in balance, Charles pleasantly keeps Paul engaged in conversation, while the broad minded Soo-jin gets on very well with Carolyn, which prevents

Catrina being her usual rude self. Grace, who is a relaxed, sporting type, plays nicely with both Candice and Mara and Harry proves a good friend to me, playing chess into the evening.

With a light north-east breeze blowing, *Good Vibes* leaves Polace, bound for the natural harbour of Lastovo. Paul has me in charge as we sail gently across a placid sea. The rocky island of Glavat, boasting a large lighthouse lies directly on route. I plot a fairly close course so as to make the quickest time and provide an interesting spectacle, yet Paul spots this and blows up.

"What do you think you're doing? I told you not to go closer than 2 miles to any island!" he roars at me, going all red in the face with this burst of anger. It is such a calm day our guests are a little surprised at his outburst and our trip is lengthened by almost an hour due to sailing the extra distance. We arrive just before dusk and fortunately the large harbour provides a simple anchorage, which even Paul cannot complicate.

Soo-jin as usual gets up early with Carolyn and they do yoga together, before Carolyn sets about her chores, which Soo-jin wants to assist with. When Catrina awakes, it's amusing to see her putting on a false smile, having to contain her sarcastic comments, finger running over the floor and tut-tutting.

Later in the day we pull out the windsurfers, which are stored in large compartments under the bridgedeck. Paul becomes quite frustrated because he can't get the knack of sailing his board, while I flit about the bay having a great time. Luckily a fine dinner of sausage pasta, one of Catrina's strange recipes which Carolyn does wonders with, served with plenty of handsome glasses of pinot noir, calms him down, as a nice breeze cools the anchorage.

Sailing on to Korcula, (famous for being the birthplace of Marco Polo), we all head ashore to explore the old town. Soo-jin is very keen to prepare a special Korean beef dish and goes with Carolyn to the markets to buy the ingredients. Meanwhile we all buy ice-creams.

"I want plain vanilla! Everything else is horrible!" Candice demands, showing that her travels are not broadening her tastes while we all choose exciting and exotic flavours like blueberry, pumpkin seed, white chocolate, olive oil, lavender, Nutella, tasting the wonders of the world.

That afternoon Carolyn is discussing cooking with Soo-jin, asking her when she would like to start preparing her beef dish. Catrina, who is getting jealous of this friendship, overhears them and flies into a rage, dragging Carolyn aside. "How dare you talk to guests like that? You are the worker and you will not ask them to cook dinner. Also you will not make guests help you with your chores. Do you understand me?" she demands.

"But Soo-jin was offering to cook dinner Catrina! She likes to help!" Carolyn tries to explain.

"I don't want to hear any more of your lies!" Catrina shouts, her façade of being a kind benefactor slipping away.

We continue on to the ancient town of Hvar, where everyone is excited to go ashore and explore the cobblestone streets. Late in the afternoon Paul insists we depart the vibrant, safe anchorage and make for the small islets of Lukavci. We are quite happy to do this, but it's plain to see Catrina far prefers being in busy towns. Had he allowed her the night in Hvar, then perhaps she would not have been so sulky for our time in Lukavci.

Motoring fast in the calm conditions, we make it in time for an evening snorkelling adventure, which Candice and Catrina refuse to join. The rest of us whiz off in the "booffer boat" over a tranquil sea. Plunging in, we cavort in the undersea world, so pristine in the magically clear Mediterranean seawater, fresh and invigorating. Late afternoon sunlight streams through, lighting up complex rocks, seaweeds, sponges, shells and sea creatures all perched with such random neatness over fine white sand, that incredible dust from every aeon gone by.

While we return refreshed and satisfied, Catrina's conversation with Soo-jin shows where her mind is. "Hong Kong is such a tidy place, the homes are so beautiful, so big, with servants to look after everything," she waxes on sipping a little greedily at a glass of chilled Chardonnay. "When we have finished with this sailing, Paul has promised me we can go and live in Hong Kong and Candice can go to a nice private boarding school."

The Boss does not seem to have his family interested on the course he has set, of adventure and sailing the world. It seems he really needs to try tending to their desires a bit more, to fan some interest in this dream of his.

Bound south again, the guests depart from Korcula, taking with them the holiday feeling. We move on to Przina Bay on the south-west tip of Korcula Island. Here we spend Carolyn's birthday cleaning out the pipes of the five on-board toilets, which I have discovered are all thick with a grey calcium build-up. Some of the pipes are so chocked that barely anything can pass through them. Hours and hours of beating the pipes on the water and poking them with bits of stiff rope, cleans them out nicely so that when the toilets are flushed the whole boat no longer reeks of rotten egg gas.

While cleaning the pipes and the toilet components on the back transoms, I drop one of Paul's precious sockets into the sea. "What am I to do with you! You're so useless and that socket was very expensive. Now we wont be able to finish this job!" He rants away as I quickly don my mask and fins and dive into the welcome crystal clear bay. Finning down 12m I easily find the shining 7mm socket sparkling on the Adriatic sea floor. Also noticing a few pieces of fancy clothing scattered amongst the sand and weed, I quickly pick them up with the last of my breath and return to the surface.

Carolyn and Mara are anxiously awaiting my return, hoping I have found the socket to calm Paul down. It turns out the clothes are Catrina's, which she has failed to peg on properly, so she sends me back down looking for more. There are a several of her things scattered about, being examined by small fish, yet when I bring them up she shows no gratitude at all.

Later, Mara and I are allowed to take Candice ashore to explore, while Carolyn must stay behind to prepare her own birthday dinner. Having walked over the narrow spit of land in the summer warmth, we swim out to a small islet, Candice grumbling all the way, wanting to go back to watch DVDs. I open a black sea urchin, but find that without lemon juice it is undesirable, so drop it back into the sea. Here it attracts an octopus, whose tentacles curl around Mara's leg, causing her to scream. I grab the creature, throwing it up unto the rocks, thus capturing a tasty addition to Carolyn's birthday dinner. Returning to *Good Vibes*, Mara proudly blurts out, "Mama, Mama, I caught an octopus with my foot!"

"Oh, that's nice darling." Carolyn, worn out from her long hours without a break, is disbelieving, until of course we produce our prize. Paul and Catrina are disinterested, and will not even taste the dish of octopus cooked in red wine, I prepare. It does at least make this otherwise bleak birthday memorable.

Continuing south we make our clearance from Croatia in Dubrovnik, sailing back to Corfu, where we meet up with Paul and Catrina's lawyer, Ronald and his wife, Nancy. On route to Corfu, we try to reason with our employers. "Look, I'm sure you realise we aren't very happy aboard *Good Vibes*, perhaps if you could just try to treat us a bit more fairly, things would be a whole lot better for everyone," I venture nervously.

"You're so ungrateful!" screams Catrina, squinting her eyes evilly. "Look at this opportunity we're giving you! Without us you'd have nothing! Look at the good education we're giving your daughter! She'd have nothing if you weren't working for us," she hisses. Considering they had seen the nice life we'd given up to join them, it's plainly useless to argue with her.

"You should be much more grateful to us. I don't want to hear any more of your complaining," finishes Paul, parroting Catrina.

Ronald and Nancy turn out to be interesting and easy going people, but we are discouraged from talking to them. Paul and Catrina doing their best to ensure we remain aware of our worker's status, certainly not on equal footing with such company.

From Corfu we sail to Paxoi Island and anchor well out from the interesting fishing and tourist town of Gaios. After a day at Paxoi a fair wind blows and we make for the small harbour of Fiskardo on the very north of Cephalonia. *Good Vibes,* sailing nicely over a sparkling Mediterranean sea, has everyone in good spirits. We need to gybe, so I carefully centre the mainsail before bringing the helm across to set us on our new course. As the sail comes around, there is a crack high up and two of the upper mainsail battens are laying off crookedly.

"Jesus, you've broken the battens! You can't be trusted to do anything, can you!" yells Paul as we both look up at the main. "They're high-tech carbon fibre battens, it'll take months to ship in new ones, and we can't sail the boat without them. You've really screwed things up!" I'm feeling at bit stunned at this turn of events. There is no way the battens should have broken during such a gentle and careful gybe. Even a crash gybe in such a mild wind should not have damaged them. If they are so fragile in 10/15 knots of wind, they'll stand no chance in a typical trade wind of 20/25 knots. So much for *Good Vibes* high-tech carbon gear, they must have been cracked already.

"Well I should be able to repair them fairly easily Paul, and I've got to say that was a pretty gentle gybe, perhaps *Good Vibes* needs a sturdier set of battens."

"Look, this boat has already been proven by a world circumnavigation! You just don't know how to sail properly!" he roars, so it's no use trying to reason with him. Right now I am totally over Paul's unjust treatment.

We moor up in quaint Fiskardo, not along the delightful town reach where we would have to pay, but making a complicated moor to the harbour wall, just inside the entrance. Everyone goes ashore in the tender to shop and look about, while I set to, repairing the battens. Carolyn and Mara are on an urgent mission to find a telephone and ring my mum to see if our 4th month of wages have gone into our account. If it's there we've secretly agreed to pack our bags and leave this very evening.

Having pulled the long, awkward battens out of the sail, I set them up along the deck and coarse sand around the broken sections, to prepare them for glassing. After carefully lining the battens up so they are dead straight and setting up sheets of plastic under the work area, I wrap a considerable amount of woven cloth around the break, wetting it out with polyester resin, tapering the bandage so as to apply more cloth in the centre. Finally I tightly bind it all with clear tape to squeeze out the excess resin, maximising the strength of the repair.

By the time the others return from their foray into town, the resin has hardened and I have removed the tape leaving a perfectly tapered and neat repair, far stronger than the thin carbon tube. Paul merely grunts when he inspects my work and disappears inside to drink Heineken beer with Ronald, not even offering one to me for my efforts. Once Carolyn has unpacked the shopping she manages to come up on deck to give me the news.

"Well I spoke to your mum, she says some money has gone into our account, but she was in a bit of a dither, saying it was $2003. It should be over $5000, shouldn't it?" whispers Carolyn. This is a bit confusing and we dare not dash off now and risk not being paid for this last month of torture. We'd been feeling so excited at the prospect of suddenly being free of this whole nightmare and setting off on our own adventures. Admittedly the idea of confronting Paul and Catrina with this news seemed fairly terrifying, as they would surely try to over-ride and stop us. We certainly know it's impossible to reason with them, having already tried that.

Feeling a bit dejected and resigned to more long days aboard *Good Vibes* before we can find out for certain whether we have been paid, I struggle on and fit the long battens back into the sail.

By the time Paul and Catrina arise at their customary late hour and loll around over breakfast, we finally make way by 11am. Assisted only by a fickle light breeze we make slow progress, bound east towards the Patraios Gulf, which leads to the Corinth Canal and the Aegean Sea.

"Well, those battens look to be holding up in this breeze but I wouldn't trust them in much more," Paul sneers. "I'll have to order two new ones and try and get them delivered to Athens. That'll probably cost at least $2000, so you'll have to be more careful in future. At least Jacques will be aboard for the Atlantic crossing to show you how to gybe properly." I don't even bother to defend myself, knowing it's useless. This will soon be his problem and we'll be free, I think to myself, to calm my frustration at his cruel words. By late afternoon we have only managed 28 miles.

"Excuse me Paul." He's dozing at the saloon table, sweating profusely in the afternoon warmth. "I think we should anchor here, off Oxia island." Outside a dry, mountainous island presents itself several miles ahead, with a promising anchorage on its western side. "It's our best option this afternoon, our only choice really."

He shakes himself in an effort to lift his stupor, scowling at the island I have suggested. "What, that ugly looking rock! I'm sure we'll find something more attractive than that! No, lets press on," he says, settling back into his slumber, failing to study the charts to see there will be nothing we can reach before nightfall. As we enter the Patras Gulf, a brisk easterly wind blows up, generating a short uncomfortable sea, the sun getting low on the horizon.

"So where are we going to anchor for the night?" asks Paul, finally awoken properly.

"Well, we have two choices. 16 miles away we can enter the canal to Mesolongian, or we can continue another 45 miles to Trizonia, these are the only two comfortable anchorages available." I inform Paul, who is beginning to look stressed.

"Why the hell didn't you tell me that before," he demands. "We'll have to go to this Mesalongi place of yours!" After he has studied the chart for some time, he starts to look positively panicky.

"No way can we navigate that narrow channel!" he blurts out " I don't trust you to navigate there in the dark, there are too many ships and that channel is too narrow!"

"Well as I see it, you don't have much choice. You can navigate if you like, I don't mind either way," says I, fixing him with a sarcastic smile, totally over the guy.

For the next four hours, *Good Vibes* beats to windward, lurching into the steep unruly waves. As we slowly approach the narrow 3 mile channel up to Mesolongian, I must continually try to assure a stressed and worried Paul we will have no trouble. Really I don't know why I bother. Finally we motor up the channel, which proves very straight forward, clearly marked with navigation beacons and anchor in a calm basin. It's now well after midnight, everyone is asleep except for Carolyn, Paul and myself. He downs a half glass of neat whisky, grunts and heads off to sleep, leaving us to briefly savour this calm anchorage after yet another trying day.

In the morning, when our bosses drag themselves out of bed at 10.30am, they are very rude about this anchorage, which has just given us all a peaceful night's sleep. "What did you bring us here for, it's a horrible place!" says Catrina, lounging lazily at the cockpit table, while Carolyn pours her coffee and serves her hot toast, with all the spreads laid out neatly. "The homes are so ugly."

We head on as soon as everyone has finished breakfast, a fair wind blowing us nicely down the Patras Gulf, with the busy port of

Patras clearly visible on the eastern shore. *Good Vibes* sails under the new bridge stretching from Antirion to Rion, being constructed as part of the 2004 Athens Olympics preparation.

"The Greeks are lazy and hopeless; they'll never get sorted for the Olympics. I wouldn't be surprised if it's cancelled," I overhear Paul saying to Ronald, who to his credit disagrees. Now we are in the narrow Corinth Gulf, passing interesting towns on both sides. Carolyn, who spends her days down in the galley, cleaning and preparing meals and snacks, misses all the sights and has no idea where we are as the galley only has a tiny porthole too high for her to see out of.

Making anchor in the sheltered cove on the eastern side of Trizonia Island in the late afternoon, Carolyn asks Catrina what she would like made for dinner. "Oh, I don't know! Something simple, like lasagne," she replies in her usual belittling fashion. In fact a proper lasagne is a very time consuming and tricky dish. Firstly the meat sauce must be made with pan browned onions and capsicum, then the eggplant fried in slices, a white sauce carefully prepared, several pots and pans in action at once. Then a dozen layers of pasta, meat sauce, pasta, eggplant, pasta, white sauce are laid on with various cheeses in every layer. And that's the easy part. Now it must be painstakingly baked in *Good Vibes* slow and temperamental oven. Where a normal oven would take one hour for such a dish, *Good Vibes* poor contraption will take at least two, if you're lucky.

The golden glow of sunset bathes the cockpit as Carolyn lays out a magnificent dinner. Along with the fine lasagne is her usual fresh garden salad and for desert a pineapple upside down cake. We all sit around the table, enjoying glasses of Robola, a special white wine from Cephalonia, whose lemony character with a faint smoky flavour seems rather too adventurous for Paul's taste. Life should have been magnificent, except for our employers' behaviour.

Carolyn carefully serves everyone handsome slices of rich, juicy lasagne. Paul does his usual trick of squashing his dinner up like mash potato, then without tasting it, slathers on a copious amount of Tabasco sauce. Ronald and Nancy savour their first mouthful and praise Carolyn for her excellent culinary effort. Catrina, on her third glass of Robola, squints her eyes evilly, takes a tiny portion on her fork and tastes it in a reluctant manner.

"Ewww! This is why I never order it in restaurants, It's much too rich!" she exclaims, screwing up her face in disgust.

Ronald and Nancy look a bit taken aback, while Paul is too busy hoeing in to hear his wife's mean comment. We enjoy the food as best we can, hoping it will prove our last aboard *Good Vibes*. After dinner, when the plates are all cleared away and washed up, I ask Paul if we can go ashore to ring home. Jolly from wine he readily agrees and we start to launch the plastic moulded kayak.

"Take the inflatable if you want," offers Paul, unusually generous, but we have our own plans and decline his offer. In the tiny island village we find a public phone and ring my mum. To our relief she answers promptly.

"Oh, hello my dear. Look, I've checked your account again. I'm such a fool, I just got muddled up in the urgency of the moment. The money has been deposited, $5025! That 2003, I was getting confused about, is just the year it was deposited…sorry!"

"Never mind mum, that's great news, although it has been a horrible extra few days, which of course we'll not be paid for. Right, wish us luck, we plan to escape tonight!" says I, the adrenalin instantly rising. We linger ashore for awhile, discussing our plans and then head back to *Good Vibes*. Now our nerves begin to build as we must sit around chatting with the others until they all retire to bed. Forced to wait quietly in our cabin so they can all fall properly asleep, the tension mounts with every minute that passes.

It's well past midnight when we switch our cabin light on and begin to make our move. Quiet as cats, we urgently load gear into our bags. Unfortunately we have come prepared for an around the world voyage so have lots of luggage. Having thrown away one of our big suitcases on arrival, I must now sneak into the forward cabin with a torch and rummage amongst *Good Vibes* spares. Luckily I find a decent bag without making too much noise and our rather stressful packing continues. Next I creep on deck to find our snorkelling gear, stowed in the forward locker, trying to be quieter than a mouse.

In all our activity Mara suddenly wakes up, and although she is aware of our imminent escape, the stress and late hour make her cry. Desperately we try to calm her down, all the time terrified the others will be waking up. After a few heart stopping minutes she realises what's happening and quietens down. Ripping a blank page out of the logbook we hastily write a note. There are a million things we could write, like just how dreadfully they have treated us, yet in these final moments we decide against anything insulting. Simply writing-

When you find this note, we will be long gone, headed back to our own happy lives. We have decided to leave Good Vibes, as it's just not working out and we don't feel it ever will! You'll find the kayak over on the wharf.

Now we begin to carefully load up the kayak with our bags. Of course we couldn't use the inflatable as the engine would awaken everyone. With so much gear we need to make two trips, so Carolyn gently brings Mara out and she joins me in the overloaded kayak. It feels we are making a terrible noise, occasionally bumping *Good Vibes* with the kayak and scraping bags in the cockpit. At any moment surely someone will emerge from their cabin to catch us in this sneaky act. The thought of having to explain ourselves does not bear contemplating.

As fast as possible we pull towards the dock, Mara now fully awake and doing her best with a paddle. We offload all the bags, much to the confusion, amusement and suspicion of a boatload of drunken Irish revellers, partying into the night. "We-eh-ell, what's your story here me man? You wouldn't be stealing all that stuff now would you? If you are, your accomplice is a mite young!" Jokes a dapper young chap, looking slightly puzzled and amused.

"Well, actually we're making a secret escape from our employers," I reply, feeling bound to make a proper explanation. "Would you mind keeping an eye on my daughter, Mara, while I go back out and fetch my partner?"

"Massive! My, dis is grand! Of course your daughter will be fine here." I set off in the kayak, leaving Mara with our Irish friends, who suddenly look a whole lot more sober, with their new-found responsibility. Back on *Good Vibes,* Carolyn is looking nervous.

"I heard someone moving about in the other hull!" she whispers urgently. "Let's get out of here, quick!" She fairly slings the last of our bags aboard and leaps in, shipping a bit of water in her haste. As we paddle off, I look back at *Good Vibes* expecting at any moment for Paul to rush up and demand to know what we're doing.

Greatly relieved at reaching the dock, we toss our bags onto the worn planks, scramble up ourselves and finally heave the kayak up onto the wooden dock. By now the Irish have become fairly fascinated in our escape.

"So what are you fellas going to do now, you have so much baggage! Where are you going to be staying tonight?" asks our dapper friend.

"Oh, we're just going to sleep in an olive grove, no worries," I reply, beginning to strap on my share of bags.

"Steady on there me man! You can't be doing that! You've got your whole clan here! You need to treat them to some luxury. There's a hotel in town, They'll put you up for the night, no doubt!" exclaims our Irishman, getting a bit animated, sounding affronted by my suggestion. We are all rather excited at the prospect of sleeping wild in an olive grove, and of course the hotel will be the first place Paul and Catrina would think to look. It would be horrible to have them storm into our hotel room and try to drag us back. No, our plan is to awake at sunrise and take the first boat off the island, getting as far away from *Good Vibes* as possible.

"Yeah, OK, we'll head on up to the hotel," I lie to calm down our well meaning Irishman, dying to get off the dock to safety. We bid our friends goodbye and struggle on, burdened by our heavy loads and even Mara must carry her own hefty bag. Crossing the road we head deep into the ancient olive grove that surrounds the harbour. When sufficiently hidden, we toss off our weighty baggage and collapse onto the rocky, dry ground. It's quite a chilly night and the ground is baked hard by hot sun, but we make a circle of our gear and snuggle up together to enjoy a night of immense freedom and peace, our dreams soaring with fresh hope and excitement once again.

Awaking early, feeling a bit stiff and chilled, an intense sense of new adventure in our hearts, we leap to our feet, heading for the ferry dock within minutes. Munching on some plain bread, trudging through the olive grove, *Good Vibes* can be glimpsed through the gnarly olive trees. No sign of life there yet and we feel no tinge of regret to be leaving this vessel, that has far from lived up to her name. "Well, you can't judge a boat by its name!" I say, feeling deeply happy, but still very much on edge.

The timetable shows a whole hour before the ferry arrives. Waiting nervously on the weather beaten wooden seats, concerned that at any moment, our scary employers will charge up and confront us, demanding our return, time crawls along. Eventually a tiny ferry can be seen making its way from the mainland and we can hardly bear the suspense. Climbing aboard the old wooden launch, which seats only 20 people, a few islanders join us looking bleary eyed for another day at work.

Ten minutes later the lines are cast off and the ferry chugs the half mile over to the mainland. Now we have to wait another hour in the main town of Trizonia for a bus heading to Patras, still peering around in fear of being caught at the last minute. It's only when we are on the bus, feeling the miles build behind us, that we begin relax.

"We've done it me hearties!" I say joyously. "It's all over and a new, fresh adventure has begun! Woohoo!" We savour every breath of the dry Greek wind and gaze wondrously at the sights whizzing, by, as if we have just arrived in Europe. Luckily my dad has offered that if we leave *Good Vibes*, we can come and do some work on his boat, currently lying in Malta. So we have our destination.

From Patras we board one of the old passenger ships to cross the Strait of Otranto to Brindisi on the heel of Italy. We camp out on the old wooden upper deck, absorbed in the thrill of the moment, the sea rushing by far below. After our second night under the stars, becoming sooty from old ship's exhaust, we enjoy a hearty breakfast in the dining saloon, its rustic condition feels 5 star to us. During the voyage, my heart soars to see Mara making friends with a fellow passenger, a young Italian girl, who is fun, gentle and caring.

On arrival in Brindisi, we lug our baggage up through the town to the railway station, purchasing tickets that will take us right down to the toe of Italy and on to Sicily. While Carolyn minds our luggage, Mara and I walk back to the waterfront, where we find markets in full swing. Wandering through we marvel at the glorious fresh produce; bunches of artichokes, flowering courgettes, strange mushrooms, green cauliflowers, crates of mussels, wooden cases of grapes, this is certainly a region that knows food. On our way back we buy the cheapest and most simple Italian pizza - Neapolitan. For a single euro, the base is expertly whirled out, slathered with tomato paste and grated cheese and then tossed into the hot oven. Somehow it seems the tastiest pizza I have ever eaten. Here lies the beauty of shoestring travelling, the simple things can seem so intensely special.

You may wonder why we are not splashing out a bit after our ordeal? We still feel so far from home and would dearly like to return with a handsome amount in our account to start this dream boat of ours. It's a long uncomfortable night on our 2nd class seats, but we are deeply happy and enjoy the adventure.

In the morning we must change trains at Reggio Calabria. This next leg is rather unique, the train driven onto a big passenger ferry, which then makes the 7 mile sea voyage across to Messina on the north-east coast of Sicily. While enjoying the sights from the viewing deck, a friendly Italian woman falls in love with Mara and treats us all to the Sicilian speciality, arancini, crisply crumbed fried balls of rice stuffed with mozzarella and fresh herbs.

As we rattle down the Sicilian coast the train is held up for several hours in Taormina. Everyone is given a mortadella roll and a bottle of water for the inconvenience, a nice Italian touch. Late that afternoon, after almost three days of travelling, feeling a bit worn out and in need of a rest, we arrive in the sprawling ancient town of Catania. At an Internet café we discover that the ferry for Malta doesn't leave till the following evening, so we have a day to explore the vast metropolis, which dwells in the lee of a smoking Mount Etna.

Rather alarmed, we find our cheap hotel doubles as a nightclub, the dark entrance and stairs, lined with skeletons, mummies and various monsters. Upstairs we reserve our room from a gentle old lady. For ten euro it's grand in an ancient fashion. The furniture, luxurious 50 years back, still retains much of its grandeur, although the mattress on the four post bed is so collapsed, it's impossible not to roll into the middle. Nevertheless we are in heaven and after stowing our bags and taking a shower, we head off to explore the town.

Emerging from our gore filled foyer, the dark cobblestone streets feel a bit creepy, lined with dilapidated old buildings, making the town feel scruffy. Yet the promenade of sophisticated locals in the main streets soon changes our tune. Entering a magnificent café, serving the *World's Best Gelato and Pastries*, we are overwhelmed by the fine aroma of fresh coffee. I order a couple of Nastro Azzurro beers and a Sicilian speciality- Granita di Mandorle - almond milk drink for Mara, accompanied by a plate of sweet ricotta pastries. The pain of our ordeal is quickly slipping away.

Back at our bizarre hotel, fittingly we sleep like the dead. Exploring more as the town awakes, we wander past the grandiose Palazzi Tower and baroque piazzas, down to the most remarkable fish market. Baskets of sea urchin, cockles, great swordfish, hunks of fresh tuna, tubs of live eels, vendors calling out amidst a sun drenched sea of strong aroma. All too soon we are boarding the high speed ferry to Malta, bound for a new adventure.

*

Ever since the days of our memorable escape from the clutches of the *Good Vibes* owners, we have wondered what happened on the morning they awoke to find us gone. Perhaps it went something like this:

Ronald and Nancy of course are the first to awake, puzzled to not find Carolyn with a pot of fresh coffee and breakfast laid out on the table, but too polite to call us. Fetching glasses of water, they sit patiently in the quiet cockpit. Half an hour passes and a bleary eyed Candice emerges from her cabin.

"Where's my breakfast?" she demands, but seeing only Ronald and Nancy, she changes her tone. "Where are those guys? Why aren't they up working? I'm going to bang on their door and get them."

"No, no Candice, please don't. They must be very tired, let them rest," says Nancy gently.

Even so, Candice does her best to make as much noise as possible, which only serves to wake Paul and Catrina earlier than usual and in a particularly bad mood. Catrina is first up, sleepily trying to straighten out her bed hair. "What's going on? Where is Carolyn with my coffee and breakfast?" she manages, shaking off her morning slumber.

"They must be very tired this morning, having a bit of a sleep in. We didn't like to wake them. We've been quite happy sitting here enjoying the morning," says Ronald.

"This won't do! I'll get the lazy things up straight away," threatens Catrina, her temper rising as she marches down to our cabin, banging loudly on our door. "Come on you layabouts, everyone is waiting for breakfast!" Her demands greeted only by an eerie silence. Perplexed, she slowly pushes the door open and peeks in, gasping as she sees the room starkly empty. "Paul, PAUL, come quickly!" she screams. He emerges promptly from his cabin with his two Speedos badly out of alignment.

"What the hell's going on?" he calls, hearing Catrina cursing in our cabin. Entering, he finds her reading our farewell note, the low voltage alarm from the inverter, buzzing weakly, meaning the batteries are getting very low and the fridge contents warming.

"Those ungrateful animals have left us! Can you believe it?" she cries, handing Paul our note.

"What? You've got to be kidding! But...but why have they gone? What do they mean - 'It's never going to work out between us'? Everything was going so well! Why this... after everything we've taught them?" Paul begins to reflect on the future of the trip without us to help. *Good Vibes* is low on fuel and has to dock up and refuel today. "How will we moor up without them? And then there's the Corinth Canal. Oh my God, how will we manage?" He gets Ronald to help him launch the inflatable and they roar across to the dock, where he can see the kayak. Our Irish friends greet them as they tie up.

"We-eh-ell you must be the evil owner, who was so unfair to that lovely family!" declares our friend, a bit hung over from partying late.

"What? What are you talking about? Where are they?" demands Paul.

"Now, now, please simmer down, for me head you know. They took a room in the hotel, but I don't think they want to see the likes of you!"

They walk fast into town, Paul feeling hungry and desperate for a coffee. The hotel receptionist knows nothing about a family with a young girl. Slowly the reality begins to dawn on Paul, the crew have run off and he'll have to be totally in charge of *Good Vibes*. The holiday is over! Ronald too is ruing this turn of events as he knows it will be him, the most capable cook, who will have to produce the meals from now on.

Returning to *Good Vibes*, kayak in tow, the feeling is low and neither Catrina or Nancy have tackled making the coffee yet. Paul's shoulders slump as the weight of responsibility hits him. "Perhaps we'll have to dock up in that marina before the Corinth Canal. Then we can fly back home, get back to work and start looking for a new crew," considers Paul feeling grim.

"I don't wanna go home, I want to stay on *Good Vibes* and play with Mara," cries Candice.

"No Candice, we'll get you back home and into a proper school. I'll buy you a new DVD player too," simpers Catrina, secretly pleased at this turn of events.

CHAPTER 14

WORKING UP TO A DREAM

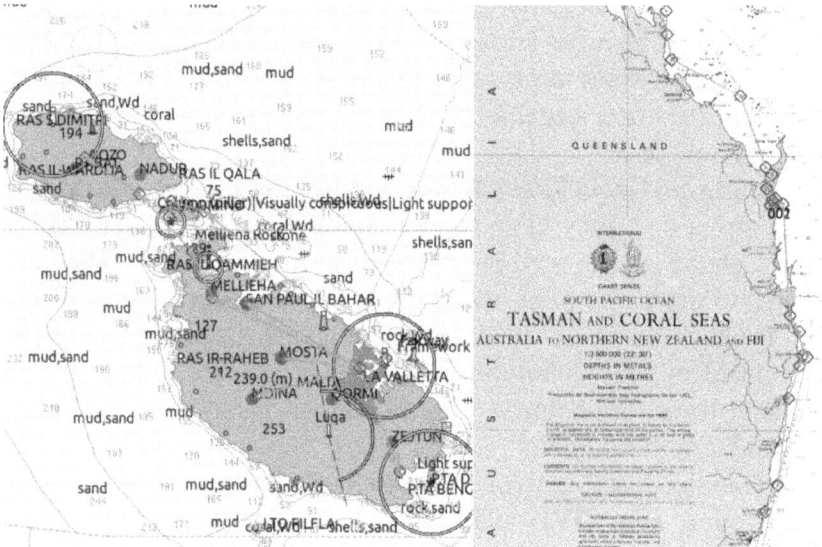

Tyres squealing, our Maltese taxi driver recklessly negotiates the dark damp tarmac that winds down from Valletta. "No worries mate! Your luggage is safe in the boot, that shock cord should hold it in. Relax!" he says in a flippant manner, tearing into a corner so we all have to hold on for our lives.

Having dragged our heavy luggage half way around the Mediterranean, we're feeling worn out and not confident in his loose elastic. "No worries you reckon! That's OK for you to say, but I'll hit you if any of that luggage falls out!" I snarl at him, tired and cross by now, to which he looks alarmed and slows down substantially.

Dad welcomes us aboard, full of cheer and his usual good humour, having spent the season cruising around the Italian coast. "Mmmm, smell this! Good peasant food for you people. Rabbit and vegetable stew, a Maltese speciality. Ooh that's good! Needs a bit more salt though." He tosses a generous amount into the simmering pot. "Right, where are the wine glasses? Try some of this Gellewza Rosé. Now have I told you the bunny rabbit joke Mara?" Dad proceeds to draw out his act, cleverly folding a tea towel into the likeness of a skinned rabbit, while we settle our nerves with the excellent rose`.

His current partner, Kazumi, a taciturn Japanese lady seems less pleased to see us, yet even her ghostly smiles can't dampen our relief to be comfortably aboard our old friend *Yanada*. The luxurious, seaman-like mahogany interior, exuding homeliness. We know Yanada intimately, having worked on her from 1990 to 1994, fitting her out meticulously for my dad.

Sleeping like the dead, we're awoken at the crack of dawn by Kazumi, crashing about the deck with a stainless steel bucket, doing heaven knows what! She seems to bustle around constantly, making a lot of noise and achieving very little. Perhaps fortunately, they are booked to fly out this very day, although we are sad not to to have the chance of spending more time with my dad, who is always good fun. Before departing on his merry way back to Australia, he points out numerous jobs we might like to tackle. Before we know it they have set off and we suddenly have the freedom of our own boat and no end of well paid work before us.

Prior to hauling *Yanada* onto the hard we decide to take her for a trial sail in order to discover any issues. Setting sail up the east coast in a modest breeze, there are muffled thuds coming from the engine room. Entering the greasy den, I pin down the source as being the gen-set and lift the fibreglass lid, "Gosh, it's a mess down there! The gen-set motor has broken off its mounts and is sliding around in a black sludge!" I call out to Carolyn.

We make for Comino Island, a small barren place between Malta and Gozo, finding a beautiful anchorage nestled inside Cominotto Islet, over shallow crystal blue water and sand. It's a battle trying to pay out the heavily rusted 13mm anchor chain, virtually welded solid from lack of use, not aided by the corroded winch. The jobs are stacking up.

Finally we manage to lay out enough scope and sit down in the wheelhouse with a glass of cheap local Shiraz to enjoy the sunset and peace with the tourists gone for the day. Carolyn serves up some fresh green Maltese olives and a plate of hot cheese pasties to accompany our fruity Shiraz. "Well, this is certainly a great chance to scrape together some more money to make this mad adventure worthwhile," says I, taking a delicate sip of my wine. "I feel most grateful to Dad for giving us this opportunity. We'll have to do our utmost to repay his generosity."

After a few days refreshing our spirits in this aquamarine haven, bathing regularly in the clear sea and exploring the herb scented, rocky island, we set back to Marsamxett harbour, to have *Yanada* hauled out onto the hard-stand at the Manoel Island Boatyard. *Yanada* has sailed half way around the globe, with an owner who leaves her every six months to decay in foreign ports. While this is a good practice for refreshing one's purse, no ship likes to lie dormant for such periods.

We replace the gen-set engine mounts, overhaul the anchor winch, repair a section of the deck where Dad's charcoal BBQ has burnt a hole, varnish, paint, scrub, supervise the building of a stern duck-board and generally undertake the hundreds of small jobs that a boat is constantly in need of.

Mara struts confidently up the worn sandstone stairs, her blond hair standing out from the dark haired Maltese. "Ahh, here she is, the Princess of Maneol Island!" greets the boatyard foreman. "You're off to watch the start of the race no doubt!"

Enjoying a fine vantage point atop Manoel Island Fortress, we gaze down at the yachts milling about for the Middle Sea Race. Across the narrow harbour the magnificent stonework of Valletta, heavily bombed during WW11 has been immaculately rebuilt. Super maxi *Alfa Romeo* dominates, building amazing apparent wind in the very light airs, zooming around at over 10 knots, while every other boat drifts about at less than 5. Mara's boldness vanishes when they fire a real cannon to start the race, her cries of indignation carrying clear across the fleet.

Malta's currency is the pound, appealing to my well developed sense of thrift. One single cent can still purchase a Maltese boiled sweet or a few cents can buy a fresh baked cheese pastie or roll from the local bakeries. Maltese life is steeped in tradition, with Sunday truly a day off, so we too adopt this holiday. Excellent old buses at an economical fare take us all over the island. We travel to Mosta with its famous rotunda church dome, Marsaxlokk with its pleasant beach overlooking the container terminal, Mdina whose inland fortress springs out of vineyards and fields, then bus and ferry to Gozo, visiting a family friend who has made it his home.

Our jobs on *Yanada* gradually dwindle, and the confidence that our previous employers tried to drag out of us has all but returned. My laptop computer, which died when Paul tried to use it, mysteriously comes back to life. Fortuitously a yachtie gives me a pirated copy of C-map, heralding a new era in my sailing life. This digital mapping program comes with charts for the entire world, so my days of navigating from the *Times Atlas* promise to be over.

When *Yanada* feels ready to tackle the high seas again we book our tickets back to Sydney. Our stay in Malta has been a great success, earning $5000 for our labour, so we now have $25000 in the bank. I for one am certain I do not want to continue working for others, ready to set about building this boat that has lingered in my dreams ever since I can remember. Perhaps I will never be able to convince others that I can achieve this aim, but at least I have convinced myself.

Our connecting flight to London's Heathrow airport soars NW. "I'll miss those boiled sweets in paper bags!" says Mara, sipping her final glass of *Kinnie,* Malta's far superior version of Fanta, full of herbs and spices, a taste once acquired that makes other soft drinks seem disappointing. "And that performing monkey who loved me but was beastly to you two! Oh yes, the Manoel Island's duck palace and the race horses who came to bathe."

"We'll miss the local bread, crisp and cheap and the affordable lampuki fish. I'm most keen to get back in command of my own ship though!" I perk up, delighted to see Mara so full of happy memories.

After a long stop-over in Bangkok, we fly to Sydney staying with Carolyn's family for a pleasant reunion. Then my mum drives us back to Tin Can Bay to be re-united with the securely moth-balled *Longnose.* We've paid up for two years and unfortunately the marina will not refund our money, although after we complain bitterly, they agree to credit us some time in the marina.

With our house rented for a further 5 months we naturally want to set off cruising straight away and they agree we can use this credit at a later date. A term that is to prove handy sooner than we think.

*

It's the beginning of 2004, summer heat is shimmering over pristine blue ocean flecked with sea lettuce and kelp. *Longnose,* heading north from Sydney, has just motored out of Lake Macquarie and hoisted sails, when there is a nasty "CLUNK" in the gearbox.

"Uh-oh, looks like we don't have forward drive any more!" I'm fiddling with the gear lever, sweat beading on my forehead. "Ahh, but it seems reverse is working still. Must be a gearbox issue!" Fitting the autopilot drive I nip inside and reach into the engine compartment, shutting off the engine. "Wretched Volvo Penta!" I exclaim, rushing up to trim the sails. "Looks like we'll have to haul out and remove the saildrive!"

"We've still our credit with the Tin Can Bay marina," suggests Carolyn, looking a trifle concerned. "It's got to be close on 500 miles of tricky sailing to get there though. Do you think that's possible?"

"I suppose so. There goes our leisurely day sailing voyage! Well, it'll a good challenge for us. To be fair that gearbox is 24 years old, so it has done fairly well."

That night we roll around uncomfortably off Sugar-loaf Point, due east of Port Stephens with barely a waft of wind to propel us, praying that the parade of coal ships can see our tiny vessel, helpless in their path. To our intense relief the night draws to an end and we make good progress throughout the daylight hours. Endeavouring to avoid the shipping lane on the second night, we set in towards the coast off Yamba. With the breeze faltering once again, we have to endure crawling through a fleet of unpredictable trawlers.

Late the next day, closing in on the Southport bar, a modest easterly breeze blows us in. With a weary sense of achievement we sail in to anchor off Currigee. While we have slept poorly during this voyage, Mara has enjoyed a wonderful rest and is full of beans to go ashore for some fun. Swimming to the beach and playing there until the mosquitoes drive us back to the ship is more than we would have elected to do but a refreshing end to the day.

Through the intense shallow maze of islands that separate the Gold Coast from Moreton Bay, now our home waters, we pass through without so much as a nudge of the keel. On we sail, across the wide expanse of the Bay, up towards the infamous Wide Bay Bar, which we cross without incident, thence down the straits towards Snapper Creek. At the marina we will have to find a way of docking without the engine and this lays heavily on our minds.

The breeze being fairly light we ring the marina and suggest that we would like to come straight in, to be hauled out by the travel lift, and would they please have the slings down, ready for us to arrive within the hour. Feeling very nervous, armed with no real plan we sail into Snapper Creek, where the breeze dies off totally behind the point. Hastily we drop all sails, launch the dinghy and set Carolyn to work.

Labouring tediously at the oars, she pulls the 9 tonne *Longnose* steadily into the creek, much to the amazement of various town folk who clap eyes on this strange sight. Fortunately the breeze holds off and we are able to tow straight into the slings without a hitch. Before long I am uncomfortably crammed into the engine hole, wielding spanners and cursing *Longnose's* tiny engine compartment, vowing to build more spacious ones on the new boat.

With the gearbox shipshape once again and our credit exhausted with the Tin Can Marina, we set off on what is to be the final long voyage we make on *Longnose.* It's that classic passage running north with the south-east trades along Queensland's pristine shores, cumulating in a delightful tour of the Whitsunday Islands. This is a special opportunity to show Mara, now 5 years old, the real joys of cruising. Although she made the most of the 'Candice Adventure' and remarkably savoured all the good things, we hope to erase the evil vibe of our employers.

*

Over the past quarter of a century, the Joe Adams designed 13m *Longnose* has served us so admirably, with more than 50,000 sea miles under her keel. The narrow beam gives her the wonderful ability to surf straight and true down a wave, with never a hint of broaching, yet also means she lays over to her gunnels in a mere 10 knots of breeze. While I hope to retain all of the Adams 13's qualities of sea keeping and simplicity, the remarkable stability of a big catamaran remains a factor of which I barely understand but deeply desire. Busily I work out an extensive costing of materials and equipment, endeavouring to think of every small cost, hoping not to be overlooking some unseen cost which could put the project out of my reach.

With that excellent sense of well being and health one develops during a cruise, we make our way south rather early in the season. Our tenant has contacted us asking if she can break her lease to be able to attend her sickly mother. I for one, am bursting to get things sorted with the house and begin this massive project, so we edge our way south against the prevailing breeze. Once down to Harvey Bay one can generally rely on a day or two of east or north-east winds, which blow in on cue, escorting us back towards Moreton Bay.

It's been a hot day with storms brewing in the SW, sucking away our wind. Moonless darkness is illuminated by great flashes of lightening striking Moreton Island, followed by nerve wracking crashes of thunder. A lightening fire burns as we storm through the tricky NE channel, running before a freshening northerly breeze. "I'm simply amazed we're able to run down this channel in these conditions. Just look how accurate this new C-map shows our position on the laptop! That port marker is positioned exactly where it should be!" I exclaim dashing outside to point out a rhythmic flashing red a few cables to our east.

"It is pretty amazing!" says Carolyn, sitting in the cockpit keeping a constant lookout. "I doubt your dad would have entered such a channel at night in the days of using a sextant."

"Oh God no! Even making landfall in the daytime was nerve wracking in those days!" I reply, using the autopilot buttons to alter course by the few degrees indicated on the computer. "Even in the 90s when GPS first began and we had the Satellite Navigator, 'Marvel of Marvels', that machine only gave a position every few hours. You know what happened when Dad took on the Palm Passage in the dark!" I sit back savouring the technological wonder of the dimmed night screen, showing our track instantly updated on a digital vector chart. "What a wonderful period of time to be living in!" Darkness lights up with a flash, followed almost instantly by a powerful boom of thunder, blowing me out of any complacency.

*

Certainly our Russell Island mooring is situated in one of the safest locations on all the coast, well protected from every direction and free of much tidal flow. From our house, the *Butterfly Lodge*, *Longnose* can be seen through a gap in the thick she-oaks and gums, that stand between our abode and the island's only sandy beach. I sleep uneasily in our fancy Sealy Posturepedic bed, feeling disconnected from my ship laying to her questionable mooring gear, without us aboard to tend to her if it should fail. This is the path I have chosen, knowing the road will be full of difficulties.

Mara enrols at the Russell Island State School as a new chapter begins in our lives. For this promises to be the highest bar I have looked up to, standing almost out of sight in the clouds. To have conquered the challenge of circumnavigating the world on one's own ship or to have fitted out boats from bare hulls seems scant preparation for what lies ahead. The fact that others have gone before me and the history of man is filled with far more amazing feats is the stuff I lay my hopes on.

CHAPTER 15

TACKLING A DREAM

My plan to design and build a fifty foot catamaran certainly feels like climbing way out on a limb, a rather skinny limb at that. "Why don't you just buy plans for this big cat of yours Andy? Save yourself a whole lot of stress and heartache!" inquires one of my new-found island friends. "Man, if you get it wrong, that'll be a really costly mistake!"

"Well, for one, a set of plans will set us back around $20,000! That's virtually all the money we've got and I don't really like any of the plans available. Also, I've spent the last 10 years figuring out my own design, so I'd be crazy to throw all that away. I've just got to bite the bullet and trust my own ability, 40 years worth!" I reply, perhaps more to myself than my doubting friend.

One of the issues with the *Butterfly Lodge* is the tendency of the lower level to flood during heavy rains, potentially damaging during the build process. We've dug drains, put in underground drainpipes, levelled out low ground with gravel and earth, diverted roofing downpipes. For all this work it still floods during heavy summer rains. So many dangers to guard against!

"Ok Sprat, I've lifted out all 60 of these great big hardwood sleepers! Now I'm levelling the earth and rocks and tree roots. Then I'll secure them all in again with hardwood edging and make a beautiful smooth driveway!" I ramble to Mara, smartly dressed in her fancy new school uniform, slightly crumpled after her day at school. She's prancing happily about the lawn doing cartwheels and round-offs.

Heading out onto the lawn I join Mara in a few handstands. "And when the drive is all covered over like a giant tent, we'll start building our mega sailing cat to adventure the world in!"

"That will be wonderful Puppi! And each day after school I'll be able to inspect all the work you've done!" she replies positively, walking around on her hands.

*

During the last few months, a 10:1 scale drawing set out on a piece of plywood consumes any spare time. Having rolled on a smooth coat of white house-paint I set to with a will, drawing up the hull lines using the methods outlined in my boatbuilding bible, the *Gougeon Brothers on Boat Construction* book. Enthusiastically the sheer line is worked in, this being the all important run that the deck makes from bow to stern, the defining shape of a boat, its profile from side on. The run of the keel line is the other vital line, defining the under-body shape and having a huge influence on how a vessel behaves as it moves through the sea.

With an artistic flair I attack these lines feeling there's plenty of time to develop and change my ideas, delighted to be inking in the long sweeping curves. I've spent my life studying beautiful shapes of dolphins and fish, the amazing designs of birds and their feathers and countless hours fascinated by yachts and boats of every kind all over the world. Now I hope the lines being drawn are inspired by these memories and I will be able to forge a masterful creation for this world. While the graphics make great sense to me, a visiting friend illustrates how strange it all appears to the onlooker.

"So Andy, what are all these lines you are so excited about?" he asks with a puzzled expression.

"Well, they're simple really! These are the waterline sections, while the buttock sections cut through parallel to the centreline and these diagonals are views of sections cut through at various angles." I explain, enthusiastically jabbing at my work.

"Buttocks you say! I know what they are, but all that other stuff, that's not simple at all!" he blurts out sounding a bit annoyed, "So what are they for anyway?"

"Well, all these different sectional views should flow nicely. When I do the full scale lofting I will be ensuring the hulls are perfectly fair before I build them." He still looks puzzled and I feel stung when he hurriedly starts talking about this weekend's local cricket match.

New Year's Day 2005 rolls up, finding me gazing down the 17m x 5m shaded work area. So much effort has been required already, just to dwell on this empty site. Sixteen treated pine posts, 34m of 4'x4' wood, 100m of decking and two 7m x 9m canvas tarps have created quite a delightful space, cool and airy. "OK, This is my New Year's resolution! Six months will be ample time to loft the design! In 6 months actual construction will begin!" I vow.

During this period I've been also labouring away on another project, writing up our adventures on *Longnose,* deeply hoping that it can be published, to win us a bit of money to further this dream. Getting a book published proves a demanding and time consuming task, as I spend endless hours sending carefully printed sections of *Escape Under Sail* out to the big publishers like Pan McMillan and Sheridan House.

Perhaps I aim too high, dreaming of big sales on the popular market, because the rejection letters are a sad blow doing my confidence little good. Probably I should have aimed my book at a smaller publisher and the purely nautical market, but by now I'm quite discouraged and decide that it's not worth the effort, figuring my time will be better spent dedicated to working on the catamaran design. A disappointing defeat with which to commence such a testing project, itself so fraught with the prospect of failure.

By late January my sheet of plywood lofting has become quite messy with lines changed, rubbed out and smudged so frequently that it's hard to follow clearly any more. 10:1 lofting No2 begins on a fresh sheet of ply. I begin to realise I'll have to truly galvanise my design this time. The artistic flair and fun of dashing off lines with little consequence begin to make way for a more serious, nervous and careful plotting of neat lines. "These lines will actually form into a vessel to take on the wild seas with the lives of my family at stake!" I nervously mumble to myself.

While on a rare holiday to visit my mother we stop off at the Kyogle plywood factory and purchase 10 sheets of 15mm seconds Hoop Pine ply, then order 20 sheets of 16mm Medium Density Fibreboard to be delivered to the island. The plywood is carefully sawn up to form a 17m x 2.4m x.4m level base on which to lay 14 of the MDF boards and thus create a giant, full scale lofting table, where the full side view and top view can be drawn. Inside the garage I set up another base with two MDF boards laid on top, to draw on the all important front views of the hulls from which the final frames will be cut.

By now the 2nd 10:1 scale drawing seems to have gone as far as it can, neater, yet still far from conclusive. Now I'm eager to begin drawing on my full scale lofting table. Mixed with this sense of eagerness is an underlying dread in knowing this time I have to actually draw out the real lines and truly finalise my design. Still, I have almost five months and feel surely things will become clear by then, for at present I am decidedly uncertain of how various lines should go.

Like any project, such a vast aim is made up of endless small and simple tasks, which need only be tackled one by one with infinite patience. Firstly the base line needs to be drawn in, and for what seems a most simple step, it is surprisingly difficult. Fencing wire is tightly drawn, clean across the 17m table span, slightly below the desired line, tensioned with a wooden lever. Next a specially made spacer is carefully held up exactly to the wire and a mark made every metre or so. Then a straight edge must be used to carefully pen in a 17m perfectly straight line.

Several hours work simply to draw a straight line you may exclaim! While a computer design program can lay out any length straight line within seconds. Yet there is something calming and enjoyable about drawing out a design full scale in the open air. There's the pure physical exercise of the feat and the joy of seeing what you wish to create in the size it will be.

High above the work area in the comfortable lounge of the *Butterfly Lodge,* free of midges and mosquitoes, my design software gives me less joy as I struggle to make any progress with its quirky habits.

Using a steel tape I measure out stations every 500mm and from each of these a perfect right angle must be drawn. For this I have to build a huge protractor and bisect arcs to determine a precise square. At the end of day one it's obvious this giant, full scale lofting is going to be a momentous project, yet its accuracy is curiously satisfying.

The first big purchase, wood to plank the hulls, bodes ill for just how complicated a job sourcing materials will be. Having settled on 20mm thick Western Red Cedar as the finest, lightest wood to use, I scour the market for the best deal, determined to get the most for our hard earned money. With two mills offering good deals I finally decide to go with the prominent Cedar Sales and transfer the $15,000 into their account.

Shortly after, the competitor, Oregon Sales, rings me, wondering if I am still interested. When I tell him the deal I have gone for he politely explains to me that because he uses a fine saw, rather than a thicknesser to dress the wood, the extra thickness and width he offers is actually a far better deal, the fine saw finish as good as the thicknesser. Well, I set to with a calculator and soon realise that what he says is quite true and his offer better by some $400. Also, instead of 19mm planks we would have 20mm planks, a matter which weighs heavily on my mind in terms of strength.

Most uncomfortably I ring Cedar Sales and tell them my backers have pulled out and I do not wish to go ahead with the deal. They are fine with this and return my money less $50 for office fees. Within the next week, 5 cubic metres of western red cedar fills half the floor space of our house's lower studio where Carolyn planned to conduct her Yoga classes. "Mmmm, that's so aromatic! What a spicy, woody, sweet fragrance!" I sigh with pleasure, imagining our boat forming out of this great pile.

A golden red glow heralds the rising sun over North Stradbroke Island. I stir reluctantly in my bed, gazing dreamily out at the new day. It's hard living in a house again after all those years of freedom, cruising the world on a yacht. It feels uncomfortable to hear the wind begin to blow in the trees around the house and not be aboard our trusty Adams 13m that lies chaffing at its mooring off the sandbanks, south-east of Russell Island.

"How did we end up here and what happened to that idyllic life?" I ask myself yet again? We could still be out cruising in paradise, but no, now we are trapped by my own plans and dreams, a predicament of my own making.

Carolyn is already up doing yoga, so I throw on my clothes and stroll out onto the veranda to survey the world. It's winter so sandflies and mosquitoes don't pounce on me as I peer down on the beginning of the dream that will make or break us. A long tarp covers the drive and a large empty lawn is all that greets my eyes. I stare wanly about me at the forest of she-oaks and blue gums that protect us from strong winds, out through the cleared section of trees to the open reaches of the Canaipa Passage. *Longnose* can be seen through some scattered trees so I know it has survived another night without me to guard it.

Having prepared myself a steaming cup of brewed coffee I wander downstairs to the studio savouring the delicious taste of the fresh ground beans and the heady aroma of cedar. An almost impossible task stretches ahead, yet it seems man is an optimistic creature and can find comfort in many guises. It will take everything I have to overcome this task and return again to the freedom of the sea on this new ship of my dreams.

*

Weeks trail into months, busy with the unwieldy 18m lofting stick, scarfed up from 3x 6m planks of the very timber the hulls will be planked from, a fact which should ensure the timbers lay on nicely. Month after month the fascinating lines are carefully eyed up and adjusted with the use of cloth covered bricks and clamps to manipulate the run of the lofting plank. Painstakingly these lines are transferred via carefully marked 'pick up sticks' so that the all important front view can be lofted up in the shed.

Locals occasionally drop by to peer at my work, generally seeing no boat at all in my lines, no matter how hard they try. One enlightened fellow exclaims in delight, "I can see it, looks like a giant long surfboat!" which I take as a fine compliment. Generally the mosquitoes and sandflies keep too many visitors away and life is peaceful in our pleasant home on the far edge of suburbia, except when it rains.

Late February an east coast low forms off Stradbroke Island with wind and rain lashing the coast. The news is full of floods around Brisbane and the Gold Coast. A roll of shadecloth, bought in a vain hope of keeping the midges out is draped up around the sides of the shelter in an effort to keep the driving rain from wetting the MDF boards and my huge delicate drawing. Water pours off the house, the garden floods, the street drains are overwhelmed and our road goes under. The view from the kitchen is bleak and discouraging, yet inside the canvas shelter the lofting is fairly dry and the raised work area is proving a sanctuary from the surrounding streams of water.

Four months have passed before the basic lofting seems complete. Now the serious task of calculating the underwater volume must be undertaken. This involves the painstaking effort of working out the area of each submerged section and multiplying this by the distance between frames. With the centre of volume worked out, it needs to be close to the centre of the calculated ship's weight, which is another task where endless patience is called for.

Each piece of equipment and every structure in the boat must be weighed or its weight calculated. Equipment is easy enough to weigh and my list is exhaustive, containing everything from acrylic windows, charts and cabling to the windsurfer and workshop vice. The structural pieces of course have to be designed, then the thickness of the material decided on and the relevant layers of glass cloth calculated. Next mathematical calculations must be applied to work out the weight of each piece of wood, ply or foam, fibreglass cloth and resin for the entire project. This of course proves a monumental effort, yet I become very snappy at calculating the weights of all the bits of cloth and resin and applying the specific gravity of the cedar and ply to work out panel weights fairly quickly.

Unfortunately the result of all these calculations shows the structural weight to be well aft of the centre of buoyancy. Having based the design on an open deck cat I conclude the extra weight of the bridgedeck cabin has put a spanner in the works. So it's literally back to the old drawing board, no small task at all!

"So what are you going to do about it?" asks Carolyn, who seems to be enjoying our time on land, busying herself about the garden and finding regular work on the island to keep our funds rolling in.

"Well, I'll pull out the waterline to widen the stern up. Of course this will mean adjusting all the other waterlines, diagonals and buttocks, the most tedious effort imaginable! It'll probably take me more than a month, by the time I've recalculated the volume," says I feeling somewhat daunted at the prospect.

"You can do it!" giving me a big hug she heads off to re-plant some hippy-astrum bulbs. Although she is not thoroughly convinced this huge project is a good idea, her encouragement is unfailing.

While carrying out this tedious modification to the design I busily study the fore and aft position of structural weights to see what things could be moved forward. Obviously movable objects like the windsurfer and passarelle will need to be stowed forward, but the inherent problem lies in the accommodation needing to fall in the comfortable aft areas. The obvious conclusion is that it will be necessary to strive in building the accommodation as light as possible, especially the aft cockpit.

"Have a look at at our new boat on this computer software, Carolyn," I say, encouraging her to view the screen. "The best part of Hullform is this hydrostatic feature. Say if I program in that our boat will weigh 8000kg. Voila! See how it will sit nicely on the waterline!"

"Well, that's impressive. Are you sure it's right?" she asks.

"Not really, but it does kind of agree with my latest longhand calculations. We'll just have to hope it's correct!"

It's nearing the end of June 2005, the allotted 6 months design time is rapidly drawing to an end. I'm still far from sure about the design and calculations. In truth I had been hoping for something more conclusive. With a project of a lifetime one would hope for glowing confidence that everything has been sorted in the design, like "Yes, yes, let's build this beauty!" kind of enthusiasm. Even though I'm vaguely pleased with my efforts, I feel sure a further 6 months would iron it out to true perfection. It's an uncomfortable place to be, for I have vowed to commence building by now.

In a high state of unease I set off on a long walk, hoping the fresh air will clear my mind. Down the dusty dirt road to Sandy Beach, that familiar smell of the sea calming my nerves, through the wild mangroves, up through the native forest full of ghost gums, tallow-woods and banksias, breathing deep gulps of life giving, gum scented air. The more I walk, the clearer the breaking concept in my mind becomes. Nothing is ever perfect, everything can be improved. To get stuck in the perfection trap would mean endlessly striving for a goal that can never be achieved. I have to move on, create my dream and begin the real hard core work, now or never.

CHAPTER 16.

OUT ON A LIMB

The hum of a jigsaw slicing steadily through MDF board, releases an aroma strangely like fresh baking bread. Painstakingly all 18 frames are sawn and shaped up, then erected on a strong-back to resemble the vast skeleton of a dinosaur. "My God, I hope I'm not creating a huge white elephant!" I murmur to myself, peering along the frames with a mixture of pride, but also an uncomfortable feeling this may all be a grand mistake.

Each morning I walk Mara to her bus stop, kicking a soccer ball down the grassy path, then dash back to begin work. My greatest fear is that Mara will finish primary school with me still struggling to finish this boat, her passion for the sailing life gradually eaten up by the lure of teenage desires. Thus driven by a variety of deep seated fears and dreams of exotic travel, I set to with a tremendous will, chipping away at this mountain of work, whose pinnacle stretches way beyond infinity, shrouded in dark clouds.

After several weeks of toil, edge gluing planks into place, Carolyn runs a critical eye over my work. "Wow, the shape looks really smooth. It's beginning to look like a boat now."

Working with the western red cedar is a true delight, something about its strong aromatic scent seems quite uplifting, which is a Godsend as otherwise progress is painfully slow. Looking like a long sleek dolphin, the under-body is curvaceous and complex to shape with planks.

Like most challenges in life, the thought of them is usually more difficult than the actual execution of each individual task involved. When the method has been carefully decided on, mostly the physical work is so simple it becomes quite tedious, yet intense all the same. The enormity of the task blows one's mind away though. Every time the poor challenged brain cells attempt to reach forward, striving to comprehend what is involved to reach the end, the mind just goes into overload and stalls, leaving the body in a cold sweat, for what it has committed to.

The understanding of visitors and passers by is far from encouraging. "It looks very skinny! Won't it just fall over?" says my neighbour, not realising it's to be a catamaran.

"Will you be able to fit inside that hull, it looks so narrow!" worries a pessimistic plump fellow as I madly work against the clock trying to wet out a section of fibreglass draped around the hull. He interrupts my daydream of putting a winter coat on a sleek racehorse, making my imaginary horse seem skinny and frail.

"What? you have to now build another one of those! That'll be boring, you'll be forever building this thing!" Just the sort of comment one needs while painfully sanding up hull number one, trying to get it beautifully smooth for painting, a process infinitely tedious, unrewarding and slow.

Nevertheless by July 2007 both hulls are complete and roughly faired, now perched out in the open, lashed awkwardly with green tarps. Whenever it rains they act like giant rain-catchers, creating a great deal of additional labour in the way of bailing them out. Two hull shells completed seems so far from a finished boat, yet already I am finding by far the most common question interested visitors ask is, " How are you going to get it to the water?" This query catches me out every time as my mind is totally pre-occupied with figuring out how to build the cross beams, the bridgedeck floor and other pressing items like the rudders. They must think me a slow-witted kind of chap, not to have worked out this most obvious process.

*

While contemplating how to go about constructing the bridgedeck floor I make a rather unwelcome discovery. Checking over the weight calculations of these vast panels I find them actually a massive 200kg more than I had originally calculated. A cold sweat quickly flushes through my body, right down to my toes as I see this new ship ending up grossly overweight, sinking deep beyond its design waterline so that the bridgedeck gets close to the sea which then slaps it horribly.

This actually proves a blessing in disguise. One of my fibreglass suppliers, Gunter Heimlich from Ballina Fibreglass, comes up with the simple solution. Lightweight polyethylene honeycombed core sheets. Made in China, they are an affordable choice. The finished panels see my designed weight back on target and disaster averted for the time being. Now the option of lightweight panels takes root in my mind.

While I generally plod on with a deep sense of confidence, at times the prospect before me becomes totally overwhelming. "Why did I start such a massive project? I mean, so much can go wrong, I might become allergic to the epoxy resin, a bush fire could burn the lot! We could be here for 15 years building this huge boat, like many people we've come across in our travels. Mara will have left home with us wasting our lives, throwing all our efforts into a boat which may not even sail properly!"

Some nights I just can't get to sleep, the hum of mosquitoes whining for my blood outside the screen door or the wind tearing at the leaves in the ironbark trees, the fragile tarps threatening to blow away. All the while our trusty yacht *Longnose,* which has taken us so faithfully around the world, neglected and tugging steadily at its mooring fittings.

On other days I wake up with boundless enthusiasm, racing down to the shed even before the sun makes its way over Stradbroke Island. A steaming mug of coffee in my hand, eager to inspect yesterday's glassing projects. With tentative delight I gingerly finger the rock hard cured resin, savouring each tiny section of progress. Today the 8.45m wide main beam lies flat on a huge construction table. It's made from panels of 25mm plywood scarfed together, reinforced with a layer of heavy cloth. Our beautiful black and white cat, damp from hunting in the dewy grass, bounds onto the frame for his customary inspection of my work.

"Good morning Pandora, caught any rats?" He looks at me disdainfully as he always catches a rat. "Well, plan for today is turn that beam over. Might need to call on some help, then glass the other side. With any luck there'll be some spare time to work at shaping up the rudders. That's the job I love the most, like you love hunting!" Pandora smooches up to me, angling for second breakfast. Even though he has already eaten a rat, his appetite is endless.

Life is in a delicate balance. "I'm minding Gary today at the Jacobs'," says Carolyn, come down to admire the pitiful progress. She is managing to keep our coffers alive doing various jobs on the island, while studying a comprehensive Satyanada Yoga Teachers course. Mara is happily progressing at school, making nice friends with the island children, still eager to go out for weekends away on the "Cosy Boat". Yet I know that each day I must go for it, make progress, even when I am at a loss for what to do. I know I must at least be sweeping up wood shavings and glass dust or doing some monotonous sanding while pondering the next hurdle. Such a project requires endless amounts of thought, yet only the hours of hands-on work, building the hard core structure create the ultimate, desired result.

"Do you want to go out sailing in the 'Glue boat' this afternoon Sprat?" I ask Mara as we skip home from the bus stop, her white school socks red from playing in the Russell Island dirt.

"Yes, Puppi, let's sail over to Stradbroke and slide down the dunes and go on the big tree swing!" It warms my heart to see her still keen for sailing, when many of her friends spend their afternoons taking on the imaginary world of computer games. I let her take the helm as we glide peacefully across the channel, the gentle breeze never failing to blow away one's cares. After a frolic on the sand dunes, covered in yellow, red, brown, black and white sand, our skin stinging from sandfly and mozzie bites, we dive into the murky green water for relief, quickly gambolling about before our fear of bull sharks drives us out. Jumping back into the 'Glue' we're fully refreshed after a nice taste of the wild, the delicate balance held in check for the time being at least.

*

After two years the beams and bridgedeck floor are in place, meaning the basic boat is all there, it just needs decking over, fitting out, rudders, centreboards, engines..... "Oh no, don't start trying to think of all the things still left to do!" The two hulls are spread so wide apart by the beams, that when viewed still without decks, one can easily imagine the whole thing folding up if struck by waves of any size, leaving a horrible nightmare of floating ply, cedar, foam and torn glass.

Aside from the endless grind of physical work, our greatest challenge lies in fending off the regular summer squalls and heavy rains. The huge tarpaulin rigged across the whole boat is a rickety affair, strung between a royal palm and a paperbark tree, spanning two blocks of land. The sagging centre is supported by cross beams propped off the boat so that when the breeze gets up it flogs around alarmingly, rising up and beating down with each wave of wind.

In one of the fearsome east coast lows, a regular feature of our winter weather, the wind is recorded at over 60 knots out to sea. I am forced to spend my first night up on the sparsely fitted bridge, tending to the props and making sure no major ropes give way as powerful gusts of wind wrack the tarp, shaking the whole boat. It's a beastly night, but our faithful Pandora keeps me company the whole time, managing to sleep fairly peacefully amid the raucous.

Having a 160 sqm tarpaulin rigged up feels not dissimilar to sailing along with a spinnaker set 24/7 for years on end! These great billowing sails are fun while the wind is moderate, but when it starts to whistle up they are stressful and better stowed below. Unfortunately there's no taking down the tarp, precariously lashed with nigh on a hundred bits of old rope. The desire to get the deck on

181

and the boat all sealed up, becomes a huge driving force, so the unruly tarp can be finally stowed.

As the days, months and years tick by, it begins to feel like life is passing me by, with virtually every waking moment swallowed by this enormous craft, so uncertain in its design and construction. Meanwhile one gets the feeling the rest of the world is off enjoying themselves. Painstakingly the hull floors are glued in, some shelves are framed up in the hope of creating a little working space aboard. Steps into the hulls and up the transom are fitted to help the thousands of trips in and out of the boat gain some ergonomics. Under the house the centreboards are being slowly whittled out of a vast laminated block of cedar. Progress seems remarkably slow and meanwhile houses pop up around the neighbourhood, knocked up in a matter of months, highlighting my apparent lack of headway.

"So Andy, what have you achieved since I last dropped in? It's been a solid a few weeks now!" asks my mate George, handing me a bottle of Corona in a stubby cooler. It's twilight so I take an appreciative swig and begin to show him over my meagre achievements. His eyebrows arch up, seemingly amazed by how little I've done, a common scenario with most of my visitors.

George is renovating an old wooden house, which he had trucked to the island, funding the whole project on a endless cascade of credit cards, so I don't envy him on that score. He's a wealth of advice on how I should be building my boat, "Why are you building this rabbit warren here?" he asks casting his gaze around the saloon seats I've started to build into the bridgedeck. "I'd leave it more open, keep it more spacious," he adds breezily, aloof of my annoyance. Even though he can be inadvertently bothersome, I enjoy his visits and the perspective of a non sailor.

It's a steamy still night, lightning occasionally illuminating the forest of trees around us. Limbs aching from a hard day's work, we sit down to a roast dinner with friends. The succulent lamb is carved, the gravy steaming in its dish, the potatoes, onions and pumpkin baked to a perfect crispness, our taste buds crying out for a hearty dinner. Suddenly the windows begin to rattle and a powerful thunderstorm with savage driving rain is upon us.

Abandoning our guests we dash downstairs. The roar of rain is deafening, the tarp is rapidly filling with water, one huge sagging area is looking like a vast children's swimming pool. It threatens to either rip the tarp to shreds or crush the boat as tonnes of water build up with alarming speed.

Clambering inside we try to push up this enormous volume of water, which now contains several tonnes, so of course it's futile. "I'LL TRY AND LET GO SOME OF THE ROPES TO RELEASE THE PRESSURE!" I yell at Carolyn, trying to raise my voice above the rain beating down like a waterfall, deafening on the now highly strung tarp. "SEE IF IT LOOSENS UP AND YOU CAN PUSH IT!" Scrambling out into the stinging, blinding rain, it soon becomes obvious it's too hard to release any ropes, they're out of reach, but something must be done fast, otherwise the boat will be structurally damaged by such weight pressing on it. "WATCH OUT BELOW!" I scream, reaching into the pool to slash a hole. The instant I touch the tarp with my knife it rips clean across, instantly releasing thousands of litres of sky fresh water onto an unsuspecting Carolyn, who is flattened and half drowned in the hull.

Darting inside I find her coughing and spluttering, looking indignant. "WHY DIDN'T YOU TELL ME YOU WERE GOING TO CUT SUCH A HUGE HOLE IN IT! GIVEN ME A BIT OF WARNING!"

"Sorry dear," I mutter sheepishly, concerned now that the hull contains several extra tonnes of weight on the supports and is draining fairly slowly through the centreboard holes. Nevertheless the danger has been diffused so we trudge soggily back upstairs to our guests who are guarding the now decidedly cool roast from a persistent Pandora. Swigging a few glasses of cask wine, this food is now savoured even more for our pre dinner adventure.

*

Several weeks later I'm showing Carolyn over my daily progress, enjoying a beer at day's end. "Oh NO!?*SUGAR! I've glassed this seat frame into the wrong place!" I cry out in frustration on seeing my mistake. Not only have I wasted time glassing it in, more time will be needed to get it out. "At least it's only a foam sandwich panel, it wont be hard to knock out." Even though we had been encouraged to use the lightweight honeycomb panels for the bridegdeck floor, I still feel sceptical that such a light core, draped with a layer of thin glass cloth on either side can be anywhere near as strong as a cedar cored glass panel.

Next morning, armed with a decent sized claw hammer, my first task is to smack out the offending panel. Nonchalantly I stroll up to it and coolly deliver a powerful hit to the join, hoping to blow it off with a single hit. POW! Not a dent. This time the arm comes back further, driving hard with the intent for follow through that will make it fly clean across the cockpit. THUNK, the only result- an arm stopping, jarring defeat of my intent and a small dent in the glass. In frustration I rain futile blows on this stubborn frame, finally staring at the offender in astonishment at how amazingly strong it is.

"I'll fix this!" I announce, striding into the shed for the short handled sledge hammer. With both hands I grip the heavy tool and drive through with all its weight. End result- a small dent. "Wow, this foam sandwich stuff is so strong!" Finally I concede and grind it out with a fine cutting disk, a beastly job, throwing fine particles of glass dust over everything. From here on, I'm converted to the amazing strength of foam sandwich construction and my faith in the meagre looking amount of glass used to bond in a panel has been solidly cemented.

In my daydreams I imagine this tiring task all done, snugly anchored in a quiet cove, gentle waves lapping at a golden sandy beach fringed with palms, lounging without a care in the cockpit reading an adventure story. Wilder dreams envisage our mighty catamaran, sails fully powered up, blasting along in a cloud of spray, winning races all around the world, inspired by stories of the Brisbane to Gladstone and Darwin to Ambon Race.

Mara is helping me clean out the shed, at age 8 she is too into fairies and acrobatics to be excited by power drills or pieces of sandpaper. All the same she inspects the progress every day and seems genuinely interested. "Hey Puppi, what's this old trophy here?" she asks, holding up a small golden sailboat, bent and dusty.

"Oh that's from the Inter Schools Dinghy Sailing Regatta. I came second racing my Laser, got too confident and capsized briefly, which cost me the win. You know I could have gone on to become a really successful dinghy racer, but I sold my Laser when I finished school and went off to see the world!"

"Perhaps I can help you win some more trophies!" says Mara in her confident, sweet little voice. It's an off-hand kind of remark, which I take little notice of.

Idly I study the excel spreadsheet printout of the table of moments, wondering if I have overlooked any vital part of the construction which could throw the whole delicate balance into disarray. "Oh no, it cant be!" To my horror I notice the considerable weight of the entire galley area, including benches, sink, plumbing, cutlery, cooking utensils etc, has been given a negative value rather than a positive, which means that suddenly there is a whole lot more weight aft in the boat than I had accounted for, a serious error.

Images of this new dream boat sitting deeply down by the stern, the bow cocked up in the air flit across my mind. This time a summer east coast low has formed offshore from Moreton Island. By now I have fitted several padded supports for the tarp to stop rain pooling and at the moment it's fending off the onslaught of buffeting winds and heavy rain. "Any more rain than this and she'll float away!" I announce glumly, peering down at the flooded lawns and road, the bleak weather and my technical concerns bringing me down.

Carolyn is happily practising Satyananda Yoga poses, she seems way above my earthly concerns. "Everything will be OK Andrew. You'll find a way," she tells me encouragingly, but I can't be placated and trudge downstairs to check on the tarp.

Some of the prop padding has shaken off so I tie it back on. Inside the shed, the floor is flooding so I make sure no materials are getting wet. Heavy rain is beating on the tin roof, "Oh why did I even take on such a massive, foolish project? It's such a long road, I'll never finish it!"

A few days later a cheery sun is beaming drying warmth out of a cloudless blue sky and the flooding has drained away. "I've been doing some calculations," I announce to Carolyn over a steaming cup of black tea and shortbread biscuits. "If we use foam cored panels for all the cockpit and galley area, we should be able to keep to the designed balance," I conclude, feeling fairly pleased with myself.

"I knew you'd find a way," says Carolyn, with a confidence she always has of me, that I often feel I don't deserve.

Now my obsession with light-weight construction takes deep root. In many ways it's aided by our shortage of money, which sees me acutely frugal with the amount of glass and resin applied. "She's very Spartan down in the hulls!" says our friend Chris, "Are you going to build doors for those cupboards?"

"No, that's them finished. It's all part of my Zen and the art of boatbuilding and living approach." Venturing this I hope to be covering up the urgency I feel for finishing this boat and the extremely low budget we are working to.

Chris, a well spoken Englishman, also holds the dream of buying a catamaran and voyaging to exotic parts of the world. "Well, if you can get the decks on by the Christmas holidays, Marian and I will come up and I'll help you get the electrics sorted." It's a very generous, harmless sounding offer, yet its ramifications prove far reaching.

I quickly realise huge mountains must be hurdled to achieve this deadline. To deck in the cockpit sides, firstly the engines have to be fitted, one each side. Biggest problem is where to get the capital to purchase such expensive items. Consequently the big move has to be made, trusty *Longnose*, our faithful friend for 27 years now, is put on the market. Still, it could take many months, even a year to sell.

When I left high school and basically dropped out of uni to follow the sailor's life, I studied spiritual visualisation of important things you want to draw into your life. Now I call on these archaic skills and conjure up two brand new motors in the hazy reaches of my mind, picturing them sitting in the shed all ready to install. "Perhaps *Longnose* will sell quickly." I suggest to Carolyn, who is also a believer in such concepts.

"Looks like you'll have to go out and get a job Andy, to get those motors. They wont just materialise out of thin air!" suggests one of my more annoying visitors, himself a long term unemployed. Now I picture a whole year of build time slipping away as I struggle at some beastly job; worst nightmare kind of scenario. Meanwhile I press on with moulding the huge bridgedeck cabin roof and begin work on the cockpit seat section that will need to go on immediately the engines are in.

My dad has shown little enthusiasm for my plan of building a big catamaran. "Why don't you build a proper boat. A traditional wooden monohull, something that will last?" That's his angle on my project, so it's with some element of surprise that I get a call from him, full of his usual enthusiasm for his own life. Now he owns a macadamia farm, his mind full of plans to improve the tree variety and I happily encourage his passions. "So, apart from all that, I've got some good news. Arrow Energy have gone through the roof. I bought shares for 50 cents five years ago and just sold them for $5.80. I've decided to give both Rachel and you 30k each!"

For weeks I'm stunned and amazed by this rare and incredible piece of luck. It truly seems I have manifested my new engines. Now though, I must labour painfully over the decision of which engines to buy and where exactly to mount them. Thus I am drawn into the challenging and trying world of deciding what equipment to buy. In my dreams it would be great to move into solar electric motors, but for now I settle for diesels. "Why did you buy Volvo's, I call them the green death! Give me Yanmars any day!" barks yet another know all, would-be sailor.

"Well, I was probably drawn in by the glossy advertisements, powerful alternator and fancy green paint job!" Hackles raised, eager to get on with a pressing glassing job, but too polite to send this chap off with a flea in his ear.

Later the roar of an ancient ride-on mower catches my attention. It's Ray Bonnell, one of those energetic chaps, well into his 70's, who's 'old school' work ethic makes my efforts seem aged and decrepit. He's just finished cutting the lawn next door, covered in sweat and grass seed. His sensible interest and ready assistance whenever we need help turning hulls or beams, has been one of the great benefits of living in a small friendly community. "Now tell me young fella, just how are you planning to get these engines up and into the hulls?" he says, looking thoughtfully up at the high topsides.

"Well, to tell the truth, I haven't thought about it much yet, but I suppose some kind of crane set-up will be needed to lower them in,"

I reply, hoping that perhaps Ray will offer some more definitive ideas.

"Now I've been giving this problem of yours a bit of thought. I've got some heavy sections of steel laying under the house, and I reckon I can build you a suitable sized gantry, that'll lift those motors of yours in just fine," he announces, then proceeds to explain his ideas, while I follow, amazed at this turn of fortune. Every now and then in life, things just fall into place!

*

Christmas day 2008 is still a week away, but the biggest gift unwrapping I'll ever have is about to get under-way. The moment has come, the event we've all looked forward to since that fateful day 15 months ago when we rigged up the giant tarp and became slaves to its tantrums and debacles, every time the breeze whipped in or some rain would chance to fall. These otherwise delightful occurrences turned evil by the tarp's malcontent behaviour.

Feverishly we tackle undoing the multitude of knots, drawn steel tight by 450 days of resisting nature's forces. Joyously the knots are prised open and gradually the taut, threadbare material flops down messily over the boat. Occasionally knots have to be cut away, but this is not the true sailor's way. With a mad urgency we push the great folds of green canvas down onto the grass and fold it up, hoping to never see the thing again. Then we look up in amazement at the great undercoat-white boat sitting on our lawn. Looking down from our veranda, it looks particularity impressive, suddenly revealed for all to see. "Wow, your boat looks awesome! It's totally wicked!" our neighbour Simone calls out enthusiastically.

All of a sudden our boat can been seen by any islander who visits Sandy Beach. "Andy, why didn't you tell us you were building such a big boat!" says one of my cricket team-mates, as I've taken to getting some competitive exercise with the local team. Even though I've constantly talked about this 50' cat I'm building to them, seeing is believing.

"Wow, your boat looks huge. What do you reckon, another two or so years and she'll be ready to launch?" A distressing comment with me hoping for a launch within a year, hating to think he could be right.

"Nice work Andy, just a coat of paint now and she'll be done!" Considering the fitout, electrics, plumbing, deck gear, mast and much else is still to be tackled, I can only dream this optimistic person will be right one day.

Chris and Marian rock up true to their promise and over the festive season the fun of installing lights, a stereo and switches begins to bring this complex machine to life. Still the bridgedeck windows are only open cut-outs inviting in rain squalls to ruin these delicate copper cored systems. Now the drive to make the acrylic windows takes hold and thus this ship forges its way ahead.

Early in 2008, with mixed emotions, *Longnose* is handed over to a new owner. This wonderful seaworthy boat, which had taken us to the far reaches of the world, 28 years old but still seemingly as solid as it was when newly launched. With 105k in our bank account I peer with concern at the extravagant construction sitting so far from completion in our back yard. "Well, there's no turning back now!" I announce to a purring Pandora, striding downstairs to continue wading away at the endless list of tasks, which still extend well beyond my known horizon.

*

"You know, I do believe making all these decisions about what equipment to buy is actually way harder than the plain hard yakka of grinding, glassing and sanding!" I complain to Carolyn and Mara as we sit on our veranda cooking lamb chops and sausages over a small wood fire, basting them with rosemary sticks, while Pandora smooches up to us, hungrily eyeing off the sizzling meat. The year I had sworn to get this boat launched in is rapidly ticking by.

"For instance there are over 120 deck fittings we need to buy! That's just for the deck jewellery! Why no woman on earth would be able to decide on so much jewellery in such short a time. Each piece is a complex balance of cost, strength, weight and practicality. Now I'm also considering buying a mast rather than building one, otherwise we'll be here building this boat forever," I ramble, hooking chops off the heat and laying them on plates with salad.

"If you think we have enough money, it would certainly take a lot of pressure off you," says Carolyn. She pokes some Eucalyptus sticks onto the fire, the sharp spicy scent of the smoke driving off inquiring mosquitoes. Pandora is busily entertaining us, re-killing a searing sausage, savaging it with his claws. Sipping some box wine, I try to cast aside the overwhelming range of equipment choices and focus on the tranquil beauty of the moment. Mara, so proudly wearing her Russell Island school uniform, munches happily on a chop bone, while cicada's and spiders make music in the bush.

Having moulded up a centreboard case over a finished board, Carolyn comes down to help me pull it off. In vain we tug at the stubborn case, the plastic covered vinyl spacer jamming the thing in place. We hose water into the space and squirt in detergent, hoping to get the unwieldy structure moving, all to no avail, even with us both tethered like ponies, tugging with all our might.

"What if it just tears the case to pieces?" says Carolyn looking a trifle worried as I prepare to use the 100hp Mercedes to rip the case off.

"I'll be hopping mad!" says I feeling frustrated that such a simple job is taking up the best part of a morning and may yet result in a step backward. With a heart stopping wrench the case pops off in one piece and progress crawls from one testing challenge to the next. Incredulously 2008 slips away in a haze of sanding and grinding dust, toiling endlessly at the list of jobs, which seem cursed into having no end. It's the monotonous task of fairing the acres of glass panels and countless corners, undercoating, sanding them, undercoating again, all in the vain hope of turning the coarse weave of cloth into a smooth surface, that seems guilty of the being the great time thief of the modern boat builder.

Ambushed by 2009, Mara is growing up quickly, the hair she refuses to have cut stretching way down her back. She is a popular playmate to her ten-year-old schoolmates, who all seem to be going on fourteen.

"Hey, you know our friend Stephen, building the 50' Schoinning cat; he fell off a ladder today and broke his leg!" I announce to Carolyn, feeling glum. Our friends building a 60' cat are finally preparing to launch their boat after 10 hard years, a time frame which gives me the horrors. To escape my thoughts I dash down to tackle the composite forebeam, one of the final major pieces of this zillion piece jigsaw.

Electing to forego the complexity and stress of building our own mast, I decide we can just afford to buy a rig, little realising how painful the choice will be. It's a complex weighing up of cost and features which confronts me for months. Forced into a decision by end of financial year considerations I decide on the heavier section recommended by Allyacht Spars.

When the huge chunk of aluminium section is delivered to our house, I am shocked by the sheer weight and width, as I see 20 odd volunteers staggering along with it, helping to settle it down on some 40 gallon drums. Putting on a brave face, I feel gutted, concerned this massively heavy rig will throw our boat around jerkily in any kind of waves, almost certain I've blown our money on the wrong rig.

Feeling further out on a limb with each passing month I commit to some more nerve wracking decisions. From a 10:1 scale drawing of the mast, penned up in the shed, I take the risk of trusting what needs to be a precision measurement by having the fore-stay wire cut to length, the ends machine swaged. If it's the wrong length, by more than a few centimetres that'll cost us $1500. Also from these measurements the sails are ordered from a discount sailmaker down in Melbourne. It'll mean a major setback if these calculations are out by the smallest degree. The cards are really needing to fall well for us when the rig is fitted after the launch.

"So what are you guys going to call this boat/house? *Longnose 11!* asks our friend Kristie, famous for naming her children Tealya-Belle and Nace Lecic Train.

"Good question! Well Carolyn likes *Isis*, Goddess of love, Is-Is being a double barrelled name, but there's already a few of those. Mara's keen on *Zingara,* the gypsy girl, which is nice but that's taken also. I fancy *Hard Core,* because it's got cedar cored hulls and we're the hard core sailors, but Carolyn doesn't like that. So like the rest of the boat, the name is still a work in progress."

Our future hangs on the outcome of this real life puzzle, where so many vital pieces must fall into place or perhaps the whole thing falls down like a house of cards. The cost of the deck jewellery is proving the key area where I failed to understand just how powerful the gear needed to be. The price of big boat blocks, travellers and winches is quickly cleaning out our bank account.

Sitting upstairs, sipping a cup of tea, poring over the latest *Australian Multihull World* magazine, studying the enviable deck gear of other boats, I find myself deeply wishing for a stroke of good fortune. Then the phone rings, breaking in on the peaceful sounds of nature at the remote *Butterfly Lodge.*

"Hello, is that Andrew Stransky? It's Alan here from Allyacht Spars. Well I know you're going to like this. You've won the prize draw! You guys get $3000 off your bill. How's that for a welcome bit of news!" Everyone who purchased a mast from Allyachts in the Boat Show month went into this draw, one chance in thirteen giving us a much needed push towards the sea. To begin with, this project seemed distinctly out of our budget's reach. Somehow, bit by bit, the money has rolled in. It seems a remarkable phenomenon how money can flow in when you are driven to pursue a dream.

*

The ridge behind our house means the sun sets early, taking the sting out of a hot summer's day, and protecting us from cold winter westerlies but also means the sun's warmth leaves us early on winter's days. It's late July 2009, the afternoon chill has set in and I'm happily admiring my day's painting which has cured enough to fend off any dew. Joyce Bonell, is taking her evening stroll with her grand daughter. "She looks magnificent! It's been such a big part of the neighbourhood for so long, it'll be sad to see her go." I'm a little surprised Joyce is thinking about it being gone, with me so caught up dealing with the never ending details. "The white paint looks very smart!"

"But Joyce it's not white, it's 'Golden Sands', it must be the light making it look white," says I, squinting now to try and make out the creamy tint of the paint.

Now in earnest, the roller coaster ride towards launch day seems to have begun. With the finish in sight, it feels like I've taken a deep breath, then relentlessly pressed on with the aim to launch the beast before exhaling. Driven by what seems now a tangible goal, it's easy to put in the long days, with the excitement of launch day rapidly approaching. Yet after many weeks of this almost incessant work a toll is extracted from my body.

Throwing myself into bolting on the deck jewels, a meticulous process with more steps than one would believe possible, each day my back develops more pain. Eventually I can barely bend down to drill a hole without a nasty screaming pain in my lower spine. "I've got to do something about this!"

The next day it's but a short drive up the road to visit the father of one of Mara's school friends, who practices his own form of natural healing. "Hello Matt, I'm not sure if you can do anything for me. I mean the pain in my lower back has reached a stage I can't work any more. Doris said you may be able to help, but perhaps I should just be resting."

He gently bids me lay down on a massage table, gives my back a powerful work-over, mutters some incantations, uses pressure points to delve into my past, then makes me do some specific exercises. "Your quadriceps have contracted, which is putting your back muscles out," he states matter-of-factly as I lie on the floor twisting my spine, stretching my thighs. To my absolute amazement I walk out the door totally free of pain, the way clear ahead again.

Later that evening, I lounge back on the couch watching *The Never Ending Story* with Mara and Carolyn. In this iconic German film, the Nothingness is eating up Fantasia the creative world. Atreyu the young hero, set the task of saving the world asks, "How many wishes do I get?"

The beautiful Childlike Empress replies, "The more wishes you make, the more magnificent Fantasia will become." I'm liking this epic struggle between evil and good, pained by Arbatax his faithful horse, sinking into the swamp of sadness, flown high on the back of Falcor the luck dragon.

A pheasant coucal hoop-hoops in the still morning air, cool and crisp in the last days of winter. "Hey, what do you guys think about *Fantasia* for a name?" I blurt out, unable to hold back my excitement. Carolyn is busy making Mara her school lunch, while Mara dances about doing handstand against the wall.

"Not really, it just makes me think of the Disney movie musical, with that silly Mickey Mouse!"

"Ouch! Ok, but that comes from the dictionary definition, an imaginative, improvised piece of music. That's only one of the meanings of this enchanting word though! It means a beautiful intelligent girl, something exotic or unreal, an amazing show and think of its meaning in *the Never Ending Story,* or in those acid jazz lyrics 'dip trip flip fantasia,' don't know what that means but it sounds cool!" Succinctly I wrap up my case, but Carolyn remains nonplussed. Mara likes it, but she wanted to have her name changed to Amethyst Gold Chain!

Gradually the 30 interior lights are being installed and the heavy cabling for the motors fitted. It seems we may well finish this boat after all. Yet I'm filled with a mixture of excitement and dread that launch day will be a disaster, the boat sinking deep on its lines, highlighting some simple mistake in my hydrostatic calculations. Nevertheless I can only hurtle on to this unknown destination.

Wanting to have our boat on the Australian Register of Ships so we will be able to voyage overseas, we need to decide on a name urgently. Somehow the passage of a few weeks has quite warmed Carolyn to the charm of *Fantasia,* so we submit our list, with *Freya* and *Zingara* the two reserve names, along with our fee of $900. A week later I receive a call from a stubborn female bureaucrat at the Ships Registry, telling me we cant have *Fantasia,* because there's a boat called *Fantazia.* "But there are lots of boats with names that are spelt quite similar! I've been through the whole list and there are hundreds," I protest.

"Well it's too similar and you CAN'T have it. That's my final decision!" Sounding like she is enjoying wielding her power, I'm forced to consider *Freya* as a name. Now that we are denied *Fantasia,* both Carolyn and Mara are quite upset, as it seems their hearts have secretly become quite set on the name.

"I know what we can do! We've never let bureaucracy dictate to us before. Let's call her *Fantasia 11* on her ship's papers, but of course we'll always refer to her as *Fantasia.* This warms all our hearts, a pirate like defiance of foolish laws. Soon deep blue vinyl names are applied in traditional Georgia font. *Fantasia* has arrived, but will she sail, will I be able to handle the shame and pain of failure if she floats poorly or behaves badly on the water?

CHAPTER 17

PIVOTAL MOMENTS

Saturday the 9th of September 2009, friends and family are rocking up thick and fast now; cousins, aunts, uncles, nieces, nephews, long lost friends, even people we don't know. Anyone who's been down to Sandy Beach over the last 4 years, 3 months and seen the ambitious boat slowly taking shape, seems keen to come see how this day may unfold. "Will that boat float?" is the question on everyone's minds.

7.30 am, *Fantasia* sits balanced on a trailer in front of the *Butterfly Lodge*, waiting for its moment of truth. Ray Bonell has been working with me for the last two weeks, bolting together a scary looking framework onto this trailer we managed to extricate from under a derelict lifeboat, hidden in the back blocks of Russell. When we first lowered the full weight of *Fantasia* onto it, the back wheels looked set to burst so we were forced to build on another set of wheels behind them.

Ray's 'old school' work-ethic, working from the crack of dawn until one can't see enough to drive a bolt in, has me feeling spent. Yet I know deep down I'm going to need more energy than I've ever had, to handle the days ahead. For the last 48hrs we've gradually tested our rig, using only Ray's rather underpowered dual cab ute to slowly turn the whole mad show around and drag it out onto the street. Now it sits ready for the tractor to arrive for the 800m tow to Sandy Beach.

Carolyn's friend P-line arrives, hippy style Indian dress, prayer beads and headscarf. "The ninth of the ninth of O-nine, sounds very auspicious for your *Fantasia*! It must have something to do with the nine lives of cats!"

"Oh yes, none of us noticed that. I do hope it will be an auspicious day for all the right reasons!" I declare, feeling ultimately on edge, wondering if I'll have enough adrenalin to get me through the day because it's coursing through my system already and *Fantasia* is still sitting peacefully in front of our house.

At 9am a big blue tractor chugs down the road, driven by my cricketing team-mate Tom Fagan. A lot will depend on Tom today and I'm hoping his driving skills are up to this big job. Total cost for the towing service, a case of Jim Beam and Coke. In fact this looks like being the entire expense for the launching, so long as everything goes smoothly. Those who build their boats inland are up for 10k and more for cranes, low loader, and police escorts. Money saved is money earned, but it's no time for mottos as we're ready to roll.

A good crowd has built up now, unfortunately there's a few naysayers, "That trailer is way too small for that huge boat mate, It'll break up as soon as you get going! I hope you've got an alternate plan, like hiring a big crane maybe, lol!" Considering we have barely scraped together enough to pay for the boat registration, the huge cost of a crane sends shivers up my spine. The tension ramps up as *Fantasia* begins her road trip in extreme low gear.

Her 8.5m of beam sets up a considerable sway every time the trailer passes an uneven spot in our red earth and gravel road. People are chatting happily, enjoying the unusual spectacle, while I'm deeply concerned our trailer can handle this moving load. Made from a 4-wheel rig with 2 light weight wheels tacked on the back, it's probably a bit underdone for carrying a 7 tonne catamaran. On the first corner it has to turn, I notice with horror the left back wheel axle has bent over!

Calling the procession to a standstill, we rush up to inspect. "What do you think Ray?" I ask, dread in my heart, having called friends and family from all over Australia to witness this launching, fearing it may end here.

Ray saunters over, a sheen of sweat on his forehead. He carefully inspects the wheels. "Don't you worry young fella, it should be OK if we take it real slow. I'm pretty sure the trailer can handle it." Ray looks a bit hot and bothered himself, but I put my faith in his words and signal Tom to continue. A few trees have to be trimmed back and the next corner is negotiated without drama. Then it's a tight squeeze through a corridor of trees before the smooth stretch past the Lyons Park, lined with spectators. Now comes the hard part, backing this great unwieldy load off the road into the Sandy Beach parking area.

The steeply cambered road sets our extreme wide load at an alarming angle and I can hardly bare to watch as it backs off the rough edge of the road. Considerable loads must be on our wooden framework at this point. Tom isn't putting a foot wrong though and when *Fantasia* is safely on the grassy beach edge, I know he is worth every can of Jim Bean and much more.

For the moment I'm hugely relieved as I climb aboard. Switching on the stereo to full volume, AC/DC unleash *Thunderstruck*. A stadium of people begin to cheer as the drummer begins to beat on his cymbals, followed by a wild burst on the electric guitar as the iconic Aussie band let rip with the bold power that thrilled me in my teenage days. The first hurdle has been conquered. In a spontaneous crowd moment, a continuous ring of people forms around *Fantasia* holding hands.

From here the plan is to wait for the tide to go out, then drive the whole rig as far down the beach as possible, unhitch the tractor then wait for the sea to come in and lift her off the trailer. Low tide's not for another 5 hours, so it's time to break out the party in the park.

Helping myself to a plate of food I contemplate my ship, working hard to muster a positive outlook, sipping on a bottle of beer to steady frayed nerves.

"She certainly looks impressive sitting there!" says our friend Kay Martin, a retired engineer who over the years has been a great help with technical issues. "It's remarkable what can be achieved by working hard each day. You stick to your task and the next thing you know there's a technical marvel produced."

"Thanks Kay, but I do feel rather nervous, the underwater part looks so small compared to the huge super structure it has to support."

"Well, you did all the calculations, so it should float on its lines," he concludes logically, drifting off into the crowd. Struggling to fend off a dark cloud of doubts, one of our more bothersome yachtie friends sidles up. Their memorable visit during the build saw his wife re-designing the layout and pronouncing all the windows to high.

"You know mate, I don't like to tell you this, but there's no way your boat's going to float on those lines. Mark my words, she'll sink well below your antifoul, just look how big she is compared to your underbody area!" His earnest prediction is exactly what I don't want to hear. The waiting suddenly becomes less bearable.

*

Late afternoon, the expectant crowd is ebbing and flowing and the tide is well out. It's time to tackle the most concerning part of the launch, hauling this heavy rig across the sand, hoping to get far enough down the beach so *Fantasia* can float off when the tide comes in. Tom fires up the big John Deer and a small army of helpers set pieces of plywood under the trailer wheels.

Having shovelled a gentle slope into the beach edge, it rolls awkwardly onto the softer beach sand. The plywood sinks in and a river of water is squeezed out as it edges along. Our team of helpers are fantastic, full of incredible confidence and positivity, while I look on wondering what to do when it all gets bogged before we get close enough to the sea.

"Is this far enough for you captain?" asks Ray as we reach the softer muddy sand.

"I hope so! Let's finish with the plywood now and let the wheels sink in to give us a few more inches," I declare, feeling somewhat relieved to have reached this point without disaster. Tom's feeling concerned about the tractor getting bogged, but pushes his tow a few more metres, where the wheels sink in and it can move no more.

Carolyn rushes up and gives me a hug. "I'm so glad that's over! I've got to admit I had my doubts."

"Yes, well all we can do now is wait for the tide to come in! And pray I did my homework properly when I designed those hulls," I announce before dashing up to get the two big bonfires going. Ray has helped me chainsaw big lumps of wood and my cousin Nicholas, an intensely positive father of 3 beautiful girls, helps me coax the fires alight.

"I'm amazed at what you've created here, it's inspiring. You rock cuz!" It's certainly an amazing day for me to be receiving such praise, I'm just deeply hoping to be worthy of it. Time crawls on but everyone is having a splendid time drinking and making merry around the fires. A blazing full moon and the tractor headlights show a trickle of water creeping up the sand. Sipping some red wine I contemplate this pivotal moment in my life, the fate of *Fantasia*, sink or swim, seems so closely tied to my own fate.

"There's more than 10,000 hours of labour there, 800 paint brushes, 1200 mixing containers, 4000 rubber gloves," I ramble to some friends.

"Not to mention a large quantity of cedar, fibreglass, foam, resin and equipment!" points out Kay Martin, clarifying my vague thoughts. The kids are off playing hide and seek, something I'd rather be doing, but my date with destiny sits heavily on my shoulders.

Blazing fires, finger foods, plenty of alcohol and a large interesting crowd has made for a buzzing party atmosphere. Everyone's pretty much forgotten about *Fantasia* patiently sitting way down the beach. Mara dashes up with a troop of friends, excited by her play and the vibe of the night. "Hey Puppi, the waters reached *Fantasia* now!"

"Oh yeah! Well, it'll be a fair while yet before she floats," says I, beginning to concede that she won't float off on my optimistic waterline. Darren Soper, who has recently launched a more sensible sized 21' Wharram cat, hands me a bottle of beer.

"You certainly picked a good night for it, full moon, clear sky, dead calm, Saturday night!" The good company helps me forget my nervousness, as we chat about boats and batteries, island gossip and nonsense. Mid tide runs faster, lapping up around the copper coated hulls, and while nobody is watching, *Fantasia* floats off the trailer much earlier than expected.

"HEY, LOOK, SHE'S FLOATING AWAY! calls out Tom, as heads pop up, amazed. A few of us sprint out, ironman style over the shallows before diving in to capture our charge. Wading along with the runaway boat in tow, I'm fairly amazed to see how high it's floating. Dropping the anchor for the first time close in to the beach is my first duty as skipper of this new ship, giddy with relief.

People flock aboard to inspect this floating creation as muddy footprints cover the decks, but I'm too happy to care. After midnight people begin to fade and *Fantasia* makes her first trip under engine anchoring out in deeper water for the night, crewed by a handsome group of adventurous souls, keen to spend the night afloat. Just as we've managed to drop anchor, it's discovered that the dinghy, ferrying passengers has been swept by a strong tide away to a distant sandbank.

We up anchor and set off on a rescue mission in the dark. Without too much drama, we soon have two rather relieved ladies aboard and the unfazed teenage skipper, Zion, who had been merrily terrifying them with stories of bull sharks. Successfully anchored again my makeshift crew whip up a fine selection of snacks and we break out the rum, sitting happily in the cockpit, marvelling at *Fantasia* afloat. Carolyn has had to forego this adventure, tending to our friends staying at the *Butterfly Lodge.* Beyond this day we never again spend a night in this island house which has served us so well. Life back aboard has begun.

The following day the party powers on and *Fantasia* makes her maiden voyage under motor. Effortlessly she carries 27 guests down to Jumpinpin Lagoon, where we feast and swim. The steering system needs improving but overall the launch has been a resounding success. Late Sunday evening, with all the visitors heading home, the big logs are still burning on the beach, with some locals happily sitting huddled around them, enjoying their warmth. I lust after a long sleep, before the next big effort gets underway. Stepping the mast promises to pose major hurdles.

*

Before we can really savour any of the joys of being back afloat the critical task of stepping the rig must be tackled. Two days later my faithful team of Ray Bonell and Kay Martin help me tow the 20m section down to Sandy Beach on an ingenious, steerable trailer Ray has made up. *Fantasia* is dried out at the top of the beach all set to have her mast lifted onto the cabin top. The task before us is formidable though, as this delicate and unwieldy object weighs in at a whopping 430kgs.

Ray has rebuilt his huge steel gantry to lift the mast up to the bow of the boat. We lash it upright, braced to some mangrove trees. After several aborted attempts at getting the angle right we manage to winch it up to the level of the forebeam. Nervously now we must slide the whole thing forward a few feet to get the head of the mast onto a ball bearing batten car, fixed to the top of the A-frame. One false move here and the delicate balance could be lost, resulting in an out of control missile smashing a hole in the boat.

With everyone on high alert, inch by inch the rig slides up onto the cabin. "Pheew! I think it's pretty much central now team, we've done it. We just need to lash it really firmly in place!" It's an awkward looking arrangement and we'll need calm seas to make the 20 mile voyage over to Manly where we have a date with a crane and a rigger in 2 days time. If it gets loose in a seaway the consequences will be dire.

My mum joins us for what is to be *Fantasia's* first voyage out of sheltered waters. All the next day a foul north-westerly gale blows, carrying a rare sandstorm off the dry interior. Thick red haze cuts visibility down to 50m and fine red sand covers our decks. "Manly's straight upwind into the eye of this storm, seas will be huge out on bay! I just hope the weather forecast is right and we can get there tomorrow." We're all sitting snugly in the spacious cabin, but with the marina, crane and rigger all booked I don't feel that comfortable.

Remarkably dawn brings a clear sky and calm. Motoring along we hose off the red sand, which has worked its way into every nook and cranny. It's a great luxury to have a deck hose, as in the old days we used the back-breaking bucket on a lanyard method to wash down decks. "Hey look! A golden dragon straight ahead!" calls out Mara. To our astonishment, the first glow of sunrise is lighting up a huge dragon's head on the bow of a ship. It turns out to be the movie set for the *Voyage of the Dawn Treader,* perched on Cleveland point.

Docking up at the East Coast Marina, Zam Bevan from Allyacht Spars is raring to go. The $400/hr crane easily lifts the rig up into place and now comes the first moment of truth. Will the forestay I had made up all those months ago, be the right length? Zam busily screws on its turnbuckle, the rig angled forward horribly, when it should be raked back at a handsome jaunty angle. My heart sinks. "Doesn't look good," says Zam. "We normally cut the forestay to length with the rig set up in place."

If the forestay length is wrong, that means the sails will all be cut to the wrong size. Mum looks on nervously from the dock. She's the one who's kindly footing the crane hire bill, and can probably read the expression of horror on my face. Rigging up halyards to the boat's stern, we winch up as much pressure as possible against the forestay. "Your mast has to sit flush on the base here." Zam is pointing to a considerable gap at the aft base of the mast. "You never know though, the main cap shrouds could still pull it back enough."

Hitching my hopes on this small chance we swage up these main aft shrouds. It's hard to avoid wondering '*What if they end up the wrong size too?*' With 2 big spanners Zam gradually tensions them up. Slowly the rig settles back to a proper rake and the mast levels out with the base. "Yes, it's perfect!" I cry out joyously, pleased the crane driver's services will no longer be needed and he can be paid off.

Before the wave of relief has a chance to settle, there's another scare. "If your structure's a bit soft, sometimes the doors jamb up when the rig goes on," states my friend Phil Wise, who recently launched his own 60' cat. I follow him inside to check the doors. "They seem a bit tight but nothing to worry about," he announces.

They don't seem much different to me, but I'm feeling weak with relief anyway.

After a hearty late lunch, we're strolling about the docks admiring our new rig. "I never thought to have the biggest rig in the whole of Manly marina!" Amid the poshest, raciest yachts in all of Brisbane, our new spar is indeed nigh on the highest about. For $200,000 we have managed to build a 50 foot catamaran, which would cost at least 1 million dollars to have professionally constructed. As the day cools down we set-up the boom and attach the mainsail. Now the big questions looming in everyone's minds; will the sails fit and will she sail?

*

Yet another glorious day greets us as we motor out of Queensland's biggest marina complex. To a chance onlooker, intrigued by this big cream coloured cat, painstakingly hoisting its mainsail in zero wind, there would be little to make them think this is such a important, pivotal moment in a man's life. It's 13 years ago now that the seed of this dream was planted. All those years of doubt, hard work and living a fugal life boils down to the success of these next few hours.

"Well at least the mainsail seems to fit, the boom's not too low that it could take out the cockpit roof!" I tick that concern off my list. Covered in sweat after hoisting the 85kg sail, even with the aid of my two strong girls, I survey the huge sail hanging loose in the still morning air. Shutting off the engines, we sit becalmed in Waterloo Bay, drinking tea and nibbling on milk arrowroot biscuits, content to wait for a breeze.

Slowly a faint zephyr of air reaches *Fantasia* and she sets off at 2 knots. "Not sure anyone else has ever been so excited at having reached such a small speed!" points out my mum, seeing the elation on our faces. Tracking nicely we pass Green Island, the speed creeps up to 3 knots, then 4.

"This light wind is a Godsend really. It's the perfect weather for a test sail!' Feeling slightly hopeful on this pristine day, the sun sparkling so magically on the gentle wind ripples. "Hey Mara, would you like to try steering?" Our 10 year old laps up the helm and with a kind of fierce concentration helms us out towards Peel Island.

"That's our new record, 6.5 knots in 9 knots of wind, under the main alone. Great work Sprat!"

"She points well and tacks nicely under the mainsail alone, not many cats can do that," says Carolyn, "I do believe you've built a good sailing boat!"

"So far so good it seems, but she has to prove herself in more wind than this before we can really be sure." Nevertheless, as we anchor over sand in the clear waters of Horseshoe Bay, for the first time in many years I feel a sense of deep relief washing over me. That evening we pop a bottle of champagne to celebrate. Yet the big question still hangs over us. How will the boat handle in a seaway with the huge 700kgs of sails and rig whipping about overhead. I have my doubts but am content to savour this small success.

Sailing back to our mooring at Russell we crack the 10 knot barrier, storming past an amazed monohull. The steering is very heavy, but that's to be expected sailing under mainsail alone, although it's evident improvements must be made to the helm connections, which appear weak under the huge loads of this big cat even in these smooth waters.

Mara's off to school, Mum's going home, Carolyn's off to work. For the first time I have *Fantasia* to myself. Anchoring close in to Sandy Beach the tide slowly goes out leaving her dried out on the sand by midday and it's time to fit the roller furler. After countless remeasures I pluck up enough courage to cut the crucial foil to length. Using a halyard, the 2m sections are joined together and hoisted up one by one. Of course I have a stream of visitors, fisherman, dog walkers and those simply out to enjoy the sea air and trample beach sand, so it's getting close to sundown by the time the unit's finally sorted.

Murky water is lapping at the hull, mozzies are hungrily looking for any unprotected skin, as the crisp dacron jib flaps its way up the newly installed foil, a last red blast of sunset dramatically colours the sky. It's imperative this sail fits exactly, so I dash back and sheet it home.

"Ahoy! Hey, wow! The jib looks good, seems like it fits pretty well." It's Carolyn and Mara, wading out to the boat, giggling at the novel pleasure of this new life.

*

"This will be the real test for *Fantasia*! We'll be beating into 15/20 knots on the way up to Tangalooma. I just hope she can handle the steep kind of waves Moreton Bay can dish out!" With the jib rolled out she tacks effortlessly out of the shallow protected waters of Redland Bay and is soon out in the open bay. "We're making 11/12 knots to windward, can you believe that? *Longnose* would only be making 7! The waves look quite big, but the funny thing is *Fantasia* hardly seems to be feeling them at all!"

As the breeze picks up and the seas build, *Fantasia* drops off the occasional wave, but there is no sense of the classic multihull hobby horsing, that uncomfortable fore and aft rocking they tend to develop in anything of a seaway. It's now blowing 20/25 knots, we're flying to windward and Mara is sitting happily at the saloon table doing her schoolwork. "Looks like she can handle the weight of her rig no problem!" I call out from the helm, a huge grin from ear to ear, joy rising in my heart. It's been a long road, but this trip is quickly lifting a lot of weight off my soul.

Arriving at Tangaloma feeling fresh, in time for lunch is a new experience. On *Longnose* we would have arrived late afternoon, worn out from sail changes and living on an uncomfortable angle. Now a glorious afternoon stretches out before us, snorkelling the wrecks, climbing the sand dunes, topped off by an evening walk to the resort to watch the dolphin feeding. It's a nice taste to remind us of our old cruising life and we're feeling hungry for more, but there's still hurdles to jump.

Late Sunday we head back to Russell to get Mara back to school. Excitedly we roll out the expensive 'Screecher' sail. The breeze is very light, yet to our amazement our speed quickly climbs to 10 knots with the helm perfectly balanced. This thrill lasts a mere 2 minutes, before there is a loud BANG as the bowsprit guy breaks and the high tech sail begins to flog about perilously, even with the wind so light. Bearing away to lose the wind, we crumple the poor sail ungraciously onto the net. "Looks like she could go pretty well under the screecher!" I gasp having tamed the runaway sail.

This powerful sail has snapped a piece of 8mm spectra rope like a piece of cotton thread. Certainly a substantially stronger bowsprit guy will be needed. Lots of other jobs are pressing, but our new life has begun and all those years of dreaming, planning and hard work are starting to pay off. "Well, we've built this boat, the question is what are we going to achieve with it?"

CHAPTER 18.

ADVENTURE BOUND

Gold Coast high-rise fills the horizon, yet the yachtsman's haven, fondly known as 'Bum's Bay' is ringed by golden sand, casuarina and native hibiscus trees, a remarkably tranquil haven in a busy world. An air of excitement hangs over *Fantasia* on the eve of our first major cruise, down to our old haunts on the NSW coast. Mara has the bosun's chair rigged up to the spinnaker halyard and is leaping off the cabin, spinning around a few times before landing on the other side of the roof. Inside it's a bit like having an elephant dancing on the roof, yet it gives her the chance to continue with her passion for acrobatics, fostered by her circus friends on Russell Island.

An inflatable dinghy zooms over to us, manned by a smartly dressed fellow who manoeuvres close to our stern, smiling cheerfully. "So it's the famous *Fantasia!* I read all the articles you wrote about building this boat in *Multihull World.* Every time an issue came out, the first thing I'd do was flick through it, wondering 'Hows that fellow getting along with his boat?' If there wasn't one of your articles I'd feel quite let down!" he says with great enthusiasm. "I was so excited when you launched her, felt like I was there watching her float off, and in your article *Fantasia Sets Sail,* I was thrilled things went so well for you guys!"

Over the course of building this boat of my dreams, nine articles on its gradual progress have been published in the glossy bi-monthly magazine devoted totally to multihulls. Thus *Fantasia* begins its sailing career with a modest amount of fame. "I read your stories and thought, 'Well if he can build that huge catamaran I can renovate the galley on my boat!" After my early frustrations with writing magazine articles, I was delighted to find the editor of Multihull Magazine so willing to publish my work. This small piece of success gave me a measure of confidence which helped me immensely during that demanding period.

Out on the open ocean of the NSW coast the weather is mild, granting us an easy passage south. The sensation of sailing along in an airy apartment is uncanny, with windows wrapping around the entire cabin giving a 360 degree view, while generous sized open windows and doors provide an easy temperature on these warm summer days. Day hopping down the coast, weaving down waves to the gentle whine of the autopilot I sit at my leisure. "Gosh, I don't even have to tinker with the windvane any-more and no more swaying about off our course! We have come a long way!" I exclaim to my crew, who are happily lounging about reading.

Pittwater, a magnificent natural harbour just 15 miles north of Sydney becomes our base for the month. Surrounded by well established houses with generous gardens and vast areas of national park, forested by glorious gum trees and native bush, it feels a remarkably wild and natural haven, so close to the 5 million strong city of Sydney.

Late on Monday afternoon I'm sitting thoughtfully at the spacious navigation table, taking in the view, when a building fleet of race boats milling about captures my attention. Enraptured, I look on with a growing sense of disquiet as the various divisions set off. Last but not least, a substantial fleet of multihulls tear off down the glorious protected reaches. My mind is driven out of its peaceful slumber, uncomfortably challenged by testing thoughts. "It's all very well to be telling people how fast our new boat is, but the only way to really prove it, is out on the race course."

Pulling out the binoculars, most of the boats look super fast out and out racers, the cream of NSW multihull racing, a fact which has me feeling a trifle doubtful. Amongst the fleet is a catamaran of similar size to ours, a million dollar plus Chincogan 52, *The Countess,* sporting high tech sails and all the best gear. "Hey, me hearties!" I call out to Carolyn and Mara who are contently tackling school-work, basically ignoring my muttering on about "race boats". "How would you both feel about racing *Fantasia* next Monday in this twilight race?"

"Yeah, let's do that Pup! I reckon *Fantasia* would do pretty well!" says Mara, happily dropping her school books to join me goggling at the race finish, where the bright red hulled *Indian Chief,* with her fancy black carbon sails has come home the clear winner.

"If you want to, but we'd have to find some crew," says Carolyn. "How do you think *Fantasia* would go?"

"Well, it would be interesting to see how we go against *The Countess!*" I reply as she crosses the line, 6th home this evening.

By the time race day rolls around, my nerves are on edge, not helped by a blustery south-east wind which is gusting as high as 31 knots. Fortunately our crew are showing no such fears, simply looking forward to the action. From Carolyn's Satyananda Yoga Ashram, she has enlisted Richard and Jayatma, who have sailed extensively aboard their Hanse 54. Chris, who helped us so profoundly with the electrics is raring to go with his teenage son Patrick. We break out some light beers to calm my nerves, then set off. It's a handful controlling *Fantasia* in such restricted waters with 90 boats tearing along every which way. Determined to keep clear of other boats we make a conservative start, last multi off the line in fact.

There's no time to be disappointed as a strong gust has us surging along and within minutes we have stormed by *The Countess,* and thread between B*ig Bird* and *Bella Isolla,* who allow us through in a very sporting fashion. My nerves fade a touch as we roar down the first leg, creaming past boats at a fine speed. On the short reach we rip by the spindly Crowther trimaran, *Twiggy* before hauling in our sheets to begin the final leg into the wind.

Beating upwind has traditionally been considered the almost sacred realm of monohull boats and a weak point in a catamaran's sailing abilities. We seem to be doing so well that some of the keel boats try to squeeze us up high into the wind, expecting we'll surely stall and stop passing them so quickly. To everyone's amazement *Fantasia* is able to point up into the wind as high as the best monohulls and still sail past these expensive yachts with their crackling, carbon cored mylar sails, the best money can buy.

Rather shamefully we rejoice to see the leader, *Indian Chief* falling by the wayside, limping under jib alone with its mainsail ripped. Now there's only *Quicksteps* ahead of us, if only we can hold our position, with *Bluey Zarzoff* clawing at us from close astern. Cautiously I must steer very high to the wind, not wishing to risk a quick port tack sally back across this fleet of yachts all converging on the finish. Just before the line a yacht tacks close under us and tries to luff us up. Squeezing up hard our bowsprit is looking uncomfortably close to the skipper of a sportsboat, finishing barely ahead of us.

When our nerves settle over a few more beers, it's nice to reflect that *Fantasia* finished the 2nd fastest mulithull, admittedly with a fair degree of luck. Out of the entire fleet she recorded the 3rd best time beaten also by the maxi *Red Hand*. "Cheers, here's to *Fantasia*, she certainly is fast! Are you planning to do any more races?" asks Richard, who has just bought a brand new Shipman 72 in the Mediterranean.

"Well, I kind of only dreamed about racing before, but on today's performance perhaps we'll be inspired to do some more." I'd often felt that the plain cruising life, sailing from one beautiful anchorage to the next made one a bit too relaxed, which for me led to a certain uninspired laziness. Thus the concept of cruising with a bit of racing thrown in to get one more motivated takes root.

Some weeks later we're heading back north, a huge swell is being generated by a distant Pacific Ocean cyclone. These long rolling masses of sea are spaced quite far apart so it's quite comfortable aboard, but constantly watching these great swells coming at you seems inexplicably tiring. I'm quite amazed really, as this type of swell would most certainly make me seasick on *Longnose,* yet I'm feeling fine. In fact not once have I felt sick since the launching of *Fantasia.* It's late afternoon, half way up the coast as we round the aptly named headland of Point Perpendicular, hoping to enter the sheltered waters of Camden Haven and escape this disturbed ocean for a peaceful night's sleep.

To our horror the narrow barred entrance is a tumultuous jumble of white water. "We'll head in a bit closer and see if we can pick a decent break in these swells," I suggest to my anxious crew, none of us feeling at all eager to spend the night out here, but realising the consequences of a mistake on this bar could spell the end of our voyaging before it's really even begun. The big swell is heaping up and beginning to crest and break so far out it proves impossible to hang about for long. Spying a modest lull, I impetuously decide to gun the engines and go for it.

Within seconds a huge wave is rearing up and it's too late to pull out as it picks us up and we're surfing at breakneck speed straight for the narrow entrance. With a great wall of surf cresting high above the cockpit, *Fantasia* screams down the front of the wave. If she veers off course or the steering happens to fail, like it has done lately, we'll crash onto the boulders of the breakwater. In one extended, surreal moment we surf our house for 100m, sitting on 20 knots, going at the speed of Usain Bolt. In 9 seconds we're suddenly shooting through the entrance to the applause from dozens of fishermen and fascinated onlookers.

Extreme calmness and serenity assail our senses as we motor up to the town feeling light headed with relief. "I really need to sort that steering system out once and for all!" I declare, feeling guilty for having risked so much, yet realising at the same time that danger is very much a part of the sailing life.

That night a lightening storm swoops over bringing strong wind and heavy rain, which beats loudly on the foam sandwich decks. The cabin deck has a low rim with a drain off both corners, leading to pipes, so there's a steady trickle of water filling our tanks. Unable to sleep, hoping this driving rain isn't finding any leaks, my mind ticks away on possible future voyages.

It's one of those wonderfully peaceful mornings aboard, doubly tranquil after the wild night. Kookaburras laugh in the still air, the haunting 'Aaaaaarhh' of the Australian raven, the distant hum of car engines, cicadas buzzing in the trees, all make up the gentle music aboard. "Last night, unable to sleep for the rain, I was having a think. We're just about ready now. What say you, we sail north this year and do the Darwin to Ambon Race, then head up to Asia and see where that leads us?" The faces of my two girls light up with excitement, making the answer pretty clear.

*

Back on the protected waters around the Bay Islands we set to, renovating the *Butterfly Lodge,* which has suffered more than 4 years of neglect, with the boat building project taking all our time. Mouldy peeling paint, blistering rust and dry wooden veranda's must be whipped into shape so it can be rented out to help fund this adventure. With a passion for racing growing in my heart, we enter the Brisbane to Gladstone race, which opens up a whole plethora of hurdles to be jumped.

Fantasia must be hauled out and accurately weighed and its sails measured so it can register an Offshore Multihull Rule, OMR rating. Two of her crew need to obtain the outrageously expensive Sea Safety certificate. Personal gps locator beacons, safety harness and inflatable life-jackets for all the crew, a comprehensive selection of pyrotechnics, the list of requirements is extensive and expensive. Nevertheless I feel it will make our cruising safer as well.

Over the years Russell Island has served us so well, its friendly community supporting us with more goodwill than I had ever dreamed of. Now as we attempt to raise money for this new campaign they flock to our day sailing trips, donating money generously. We row out 20 and more people, sail them up the bay, winding *Fantasia* up to 15-20 knots to thrill them, while feasting on the fancy snacks Carolyn piles on. Then we anchor off the glorious white sandy beach of Peel Island and enjoy a splendid lunch and swim in the clear water. Somehow anyone who makes a trip on *Fantasia,* comes away amazed at how comfortable and smooth the sailing is. "Wow, that was the best day ever! I'd love to come again," says Rose, our friendly island nurse.

"Hey Andy, your boat's awesome! You've inspired me to get a boat and go cruising too!" says Steven Marx, the local Oddjobologist. It's comments like this that really warm one's heart. An aboriginal cricketing team-mate donates a remarkably intricate and accurate dot painting of two snakes, "Fire on the Ocean," which if you look at, in the right way, does appear like a fire on the ocean. We raffle the beautiful painting, which I would have dearly loved to keep and it raises $500. On the eave of our departure, there's a pang of sadness to be leaving our friends on Russell Island, but as my life motto goes, "Nothing ventured, nothing gained."

We have an all Russell Island crew for the race. Mara's school teacher Mr Tucker, the island tiler and our photographer, Cornish born Darren Soper and Nick Lyons an engineering student at uni. Mara, who has just turned 12 must certainly rate as one of the youngest participants in the race's history. Our preparations are marred by the failure of the very expensive screecher sail to measure up as a valid screecher. This means the sail we had been making our best speeds with, can't be used. We feel very green to the whole multihull racing scene and are puzzled by particularities of the OMR rule.

It's a painfully slow start to the race with *Fantasia* sailing very well upwind in the light air, but on the downwind leg to Caloundra we lose out badly. Fast multihulls must be angled downwind, which actually pulls the wind forward, accelerating it, gybing regularly on a zigzag course. Gybing a spinnaker can end in a dangerous tangle and destruction of the sail though. Not confident enough to risk so many gybes of the spinnaker we try to sail straight downwind, the great mass of nylon cloth flopping down in a very frustrating manner.

Once out of the confines of Moreton Bay, we set off nicely under this big kite on the long leg past Fraser Island. In the early hours of the morning we pass the 50' cat *Renaissance* who rates lower than us so we should be ahead of them anyway. Sunrise sees the breeze beginning to freshen and we can make out quite a few boats several miles ahead. As the day wears on *Fantasia* shows some speed, catching and passing two boats, yet all the time we head further offshore, where unbeknown to us the adverse current is a lot stronger.

Feeling nervous about gybing, Carolyn serves up a fine lunch so we content ourselves tucking in to a hearty meal instead. By the time we gybe we're way offshore and pushing a 2 knot current, not realising we are breaking the golden rule of this race, "Stay inshore!" Crossing "The Paddock" between Fraser Island and the approaches to Gladstone our speed is good but we miss the extra speed of our screecher, yet as we converge on the Gladstone fairway beacon the action really hots up.

Out of the darkness, a blue and white spinnaker suddenly appears, it's *Free Spirit*, the Super Shockwave cat a mere 10 boat lengths astern. Battling hard they pass us during some close manoeuvres down the narrow channel, and we sight another boat ahead, seemingly limping along. Our method of running deep pays off now and we gain the upper hand by a few boat lengths, soon making out *Cut Snake* who are hastily hoisting their kite in order to fend off these fast approaching rivals.

There's some confusion aboard *Fantasia* in the final approach to the line, while *Free Spirit* and *Cut Snake* hot up their speed by sailing high and both of them pip us to the finish by seconds. Moored up in the marina, hoeing into our free case of beer, our initial downcast feeling begins to lift. "Well, 10th out of 15 seems a bit disappointing, but of course we were only seconds away from 8th and only 50 minutes out of 4th place. Considering all the mistakes we made we acquitted ourselves fairly well!" I say, cracking open another 4X.

When the handicap results are worked out we finish a creditable 4th. At the time we are surprised and impressed with this result, but later we are to learn of a mistake in our rating which would have given us 3rd. Geoff Cruse, legendary multihull racer, one of the key crew on *Free Spirit* comes aboard *Fantasia*, sniffing the heavy smell of rum wafting from our cabin, his wild greying hair, reminiscent of a tigers mane.

"Good morning *Fantasians*, what's that delightful aroma my nostrils are picking up?" It's only 9.00am in the morning but that's the aftermath of a big yacht race for you. Carolyn mixes up a special stiff cocktail of fresh lime juice, honey and rum to soothe our honoured guest. "I thought you chaps had us there at the finish, no amount of growling orders to our slovenly crew could make *Free Spirit* go any faster, and then you blew it right on the line. I enjoyed that, we'll have to do it again sometime!" Nobody other than Geoff wants to relive that moment so we change the subject.

"So Geoffrey, where are you guys heading from here?"

"Sadly I'll be on the plane back to Brisbane tomorrow. Boats to survey, wife to appease, that kind of thing, but you lucky sailors could head up for the Yeppoon to Mackay race in two days time!" Carolyn and Mara's heads swing round to gauge my reaction.

"The minute any race is mentioned, I know straight away he'll want to do it, even before he says anything!" says Carolyn. Well I certainly hadn't planned on doing this race, but if my crew thinks I am………mmmmm?

"Andy it's been an absolutely awesome race. I've enjoyed every minute of it," announces Mr Tucker in his best teachers voice. "So you guys are heading on now, bound for Asia! We'll miss you on Russell. I might have to think about building my own boat." It's hugs all-round as he heads off to catch a plane home.

*

"It'll be an easy race!" I promise my girls, who'll be the only crew "The forecast is for strong winds so we wont need to fly the spinnaker." Nothing could be further from the truth as the breeze lightens off and they spend the night gybing the spinnaker from side to side. Our inexperience making us do it the hard way. Pull the sock down over the kite, drop it, haul it all around to the other side then hoist the 20kg sail back up again, unsock the great mass of nylon so it billows out again, while I sheet it home. At least half a dozen times the unwelcome order of "you know we should really gybe the spinnaker again," is met with stoic resignation. The race to Mackay slingshots us north, past our favourite haunts, Keppel and Percy Islands.

"It was worth it in the end!" I comfort my girls at the trophy presentation in the Mackay Yacht Club. "For our $40 entry fee we got 3 free nights marina berthing, a bottle of rum for first boat to the leeward mark off Yeepoon, 3 bottles of posh red wine for line honours, beating *Wild Spirit* who got 6th over the line in the Gladstone. Then another bottle of rum and a gear bag for 1st on handicap and our name inscribed on the perpetual trophy!"

"It did seem like a lot of hard gybes at the time, but I suppose it was kind of fun," admits Carolyn, now that her rope worn hands are stinging less. For Mara it's been an eye opening experience as she actually got to do more of the crew work, without a whole bunch of men always on hand to do the work and she seemed to enjoy this.

*

"Aren't you worried your daughter isn't getting to hang out with kids her own age? We never seem to meet families with kids out cruising," says a well meaning yachting wife. It's a common cruising concern. We're hanging out at one of our all time favourite spots, that buzzing hive of action, Airlie Beach. Main town of the legendary Whitsunday Islands, the yachting Mecca of Australian sailors. Mara spies a big aluminium cat called '*Lost'*, seemingly overrun by teenage girls.

"Let's go over and visit them! Don't be shy, they wont bite," cajoles Carolyn as Mara feigns shyness. The *Lost* crew have cruised around from Darwin and the three lively girls, Tahni, Kaila and Marli prove a windfall of friends for Mara. Everyone's happy and nobody needs to feel they're missing out. It's a coolish winter, chill air pushing deep into the tropics, yet the days are sunny and the trade winds are continuing to provide a steady flow of wind driving us north. Life is a pleasant procession of reef lagoons and bays, while slipping easily by vast regions of natural woodlands.

"Did you guys know the Great Barrier reef is by far the largest living thing on earth, stretching for 2300km, made up of a staggering 3000 reef systems!" says I, reporting on the nature of my studies. "Home to a mind boggling variety of amazing creatures, it's one of the seven natural wonders of the world, Australia's prize jewel! I do believe the reef is the most beautiful place on earth."

We're anchored in Britomart Reef, next to our friends on *Lost*. The two big catamarans lie easily to a modest breeze, in a spacious aquamarine sandy patch surrounded by coral bommies. "It's like we're in a magic cocoon, far from the hustle and bustle of the land.

The ocean comprises 71% of the planets surface so this fresh pure air is washed clean by that incredible vastness. This is heaven!"

Relaxing with a green tea and Carolyn's fresh baked power cookies, we savour the stillness after a lively sail, the reef breaking the ocean waves, leaving the lagoon tranquil. A clear and vast horizon surrounds us, full of frolicking sea-birds happily fishing, the peace gradually sweeping over us. "Here's everyone's snorkelling gear!" says Carolyn, bustling up from below with an armful of gear.

Reef is so close to us we simply dive off the boat and swim over. White streams of aerated water swirl off our bodies as we plunge in and marvel at these new surroundings. The pale blue sea is crisp and clear with occasional particles of sealife. Visibility stretches along *Fantasia's* dolphin like hulls, beyond the anchoring cable, off into the sandy bottom, 8m below. It's easy for the girls to enjoy an adventure together in this playpen of the Gods, so far removed from a shopping mall. We swim down to inspect the anchor, securely dug into the firm white sand.

Heading across to the reef we break into the Australian crawl finning comfortably to cross the sandy acres that stretch to the reef, where the odd sea cucumber, starfish and shell, filter feeds on the sand as stingrays dig for molluscs and worms. We feel comfortable knowing only reef sharks inhabit this domain. Now a bommie looms ahead, greeny grey with outriders like the fusilier, snapper and coral trout lurking around the perimeter. Up closer, the explosion of colour is hard to take in, a complexity of species potentially requiring a lifetime of observation to understand.

Corals of every shape are the basis of the reef. Hard ones like the staghorn, plate and brain corals, then soft ones, so tempting to touch, sea fans and whips, more than 600 types of every colour in the rainbow. Here is the gigantic city of the tiny coral polyps who build this complex structure. Then there are the more mobile giants of this undersea world, the fish, sea snakes, cephalopods, turtles and sharks. With great excitement one is constantly casting about to see what denizen of this world is gracing your particular location in this incredibly vast maze of reef.

Tiny blue green chromis fish swarm over a clump of reddy brown staghorn coral, sergeant damselfish patrol the the busy corridors of the polyp's high-rise creations. A pair of lined butterfly fish flit by, a black-spot snapper looks at me suspiciously for man is the most fearsome predator on the reef. Rabbit fish timidly scamper away, a lionfish lurks under a blue plate coral awaiting his prey, while a clown anemone family lounge in their host anemone with its purple tipped feelers waving gently in the tide. I'm fascinated by the master of disguises the octopus, notoriously elusive to spot but there's a giant bumphead parrotfish gliding past a purple starfish and some iridescent clams. Snorkelling the reef seems by far and away the richest natural experience on this magnificent planet.

Coming across a dead bommie is a sad and bleak feeling, the once living, brightly coloured coral now a grey mass of calcium carbonate, a dead skeleton devoid of its usual entourage of fish. I have always been optimistic that man will be able to overcome his primal urges of greed and comprehend that we must nurture and feed the earth, which provides us with our lives. Further on the bommies are alive again, adorned with Moorish idols and sixbar wrasse as soft corals wave their supple arms. Mara and her friends are doing some aquatic acrobatics while a green sea turtle looks on intrigued. The amazing reef we must do all we can to help survive, for her death will be ours.

Right up to Cairns Mara enjoys her three sisters of the sea, but urgent business back in Darwin sees them flying home, putting us in charge of their most curious pet. Sid, the carpet snake moves aboard with us, leaving me slightly uneasy about this creature's presence. His license doesn't allow him to be in Queensland so it becomes our duty to return him to his home in Darwin. He only needs to be fed a rat every 2 weeks and allowed a brief jaunt around the boat each day and Mara's petting needs can be fulfilled.

Cairns being the last proper shops until Darwin, 1200 miles on, we stock up for 4 weeks and more. Trudging back through the bustling tourist town, past the shady trees of the esplanade, weighed down with shopping bags, even Mara is struggling along with her fair share of bags. At the Cairns Yacht Club a smartly dressed yachtsman, strikes up a conversation, intrigued by our lifestyle. He is dreaming of heading off on an adventure like us, but seemingly chained to the grindstone of work. "So how do you guys afford to go off on these great long adventures? Have you got like, 100k saved up to last you through the year?"

It's nice to be relaxing in the shade of the building before our row across the inlet to *Fantasia*, our sweat cooling. "Haha, I wish. No we just do it the old fashioned cruisers' way. We avoid marinas like the plague and always anchor out, so at $100/night for a 15m cat, that's a huge saving. Also we do all our own maintenance, so we're getting by on just over 10k a year." Our friend looks incredulous when I tell him this.

He turns his attention to Carolyn, who is happily eating bananas with Mara. "You guys look happy enough, but I mean even just buying food and dinning out would be costing much more than that, surely?" he pleads.

"Well, for one we only dine out once in a blue moon. When we shop we only buy what's in season, which of course means it's fresher and cheaper. Mostly we buy the specials and try and buy whole foods which are full of real goodness, rather than luxury items which are mostly not so good for you anyway," says Carolyn, full of a delightful earnestness. "And rather than needing to always buy particular products and often paying a premium for them, we're keen to try the new and different local produce. The savings add up all the time. Also we catch a lot of fish." Our friend looks puzzled and deeply reflective as he watches us row off. "Oh yes, we don't use an outboard either! More savings," calls Carolyn as a parting gesture.

After the hustle and bustle of victualling in Cairns a fitful morning breeze gradually settles in to become the steady trade wind, blowing us lustily to Low Isles. By day a constant stream of tourists flock to this tiny coral cay, to savour its shady vegetation and frolic in the cool sea and coral gardens. From late afternoon sailors have this slice of paradise all to themselves. Leaping into the inviting clear sea we wash off the dust and confusion of town life with a refreshing snorkel around the nearby reef, the fish lively in the soft evening light. "Ahh, that feels so good," I sigh, towelling myself dry. " The Darwin to Ambon race starts in a month's time and we'll need a few weeks to sort Indonesian visas, so we'll have to crack the pace from here."

*

Streaking north before the glorious trade wind, blowing like clockwork along this wild and virtually unpopulated stretch of the Queensland coast, we gybe inshore to glimpse some of the wonders of the Daintree, boasting the most diverse flora in Australia. Tropical forest meets the ocean, with the lush green of towering bunya pines, blue quandong, bull kauri pines, the rare plum pine, fan palms and pandanus reaching down to pristine white beaches. Cape Tribulation reaches out, rimmed by a dark rocky foreshore. Aboard *Fantasia* it's a remarkable sensation to be racing along, passing such spectacular scenery, virtually in a space capsule, with all the comforts of home at hand, embarked on the adventure of a lifetime.

In our 1st major race, the Surf to City, run between the Gold Coast and Brisbane, our home built *Fantasia* surprised everyone. Some who had seen my magazine articles had laughed at her traditional style, sharp sided wheelhouse and thought my efforts something of a joke. Now they had to eat their words. Some spectators watching the race gave us a cool video clip they captured of us racing by, up with the leaders. These are the excited commentators words. "Woohoo! Friggin it hammers doesn't it. That's Truckin! It's a house! It's a FLYING HOUSE! That's cruzin! That's the way to sail around the world!"

Now the "Flying House" spreads its woven wings, exploring historical Cooktown, idyllic Lizard Island, the grey boulders of Cape Melville, Princess Charlotte Bay, each day progressing deeper into the wild far north. While running before this strong breeze of 25/30 knots is enjoyable, there's virtually no turning back from here, as beating into that power of wind and wild sea would make for horrendous travel. Thus the only people sailing past this low undulating coast of eucalyptus forest, beach scrub and red earth termite mounds, are those on route to Thursday Island then Gove or Darwin.

Departing Thursday Island on the longest stretch, 333 nautical miles across the Gulf of Carpentaria we hope to make the crossing with only one night at sea. That enclosed feeling of being ashore with its myriad of concerns begins to evaporate as *Fantasia* surfs out into the wide open sea. The inner ear balance mechanism is typically confused at first by the twisting, surging motion and the body shuts down most of its usual desire to rush about. In this enforced state of relaxation a dreamy vacant feeling leaves one happy to lie on a bunk and read or simply enjoy the mind's wandering.

During the night the seas build up. "We're doing well under two reefs and no jib!" I call to Carolyn and Mara, needing to pitch my voice over the tumbling of waves and the whining of wind in our rigging. "We're averaging over 10 knots, so we should make Cape Wessel before dark tomorrow." A brown boobie has managed to clumsily land on our foredeck then strut back to shelter on the edge of our cockpit. We feel honoured to have such a guest, being very careful not to disturb our wild seabird.

"What's that flashing light to our north there?" says Carolyn, sounding concerned.

"No idea! It's that far away I don't think we need worry about it!"

"There's one down to the south as well!" she points out a little while later.

"Well I don't see what we can do about them!" I return to the comfort of the chart table and begin to doze off, fending off a niggling sense of apprehension. Suddenly our surfing ship comes to a violent, instant stop, thrusting me forward into the table, throwing any lose items onto the floor. Imagining that we have hit some uncharted shoal we rush outside in astonishment. Peering over the side, vivid phosphorescence lights up the course mesh of a fishing net, looking quite enchanting. *Fantasia* has been nabbed like an ocean fish! Dashing forward we drop the mainsail, then pull up the centreboards and rudders, which lets us float free.

"Wow, that was a bit scary!" says a wide-eyed Mara. "Who would put a net there?" she exclaims indignantly. "It's scared away our boobie!" who has kindly left us a pile of guano for his stay.

"It'd have to be an Indonesian fishing boat, to be laying a net right on a sailing route. Hopefully we wont run into too many of them up in Asia!" I reply feeling relieved.

Even after this setback we make Marchinbar Island, anchoring in gloriously remote Two Island Bay in time for sunset cocktails. Now we have entered Australia's least populated but 3rd biggest state, the Northern Territory. Dry red earth, open forests, wetlands and

Spinifex, the spiky tussock grass that thrives on arid land, gives way to coastal mangroves and some of the wildest, remote coast in all the world. This harsh place of crocodiles and heat, remains the domain of the oldest surviving culture on the planet, the original inhabitants of this country. One may find the remains of some desecrated European houses or equipment, but the land is pristine, for these people worship the land, not what can be stripped from it. So far from our usual western influences, something of their spiritual 'Dreaming' reaches out to us.

In the deep quiet of the 'Top End', the haunting ebb and flow of the didgeridoo barks at our soul, while the hypnotic song of this rich culture blends with the low pitched drone of the bull roarer, the raucous, chaotic sound of the gum leaf and the sharp percussion of the clapsticks. Our brief connection to this complex culture is fuelled by excellent results with the fishing lure, but diluted by our arrival in Darwin one still hot morning. Sid the snake, who I had always held in high esteem, believing him of exceptional intelligence, plummets in my estimation when he tries to ingest a t-shirt which he mistakes for his bi-weekly rat. Now our preparations for the race to Ambon must begin in earnest.

CHAPTER 19.

FANTASIA SAILS TO ASIA

"Hey, look I'm sorry mate for giving *Fantasia* such a high handicap! I realise it's your first Ambon, but the committee insisted. I know it's a big ask to be expected to put time on boats like *Freedom Express!* I mean he's the same length as you, immaculate boat, Schionning Waterline design, I think." With *Fantasia* dried out on the extensive low tide beach in front of the Darwin Sailing Club, the race handicapper has strolled down to gently break his news to us.

"That's OK. Who knows, perhaps we deserve such a handicap. We just hope it's a successful race and lots of fun!" What with the complexity of preparations assailing us, this bit of news is the least of my concerns. Leaving the comforts of one's homeland and stocking up for a voyage into the world's largest archipelago, the fourth most populated country on the planet and perhaps the strangest culturally, is a daunting prospect. Food, spare parts, guides, schoolwork for

Mara, cancelling our Australian phone service, fitting a new radar set, we have our hands full in the steaming tropical heat of Darwin. At the same time I feel a certain pressure looming over my head. It's all very well to have built a decent catamaran, but it would make the whole project deeply fulfilling if it registered some notable success.

Best clothes must be fished out for cocktails at Parliament house, where race entrants are grandly welcomed by political dignitaries and representatives from Indonesia. "Ahh, *Fantasia,* I love the name!" An important looking lady with glorious make-up and a fancy hat, sidles up to us, waving her glass of champagne. "So you're the cruising family doing the race. You've done some racing already I hear, and this is your lovely daughter, only 12 years old! So tell me, which boat do you think will be first into Ambon?"

"Well, we don't really know much about the other boats but I think we'll be first in," I reply modestly, taking a swig from my schooner of Northern Territory draught, while a very formal waiter offers us twisty pesto and cheese straws.

"Haha, I like your confidence! Realistically though, what about the maxi yacht *Walk on the Wild Side* manned by 15 experienced racers from WA or *Australian Maid,* who has won several times before. Even Darwin's own *Freedom Express*, such a high tech modern catamaran. Well I wish you the best of luck, but don't be too disappointed, just getting there will be a great achievement." She gives us a winning smile, quaffing her champagne and heads off for a refill.

"Lucky I didn't mention we think we're a chance for the race record!" I laugh, joining Carolyn and Mara, happily savouring the oriental prawn cakes.

Nick Lyons, who did the Gladstone race with us is our sole crew, arriving a day before the start. Flying from a cool gentle Brisbane winter, one is enveloped in the warm arms of the far north. A sheen of sweat shows on Nick's young smiling face as he winches me up the mast for a final check on the rigging. He flicks his short chocolate brown hair back, peering up to check I'm ok, his sharp engineering mind, the perfect tool for a sailor. His skin is a little pallid from working long hours at his new job but he's the kind of guy who tans easily. I'm hoping his surfing skills will come in useful if we get some fresh south-east trades and *Fantasia* can begin to surf.

"It's all shipshape up there!" I say to Nick after he has carefully lowered me down. "You must be feeling pretty excited, this being your first voyage on a yacht to a foreign land. I think it's going to be a huge thrill for you and Mara alike!"

"You're not wrong there! I can't believe the day has come. Bring it on!" His laid back attitude makes him easy to have aboard. Spending his teenage days, sailing a speedy off-the-beach cat from his family house, he brings a reputation for driving it exceptionally hard, often to breaking point. I'm hoping he's not too gung-ho out on the far reaches of the Timor and Banda Sea though.

Nineteen yachts jostle in the light southerly land breeze as a crowd of onlookers line Stokes Wharf, the excitement fuelled by a troupe of Indonesian ladies dancing to the beat of drums. The harbour is sparkling in the bright sunshine and the countdown is on with the yachts charging towards the line. *HMAS Ararat* fires the starting shot and the 2011 Darwin to Ambon is under-way, Australia's premier international offshore yacht race.

Race favourite, the 57 foot, *Walk on the Wild Side* leads the fleet off, her professional crew quick to set their spinnaker. *Even Karma*, a Sydney 38 design hold off the charging *Australian Maid,* a 55' monohull, which in her time came 3rd over the line in the Sydney Hobart. We struggle to set our striking black, orange and gold kite but soon have the muddy blue water of Darwin harbour gurgling past our transoms.

"We seem to be passing the *Maid* pretty easily," says Nick happily trimming the spinnaker sheet. "I think we're gaining on *Wildside* too and there's a bit more breeze up ahead."

Harnessing more power *Fantasia* draws up level with *Wildside,* where her smart crew in matching cream uniforms do their best to ignore this cruising catamaran, which obviously has speed on them in these conditions. One of the principal race organisers, Robyn Dix, shoots a nice photo of us edging into the lead from *HMAS Ararat* following the fleet, which the *Darwin Sun* runs for their story in the sports pages.

Our glory is short lived though, as the land breeze dies off with the heat of the day and a light northerly fills in. With the breeze against us, it allows the big monohulls who carry huge light weather headsails to forge past. This hot dry wind lightly fans our sails as we creep by the fleet of 250 yachts in the Sail Indonesia Rally, an armada of hopes and dreams setting off to discover exotic lands.

It's slow work across the 60 mile Beagle Gulf and my dreams of a record run are rapidly evaporating in the stifling heat. Late afternoon sees us battling with cruiser/racer *Sue Sea* an upmarket Martin 49, then as a welcome sunset falls the breeze drops off altogether.

"Lets have a game 21 questions to get our minds away from this frustrating lack of wind," says Carolyn producing a plate of snacks. Under a rapidly appearing canopy of stars we lounge on the trampolines, munching on chips, olives and fresh vegi sticks dipped in hummus.

"Ok, my question. Is it bigger than a bread box?" asks Mara. "Hey, I can feel a breeze on my neck!" We've only played a few rounds but a gentle south-west breeze is definitely filling in.

By midnight we pass the western most point of Melville Island, Cape Fourcroy, our speed now over 9 knots. The sea is still quite calm while the stars are so vivid it feels like one could reach out and touch them. Our spirits have risen as we can see the navigation lights of the two leaders not too far ahead.

At 3.50am the breeze shifts a bit to the south so I figure it's swinging around to the normal south-east direction, and we decide to gybe *Fantasia* onto the now more favourable course. For some strange reason the other yachts fail to change course so at 4.00am we cross within 50m of *Wildside's* stern. "I can't understand why they're not gybing like us?" says Nick. "I'd say we're officially in the lead now!" Before long the south-east breeze begins to fill in nicely and *Fantasia* starts to lift her skirts and fly.

The 9am HF radio sked shows us 10 miles ahead of *Wildside*. There's high fives all round as Nick and I settle into sharing stints at the helm, our billowing spinnaker driving us down the nicely developing swells of the open Timor Sea. "I've just calculated that we need to average 13.9 knots from here to take the record. We can forget that." I announce, having consulted the charts.

"Wow, it feels strange to be just sailing on and on, way out into this wide and endless sea!" remarks Mara, the sweet innocence of her voice wafting out happily over our distant location. "It's just so vast and amazingly beautiful out here but I wish I was old enough and strong enough to steer!" she says, energetically trimming the spinnaker, casting jealous glances at Nick working the helm to catch the glorious long swells that are regularly allowing us to surf at over 20 knots.

Throughout the day *Fantasia* streaks across the great expanse of the Timor Sea. "That's 15.4 knots you've averaged in that hour Nick. Great steering!" says I taking over for my stint at the helm. It's tiring wrestling with the wheel, lining *Fantasia* up for the next wave, then working quickly to stop her veering off in the wrong direction as she surfs fantastically down these great long swells. It feels kind of weird having one's house do what a surfboard normally does. Grey clouds are beginning to form on the horizon where we need to find the pass into the Banda Sea and the breeze is picking up, putting more strain on the spinnaker.

"Wow, that's 15.8 miles in the last hour," says Carolyn, "but do you think we might feel more under control without the spinnaker?" Everyone agrees with this call and we douse the kite and roll out the screecher, which takes the alarming drama out of our progress, yet we still average well over 14 knots. By the 5pm radio sked billowing clouds have masked our pristine sunny day and Semata Island has appeared, a dark mound on the horizon, but *Fantasia* has stormed 33 miles ahead of *Wildside*.

We are carrying a satellite tracker so the sailing world can see us chalking up a handsome lead, more than 100 miles ahead of some boats, while I'm just praying we can maintain our pace. "Hey Andy, there's a rip across the top of the sceecher. Doesn't look good!" Our expensive sail has failed for the 3rd time now, seemingly not built strong enough. We roll it up and continue on now into the darkening sky under mainsail and jib alone.

Our ocean keen nostrils pick up faint scents of earth, cooking fires and blossoms, borne on the strengthening wind, as we enter the Banda Sea. "We're in Indonesia, hooray! It feels different, wild and remote." Mara, sitting in the cockpit is peering at some dark distant islands, as we continue to make good speed on our course slightly west of north. Clouds race overhead, occasionally thinning enough to allow a waxing moon its chance to turn the disturbed sea a glimmering silver.

Into the night we glide across the seas, *Fantasia* riding so smoothly over the waves, barely feeling them. Held firm by the driving force of the sails and the lifting force of the foils, the hulls blow through the seas so easily, but squally conditions put us to the test. "Hey Andy, I think we need to reef!" calls Nick from the helm, firmly, with a hint of concern. "This squall came on pretty quick. I've had to run straight before the wind and we're still sitting on 20 knots steady!" It feels remarkably comfortable in the cosy cabin, yet out in the cockpit a powerful wind is straining the sails, while Nick urgently wrestles the helm. We dash forward and pull two reefs into the mainsail, not without difficulty. "That feels a lot better!" says Nick, sounding relieved. Obviously there was no need to think he might be too gung-ho, this far flung wild sea surrounded by savage looking islands encouraging everyone towards caution.

All night long squalls harass us, leaving *Fantasia* underpowered when they fade away. Short on crew we're reluctant to hoist the kite in case it gets blown away in the powerful squalls that regularly swoop over our course. With the first rays of dawn streaking across a clearing sky, all hands set the spinnaker and the refreshing aromas of coffee, bacon and eggs begin to waft about our cabin. The 9am radio sked shows us 48 miles ahead of our rival, *Wildside,* so our spirits are high. Looking out on the vast Banda Sea, running so pleasantly, there's surprisingly not an Indonesian fishing vessel to be seen.

"That's a day's run of 308 miles and on *Longnose* our best ever run was 208 miles. It feels pretty satisfying to have built a boat that's at least a third faster." I'm sitting comfortably at the chart table sipping more coffee, feeling I may have the best desk job in the world, enjoying the 360 degree view with the foreign looking peak of Pulau-Pulau Penyu, a distant landmark to our west. The stormy night clouds have burnt off leaving the blazing beauty of equatorial sunshine to light up the intense blue of the extremely deep seas that exist in these Asian waters. Running on a gentle caffeine high and lack of sleep I savour a rare moment of intense satisfaction, before it's my turn on the helm again.

All day *Fantasia* scoots along, scaring schools of flying fish who leap out and spread their wings to escape this great foreign beast, that must appear like two giant dolphins swimming in tandem. By late afternoon we are bearing down on the island of Ambon, gradually making out lush tropical forest dominating its hillsides. One of the most infamous legs of this race is the final 6 mile stretch into the harbour, where the wind is inclined to die off and strong run out tides have held yachts there all night.

As we harden up our sheets for the beat in, the breeze looks promising but there are surprises in stall. "What are all those things out on the water? They look a bit like little huts!" says Nick, his astonishment growing. So far we have seen very little sign of Asian life, now we are confronted by numerous little fishing huts scattered all over the harbour. "But, but... it's like 500m deep here, how have they anchored them?" Wizened brown fishermen prepare tea over coals, peering deeply at this futuristic machine which has suddenly appeared in their ancient world. We are quickly realising just how foreign a country we are entering.

With the rapid fall of dusk, suddenly our breeze falters and we find ourselves just making way in a barely perceptible breath of wind. The lights of Amahusu village can be seen only a mile away, but if we don't get there soon the tide will turn against us. On the last radio sked *Wildside* was 65 miles astern, but if we spend the night drifting back out the harbour, as we have heard many a tale of, we may yet have to duel with them again.

Fantasia struggles on barely making way, then a zephyr wafts through and we feel elated doing 2 knots as a green laser light dances on our sails. Out of the darkness a boat approaches and an on-board band begins to play the most enchanting music I have ever heard. A magic combination of many drums, gongs and exotic bells sends our emotions soaring, bringing tears to our eyes as they gently circle *Fantasia* and cheering breaks out from the shore.

Yet this proves to be something of a premature crescendo as we lose all way, a tantalising 200m from the line. The enthusiastic drums die off as our escort continues hopefully to circle us. Ashore the cheering has died away, yet we are close enough to hear the murmur of people talking. To my horror I begin to notice the gps showing us going backward. With our senses straining, we feel for any sign of wind. It's so calm on the harbour it feels like the wind has died out for the night, shut up shop and gone home. Lighting a mosquito coil its smoke rises up in a perfect line. We look at each other nervously, feeling the desire of all the crowd on shore, who'd like to see us finish, concerned we may be about to disappoint them badly.

A slight breath takes us towards the line, yet with 50m to go it falters and we must inch towards the light of the restaurant, rumbling with voices. Closing with the rocky seawall, with barely any way on at all, I delicately put the helm over and pray *Fantasia* will tack, as I can see a sad end to this story.

Around she comes and then picks up to a whole knot of speed, crossing the line in one of the most memorable events in all our lives. The roar of the crowd a surreal moment to die for. Once anchored twelve officials in spotless uniforms crowd aboard, adorned with gold epaulettes and finely polished medals, eager to be the most important. "Captain, I think you will find it's my forms you should be filling out first!" says the customs official after I had begun with the harbourmaster's paperwork. The serious nature of clearance seems more show than anything as they keep flashing us big smiles and congratulating us on our win.

Feeling a bit dazed we are now called ashore to meet a great crowd of dignitaries. Blazing lights for TV cameras somewhat blind us as we make our way up the seawall, stunned and amazed. At the race control office we shake hands with the King of Amahusu, who presents me with a finely woven blue banner. Now we feel like movie stars with everyone shaking our hands and being interviewed for Indonesian TV and radio.

Having done our duty with the media we are escorted off to the restaurant on the seawall and served up lavish seafood and vegetable dishes with plenty of bottles of cold Bintang beer. This warm and enthusiastic welcome would rival winning the Sydney to Hobart Race. We had fallen 4 hours short of the record, yet *Fantasia's* performance seemed exceptional considering the conditions. *Wildside* rock up 6.5 hours later, claiming their own glory by breaking the monohull record. Feeling deeply exhausted we are all happy to get back aboard after our stunning arrival and fall instantly asleep.

*

Carolyn, in her usual fashion is up early doing some yoga and meditation. She has the coffee made when I drag myself out of bed, so after a brief stretch I can savour the delights of this rich roasted bean. How wonderful is the planet to provide us with such a smooth, uplifting and satisfying drink. "*Freedom Express* is coming up the harbour now, just ahead of a monhull. It must be *Australian Maid,*" says Carolyn sitting contentedly in the cockpit taking in our exotic new surroundings.

Warm tropical rain explains the lush green of the village and surrounding hills, it does not stop some locals paddling out in canoes to view the new arrivals. "Lets dive in and freshen up with a swim!" I cry out enthusiastically inspiring my crew reluctantly into this deep blue foreign water, much to the entertainment of the locals. Splashing about in the remarkably clear water, we gaze up at the steep slopes, verdant with jungle, the village esplanade lined with coconut trees, thick with colourful banners, swaying gaily in the wind. Raindrops from the heavens sprinkle pure fresh water on our bodies making us feel so deeply refreshed and amazed at being transported to this strange country.

"Would you like to come and see our village?" the elder of the young boys in the canoes asks us politely. Of course we are all keen to stretch our legs, so we lock up the boat and head ashore. Coconut fronds, Java almond leaves and plastic rubbish marks the beach's high tide point as we follow a clear river up towards the village. Making our way through the wet, luxurious, mossy bush we come across two ladies washing the paper stickers off water bottles in the river to re-cycle them. Foreignness seeps in as we walk on.

A narrow bitumen road meanders its way around the extensive harbour shore and through the village of Amahusu. The houses are brightly painted in red, blue, yellow and seemingly whatever paint they can get their hands on. The gardens, where open fire cookhouses are built, grow mostly useful flora like bamboo, star fruit, cacao, limes, bananas, pineapples, manioc or flowers etc, all thriving on rich soil and plentiful rain. Our friends generously buy us bottles of drinking water as we march beyond the road into the thick forest.

"Where do we put these bottles?" asks Nick, looking around keenly for some kind of rubbish bin.

"Those? Oh just drop them there," replies our young guide, pointing to the virgin forest floor, demonstrating by gaily tossing his bottle into the thick green shrubs. There is no choice, and battling our deep seated cultural learning we reluctantly place our bottles on the path edge. As we hike up the hill, there are men shoring up the riverbed with rock-work and higher up we meet some merry fellows cutting wood. We fill our lungs with the fresh forest air as our muscles rejoice with the exercise.

From the hilltop one looks down over a sea of trees, the rusty roofs of the village blending in pleasantly. Many boats are yet to arrive and we can make one out, battling its way up the harbour. At the head of the bay can be seen the extensively built up area of the city of Ambon, fronted by shipping wharfs. "I can't wait to get into the markets to do some stocking up," says Carolyn. That's the last thing on my mind, standing on the top of this hill with an exotic foreign country stretching out before my eyes, feeling at last to be deeply reaping the rewards of my labour.

Returning from our walk there is much commotion in Amahusu as they prepare for a cultural performance, seemingly undaunted by the rain that has turned the performing area to mud. Up on the big stage an elaborate band starts up with golden gongs and drums weaving the enchanting Maluku melody and drawing a crowd of sailors and locals. As the big band plays, a tall maypole is set up in the mud and a group of smartly dressed children prepare for a dance. "But how will they be able to dance? It's so muddy!" says Mara, looking concerned for the children in their immaculate white pants and red coats.

In the nick of time a truck arrives and a team of men quickly start shovelling sand over the mud. Firstly they form a little island so the dance can begin and as the tempo of the dance increases the men have made the island bigger. By the time the maypole dance is hitting its crescendo and the children are rapidly unplaiting the banners they have carefully danced into neat plaits, a dazzling piece of skill, the men have covered the whole area with sand. "Wow, only in Asia would you see that!" says Carolyn. "It was a miracle they managed that dance at all."

Next day we are all bussed into the fast paced city of Ambon and the entire fleet are guided into rickshaws, then cycled through town, occasionally cycling into the oncoming stream of traffic feeling a little apprehensive. Arriving in a spacious park, marquees are set up with silk lined seats for sailors and dignitaries alike. "Oh yes madam, we are still waiting on the Mayor. He is very important so will make us wait," explains a finely dressed fellow as we lounge happily on the smooth glossy material.

With immaculate pomp and ceremony speeches are made, banners are presented to the sailors and gifts to the school in Ambon. The band plays and nimble girls and boys demonstrate the complex stick dance, where a false move will squash the hands of those working the sticks, which clap together rhythmically under the nimble flashing feet.

Of course no presentation is complete without a feast and the people of Ambon turn it on with a complex buffet. "Look at this!" says Mara excitedly, brandishing a bowl "you have to slurp up this sago stuff, like a thick soup!" Well, she may be missing out on formal school, but this seems a good education.

Happily we munch away on Ambonese delicacies, "Mmmm, yum this is a very fresh raw fish marinated with lime, shallots and chillis," says Carolyn blissfully. "I'm just amazed that all this presentation is just to celebrate Darwin and Ambon being sister cities."

That night we scrub up and don our best clothes to be bussed in to the Mayor's mansion on the outskirts of Ambon. "It's just amazing the amount of effort they are putting in just for a yacht race!" I wonder out loud as we stride up the steps to enter the grand manor. "I suppose, to put it in perspective, this is the biggest yacht race in one of the most populated countries in the world. The Indonesians are really showing a lot of class with this welcome!"

Finest behaviour is being turned on by the whole gaggle of yachtsmen as we are led through a hall to the entertaining wing. The furniture does not disappoint, as we are seated in grand Victorian lounges, whose elaborately carved wood is picked out with gold paint. Finely woven chenille upholstery of golden brown with a traditional floral pattern is faultlessly edge-piped to form a soft luxury that instantly swallows one up. Even the tissue boxes on the matching coffee tables are gold filigree.

Naturally we are served the major race sponsors beer, Bintang, in glasses of course. Sipping Indonesia's favourite, a clear golden lager, easy to drink with a faint exotic herbal taste, we make delicate conversation. "Hello Andrew, congratulations to your team on *Fantasia* for this victory," says one of the key race organisers Helen De Lima. She is a well travelled Ambon local, who did so much in reviving the race after the political upheaval which plagued Ambon at the turn of the 21st century. Her youthful yet mature smile is deep and genuine as she toasts our success with a draught of beer. "You have the second fastest time for our race, so do you think you'll be back again to try and break the record?" she asks the question so far from my present thoughts.

"Well, now that you ask, I suppose we most certainly will want to return and break the record. Who wouldn't want to come back to this magical place," I reply, most honestly.

"I think dinner is served now. The food will be very good I believe," says Helen graciously indicating the tables on a higher level. The spacious room with high ceilings is an Asian pink, adorned with grand pictures of the current President Susilo Bambang and his wife Lady Ani. Here we help ourselves to Ambonese delicacies such as snapper grilled to perfection over coconut coals, steamed sweet potatoes, battered rice balls, steamed squid with papaya wrapped in banana leaf, fried wontons, charcoal grilled chicken, turmeric rice, egg noodles, the choice is endless.

"Andrew, have you tried this sauce, its quite hot, but there is a delicious flavour of nutmeg and mace," says Carolyn excitedly. "Mmmm, lemongrass and ginger too. We certainly are in the Spice islands." This feast, which quietens the room down to a mere murmur is followed up by a huge selection of deserts. Carolyn, a great lover of exotic food is enraptured. "These colourful balls seem to be made from taro, they are very nice and look, this one is grilled sticky rice with shredded coconut. These buns, Helen told me, are made from fermented sago with coconut and brown sugar."

"The Rojak is good!" exclaims Mara, tucking into chilli dusted pieces of fruit. Of course we are delighted to observe her taking to foreign foods with such relish. Coffee is served in elegant cups. It has a the decisive bite of ginger and spices and another smooth flavour that is hard to fathom.

"Ahh, Mr Andrew, I see you looking puzzled at our local coffee. You'll recognise the ginger and spices, but you won't know the Keneri nut! Something like an almond perhaps," says Helen De Lima, showing keen observation. The Mayor's wife brings out their children, already in pyjamas, to bid us all farewell. It has been a most lavish and remarkable night, so revealing of the rich depth of Indonesian culture. As we ride back to Amahusu on the bus, our bellies resplendent with fine foods, the night air warm and inviting, nobody wishes they were anywhere else.

It's not all a bed of roses on *Fantasia.* In Amahusu the anchorage is devilishly deep, mostly around 45/50m. Initially we anchored on the one sandy patch and arrive back that night to find we have dragged into another boat causing minor damage. When we haul up the anchor in the morning we discover it wrapped in a ball of plastic. "We'll have to try anchoring stern in to the town seawall," says I, feeling flustered after motoring around, contemplating dropping anchor in such a deep bay. It's a ticklish job, dropping the hook on the steep drop-off, then quickly getting a line ashore over the coral reef. All in a days work for a sailor though.

In the city of Ambon we must master the intricacies of obtaining an Indonesian modem for the all important Internet connection. Then we must brave the powerfully strong aromas of old fish, meat and vegetables that waft, almost overwhelmingly about the Ambon city markets in order to provision up for our next voyage.

Lounging at *Fantasia's* spacious chart table, after yet another gala night, this time for the actual prize presentations, I sip Smirnoff Vodka mixed with fresh squeezed orange juice. Feeling quite elated, I crack small salted peanuts in a shell and crunch them up like I haven't eaten in weeks, The Vodka, a rare treat is part of our winnings and we are enjoying its sweet fiery zest.

Nick has flown home yet the vacuum from losing his enthusiastic presence is filled by the heady glow of *Fantasia's* success. "The presentation was amazing wasn't it! How they print those huge vinyl posters is remarkable, they're all around Amahusu and Ambon, and draped everywhere in the presentation hall. Back in OZ, they wouldn't be able to afford even one banner of that size! Didn't it feel amazing to be presented with these trophies, they made me feel so honoured," I ramble, lovingly running my fingers over the trophy for first on handicap.

"Yes, the Indonesians certainly know how to put on a show! The line honours trophy is certainly very Indonesian, a bit garish, I like it though, it's cute," says Carolyn, merrily taking a swig of her cocktail, while admiring the delicate silver Indonesian sailing boat in a glass box awarded for first over the line. Mara is happily snapping photos on the neat little digital Lumix camera, a fine addition in our basket of winnings. Our initial efforts at racing *Fantasia* have gone off so well, who knows what dreams this is forming in her young mind?

"Ahh, but this is the crowning glory," says I, joyously tipping a thin stack of money onto the cluttered table. "The prize-money, $750 in cash! I mean that won't seem much to most people, but for us it's a windfall. This amount could virtually cover our next two months in Indonesia. It really doesn't seem long ago that we were struggling to generate any income at all and now we've built this amazing machine the money is starting to flow," I conclude, feeling a great sense of contentment. I celebrate by pouring another vodka cocktail. It's time to sail on and discover more of this incredible archipelago, into which we have arrived so handsomely.

Chapter 20.

THE INDONESIAN EXPERIENCE

Anchored close to the shore on a slim edge of coral and sand, Carolyn's birthday dinner has been an unrelaxing affair. I scrape our fish bones into the sea, reflecting on our afternoon searching the north coast of Ambon for an anchorage less than 50m deep. Fortunately during this difficult period Carolyn managed to whip up a juicy looking chocolate cake. She cuts us generous slices and plates them up artistically on the table. We sit down, all set to sing Happy Birthday, when the chartplotter alarm sets off.

"Oh no, we're dragging anchor! I curse, dashing on deck to start the engines. "Looks like we can't stay here! It's just too deep everywhere. These steep mountains obviously keep dropping away deep under the sea. We'll just have to sail on, we're never going to find an anchorage here!"

Soon we have the sails hoisted, whizzing along, feeling happier, the difficulties of anchoring left behind in our phosphorescent wake, which lights up like a comet trail. Moist, rich chocolate cake and cups of tea are happily savoured under an intensely powerful galaxy of stars.

"Well, I know it wasn't quite the birthday you had planned for me, but it's been an interesting day and here we are, starting out on a whole new adventure. What more could I wish for!" What an excellent first mate I think to myself, contemplating the infinity of stars above, she's still content after a beastly day unable to find an anchorage. Our real voyage through Indonesia has only just begun and it's hard to see it living up to the heady first week.

Across the Banda Sea our spaceship takes us, an immensely deep body of water up to 8km deep in places. Yet the undulating sea-floor sends up strange up-wellings and every so often our skimming apartment must tackle a stretch of disturbed water, which shakes us up in a gentle warning against becoming too complacent. This is surely a good thing as otherwise we loll about the saloon in something of a sublime dream, reading books, watching dvds, resting and eating as a rich indigo sea passes by the windows. Our field of vision to the ring of horizon uninterrupted, except for the odd breaching whale, some flying fish and the occasional seabird gliding past to inspect this water-bound skimming beast, manned by humans. A crowded Indonesian ferry the *Lemalu*, changes course to pass us close by, the captain wishing to entertain his passengers who line the decks, waving enthusiastically.

On our second morning we are greeted by the sight of a prodigious number of coconut trees waving their fronds in the fresh trade wind as the first of the Wakatobi group come in to view, a south-east offshoot of the Sulawesi Archipelago. Unbeknown to us we have chosen the same anchorage as the Sail Indonesian rally, a commodiously comfortable lagoon off the main town of Wanji and it seems we are the first boat to arrive. There is a little confusion as a welcome committee rush out to greet us and we try to explain that we are not actually part of the rally.

"Doesn't matter, you are just as welcome! Our government wants to encourage yachts to visit here and you have come to our island on a yacht, so we will look after you. Don't worry Mr Andrew! You will have guides to show you around our town, we have put in special moorings for you and we will give 100 litres of diesel, all free, no charge."

It's a very magnanimous way to be welcomed and for several days we enjoy being shown around the town by a group of giggling youths, who are in turn able to practice their English, a marvellous cultural exchange really. It being the month of Ramadan, each day the various mosques use powerful speakers, attempting to outdo each other in calling their devoted to prayer. From the anchorage it comes across a dreadful cacophony of sound as the various Muezzin, turn up the volume until the speakers begin to crackle, nevertheless it does exude that exotic foreign feeling.

I dive down to inspect the moorings and find a woven basket of coral stones, not nearly adequate to hold a big cruising yacht in anything other than the present still air. The rally fleet start to rock up so we take our present of diesel and cruise on down this chain of islands.

After a pleasant late afternoon snorkel in the Kaledupa lagoon, Carolyn and Mara clamber into the dinghy, glowing with health in the soft hues of fading light. "It was very beautiful down there, those giant yellow brain corals were magnificent and green staghorns simply covered in those electric blue damselfish and I saw a beautiful emperor angelfish and another, a blue and gold one. I'm excited to look them up in our book," says Carolyn.

"I saw one of those banquillo fish you talked about. He was amazing, sort of like a snake and he could swim backwards. And I saw a lovely family of clown fish, but when I swam down to see them close up, one rushed out and attacked me!" says Mara as she pulls in the dinghy anchor and I begin to row back to the boat.

"Well I didn't see very many eating type fish, only a few emperor and they are so wary it's hard to get within 10m of them!" I complain, bemoaning our lack of fresh fish for dinner. "It's certainly been well fished this reef, beautiful though it is!"

After a peaceful night's sleep we make sail for Adunara Island, part of the main chain that leads on to Bali, Java and Sumartra. An easy overnight voyage sees *Fantasia* anchored in an aquamarine swimming pool, hanging over pure white sand, with a vivid but well fished reef fending off the gentle swell and tiny Peni Island popping out of the shallows. A few fishing boats ply these waters waving merrily to us, the towering distant peaks of mount Boleng and mount Api grace the dry and unpopulated foothills and through the binoculars we can make out a small village way off on Kawula Island. I boot up my laptop and plug in the Indonesian modem, fairly certain there'll be no signal in this wild and remote spot.

"Wow, that's amazing! We've got a decent internet connection here!" I announce triumphantly. Previously our cruises had been made quite difficult by the need to collect mail Post Restante, with the complexity of knowing when and where our ship would be, months in advance.

Having breezily dealt with emails from the comfort of *Fantasia's* chart-table, my mind wanders on, looking ahead to our arrival on the Malay peninsula. "So there's this Raja Muda Regatta, a series of races from Port Klang to Langkawi. Looks like fun, perhaps we could organise some crew and do that," I suggest offhand, dreamily gazing through the acrylic windows where a tuft of cloud gives the impression Mount Api is an active volcano.

"When is this Raja Muda? Let's do it! What boats are entered? Please Puppi, can we do it!" It's a statement not a question it seems. Mara has pounced on the computer to read up about this possible event. Her enthusiasm makes it clear she's been bitten by the racing bug.

It's kind of nice to have a race looming ahead on your cruising calendar. It drives one to get everything sorted aboard, repair ailing equipment and generally inspiring one to sail fast rather than just wandering along. As a cruising sailor my search had been for relaxation, peaceful places, the beauty of nature, living outside the system and striving to maintain the boat as economically as possible. While this led to a great appreciation of nature and the ability to live on the most limited income, it did seem to foster a sense of idleness. Unless a job is vitally pressing it will tend to get left for another time.

Now with the prospect of a race, there is that spark of adrenalin in one's centre, a drive to get those little tasks done in order to tackle a host of new jobs, which entering a race creates.

Just so you the reader, can experience more closely what it feels like to be aboard *Fantasia,* here are some pages from the log, which I felt driven to write while journeying these exotic seas.

Two men in canoes awake us early by fishing very close by and shouting happily to each other. When Carolyn shows her face, our friend from the day before rushes over and insists she buys his bananas and papaya. We only have 50000 rupiah notes which are actually only $5.50, and he has no change so buy his produce feeling a shade hard done by even though one paw paw alone would have cost more back home in Aussie.

Pitching our coffee in we hoist our anchor up from its deep home down on the low corals 28m below. I feel happy to see the anchor come up having been concerned about it being stuck on a bommie during the night. We hoist all plain sail and set off in the light southerly breeze, a decent long swell sweeping in from the east now that we have left the protection of our reef.

A lethargy steals over the boat as the heat increases, regardless of my 'spark of adrenalin'. We sloth around doing nothing much, feeling too hot and lazy to hoist the kite although we should. Later in the day we play a long game of cards to pass the time as we slowly converge on the eastern head of Flores Island. I bring up our pirated copy of 101 anchorages on the computer and select an anchorage that we can make by dusk, protected from this unusual north-east breeze.

*The guide suggests the anchorage is nothing special, but every coastal sailors needs a haven come sundown. Actually the coastline is quite exciting with impressive natural rock statues and a tangled wild vegetation. Lolling at the chart table begins to feel hot, the late afternoon sun invading my comfort, yet not enough to warrant fitting the shade screen. I'm watching **Bourne Supremacy**, hoping to boot myself out of this lethargy. Out of habit I peer back at the fishing line, desiring to spot evidence of a strike, even though we are yet to land a fish in this country. "Hey, we've got a big fish on our line!" I*

241

dash out and grab the line, giving it a good yank to ensure the hook is set and pull in as fast as I can, hoping not to lose this gift from the sea.

With Jason Bourne like efficiency and speed I have the fish aboard in seconds, a 1.2m Wahoo, clubbed with our Tongan war-club before it knows where it is. There's fish slobber and blood all over the cockpit with the anchorage approaching fast. The lethargy of the day is gone in an instant. A beautiful anchorage is found over crystal clear water and sand, most amazing of all is the complete lack of boats, which for Indonesia is a total miracle, the beach deserted except for some fish drying racks. We plunge in for a swim before sunset to fully cool off after the hot day. In the pristine white sand, garden eels play and a dozens of baby anemone fish frolic about, protected by bold parents, who Mara has learnt to keep clear of.

*Back aboard I set too, filleting our wonderful fish. We had been getting concerned about the lack of fish in our diet and now we have enough for weeks. Our hopes soar again, cool and excited after a nice swim, the delicious colour of the water refreshing just to look at. I drink the last of our line honours Vodka, in fact too much and feel a little drunk as I fry up fillets of fresh fish. While watching our favourite movie of all, **Pirates of the Caribbean**, which epitomises so much of our sailing life. Tucking into our tasty dinner, the Vodka settles but I soon crash out early, feeling satisfied but a little decadent.*

After a calm night we awake early to drink in the tranquillity and beauty of this place. Our peace doesn't last long, as a weather-beaten Indonesian arrives in a canoe, demanding coffee. Having tended to our guest we ignore him and we set to work doing some jobs aboard. I dive in and scrub the starboard hull, enjoying the crystal clear water where I can peer around and be sure no monster is stalking me. We sand up the doors and chart table which were getting a bit scruffy and begin to varnish.

Now of course a young boy approaches in a canoe and ties up astern. He asks Carolyn nicely for some swimming goggles and as she is busy with varnishing he waits patiently. Soon another weathered old chap arrives and proceeds to tie his coral anchor to our rudder in such a way that it bangs on our delicate foil with each wave. I greet the chap thinking perhaps he is the headman and he demands a drink so I give them all some cordial. Carolyn produces an old set of swimming googles and gives them to the boy.

Unfortunately now the old chap wants a set too! We try to ignore them and continue to work. Soon another chap arrives in a canoe and he too begins to tie up and motions that he would like a pair of swimming googles also. We realise we have made a mistake in giving something away without even trading. "There'll be no peace for us now!" We begin to haul the anchor, thus encouraging our guests to leave. A good breeze has been picking up all the while but as we roll out the jib it seems to die. With wet varnish on the chart table it's a trifle hard to set a course but we hoist the main and before long a nice breeze blows down off the mountain and we set off, fairly whizzing along. Mara is doing her schoolwork on the deck to escape the heat and a few pages blow into the sea as the wind picks up.

Just as the wind had settled in it dies off, then swings around so we're hard on the wind. We sail past a beautiful mountain island, its coast scattered with coconut palms and villages of thatched huts. Some miles out from our destination we feel a swell from the open sea which would roll into this anchorage. I decide to sail to the other side of this island group protected by a huge bay. No sooner have we rounded the island than a short steep sea attacks us from the opposite direction. Indonesia is proving a tricky place.

We motor on getting desperate to find anchorage before nightfall. The C-map being very unreliable and lacking in detail shows a couple of tiny islands off the main island that could have protection from these nasty seas. As we near these islands we see they are covered in houses. Suddenly shallow reef blocks our path making us despair. "How far is it to the mainland anchorage?" Carolyn asks me.

"I don't know!" I answer crossly and continue to angle towards the island. Close in there's a break in the reef and we slip into the protection of the most remarkable place. The two islands have been joined together by an amazing jumble of ramshackle dwellings. A large wooden ship is being built back from a incongruous new

concrete wharf where dozens of children appear to dance and goggle at this strange arrival. Most of the houses are built out over the water and two copper domes poke out of the middle of this incredible place.

We find bottom at 11m, relieved to drop anchor. The islands have been joined to the shore by a coral pathway, where locals pick back and forth along the rough path. It's been a true adventure finding this anchorage, somewhat in desperation. Feeling quite elated we pop open some drinks in the cockpit, gazing at the strange place, wondering how it is possible for such a small island to support so many people. You never know what the day will bring in this sailing life.

*

Yet again we seem to fall in with the loose itinerary of the Sail Indonesia rally. Being on the trail of this pilgrimage through southeast Asia has its pros and cons. In the reef guarded town of Riung we strike a party with tasty local foods and entertainment. A charismatic local demonstrates to Mara, who is nervous of flinging about in a dance, that she has nothing to fear. He flops about like a simpleton, jigging foolishly to demonstrate that nothing you do on the dance floor isn't dance. A fine teacher to top off a day in the school of life.

In a lot of the other anchorages we are besieged with locals in all manor of craft lining up for gifts. Typically one arrives at anchor worn out and ready for an invigorating swim or to partake in some refreshments. So instead, having to stand in the burning sun, straining to communicate in pidgin English/Bahasa, dealing with the demands of locals who have grown accustomed to generous handouts, while maintaining a fixed smile can be a trying affair. Yet this is all part of the Indonesian experience, one day you're a depot for masks, batteries, books, pens, refreshments and the next day, a few miles off the beaten track, you're worshipped as a rarely seen species.

Yet every day in this incredibly diverse nation is one to be remembered forever. Our route takes us through the Komodo Islands in search of the famous dragon. In the ramshackle boom town of Labuanbajo we stock up on fresh victuals. Disliking the idea of paying for a guided tour to see this prehistoric beast, we head off to explore some of the remote looking coves, determined to spot one in the wild. These steep volcanic islands sprout only the odd lontar palm in a grassy savannah landscape, with occasional forest in the dry creek beds. Remote pinkish beaches reflect a thriving undersea world of red corals, fanned by the swirling currents of the Linta Straits.

"We've been clambering about this wild scrub for days, and still we've really only seen footprints of this giant lizard!" I cheerfully grumble as we follow a promising sandy creek bed.

"We have seen all those wild boar and your cute Rusu deer and the crab eating monkeys while having tremendous fun exploring!" says Carolyn. A delicate sheen of sweat on her brow as we trudge over a rocky scree.

"And Puppi, remember what you always tell me! It's the moment that counts, not the destination!" pipes up Mara, scrambling up a deciduous tree, thriving in the volcanic soil.

Day hopping along the uniquely Indonesian coasts of Sumbawa and Lombok we begin to find the sea sprinkled with bamboo fish attracting devices. Around Bali, where the sea is more than a 1000m deep, these shacks are amazingly moored to the sea floor, presenting a dangerous obstacle for a delicate sea vessel like ours. The radar can barely detect them at close range so we increase our vigilance to avoid a destructive collision. Out into the Java Sea they fade away, yet this is a busy unpredictable waterway, where an exotic feeling hangs about us like a sea mist.

Spicing up our travels is the ominous warning on our digital charts, the dreaded spectre of all sailors. Piracy! Our guides and online forums are full of all manor of attacks on yachts, so I take careful note to avoid the hotspots and hope for the best. It's a dark night, the moon and stars snuffed out by a blanket of grey clouds, but the gentle face of the Java sea is illuminated, almost to the point of daylight by a vast fleet of squid boats, bristling with remarkably powerful lights in blue, white, yellow and pink.

"It's hard to judge whether that's a small boat close by or a big one far away." I remark, sitting wearily at the chart table sipping tea, fiddling with the radar controls. "Life is so much easier for the modern adventurer, what with fancy gadgets like our broadband radar! It's even picking up those small wooden squid boats over there. That's if it keeps working, touch wood." Still it's a long, almost alien night threading our way through this seaborne village of the strangest craft on the planet, all hauling aboard squid to feed this hungry nation.

We rejoice to sight the misty, hazy coast of Belitung, feeling slightly apprehensive as we are now heading for port with the intention of making our clearance. A daunting prospect of dealing with unpredictable officialdom. Pleasantly the clouds thin and a gentle golden light reveals a wild and beautiful island, the coast a maze of rich reef, which must be carefully negotiated. Situated bang in the middle of the spice route to Singapore, this large island is seemingly best known through its association with BHP Billiton, but we spy no sign of mining. Lurking on its north-west coast, the main town of Tanjungpandan is to prove an eye opening landfall.

A thickly wooded islet, colourful with autumn leaves and a peaceful Japanese paGoda marks the river entrance. In direct contrast the town reach is a swarming hive of activity where every type of fishing boat is crammed into its brown turbid waters. Small cargo ships give way to hundreds of wooden fishing craft with spindly outriggers. The armas of these strange craft are mere lengths of bamboo while their cabins are smartly painted in blue, red, aqua, green and yellow, neatly fitted with wooden shutters, strung with washing. The tiny low freeboard canoes, which tend them look sure to founder in the busy harbour wash. These bizarre vessels crowd the town giving it a spider like grace.

As a steaming hot sun dips welcomely down to the smoky horizon, a meandering stream of fishers head out for their night's work. Bright lights and regular traffic makes for poor sleeping but we awake early to tackle the business end of cruising. Fishermen have swarmed back into town, bringing that strong smell of fresh caught and old fish, blended with diesel fumes and that delightful scent of clove cigarettes. We row ashore, threading through the traffic and claim a rickety corner of a jetty to secure our dinghy for the day. Out of the town spews a thick black river carrying a rotting stench which takes our breath away. A crowd of locals are loitering on the bridge and banks pointing excitedly at this unlikely form of entertainment. Excuse me sir, what is everyone pointing at?" I ask a smartly dressed fellow.

"Hello mister, it's a crocodile. See it there, his head is poking out now!" Sure enough we can see it hunting about in a most unpleasant environment. Huge markets border this bleak river with hundreds of red snapper split down the centre, drying on a vast bamboo mat, adding powerful smells of curing fish to the stench of the open aired butchers that make Asia confronting to some.

We can't resist a stroll through to see what's available, impressed by great baskets of red chillis, fresh dug ginger root, tomatoes, cabbages, carrots, bags of imported garlic and the welcome aromas from the spice stalls powerfully drowning out all the other smells. A throng of locals crowd the narrow alleyways, all going about the daily ritual of buying fresh victuals. A handsome young lad is busily chopping up chickens in a tray directly above a cage full of the next victims. Blood dripping off his hands does not stop him from proposing to marry Mara, an offer she shyly but firmly fends off.

We ask about for the location of the port authorities and thus begins something of a wild goose chase as we visit several promising looking buildings, where sadly nobody knows anything about ships clearance. Just when we are beginning to despair a handsomely dressed official fellow takes pity on us, driving us way out of town to the immigration office where we are stamped out of the country then back into the port area, where I must fill out endless forms. In recent years yachts have been charged import duty just for visiting the country and even though the government is obviously doing their best to encourage yachts to visit, it's no guarantee against some greedy official.

Fortunately our paperwork from Ambon sees us through, with one chap rather amazed and disappointed we already have our "Pib and Peb" sorted. It's late evening by the time our clearance is all squared away so we buy fuel for our assistant's car and shout him dinner. This proves a good move as he knows the best place to go, so our seafood, vegetables and noodles are succulent, fresh and exceptionally cheap. Driving around the maze of back-blocks we buy diesel, siphoned out of a steel drum by a swarthy, cheerful young chap puffing on a clove cigarette.

Gratefully our dinghy is still tied up where we left it, in the dark reaches of the fisherman's docks. Piling aboard we row out to *Fantasia,* glowing vividly from the loom of the town. It's with a deep sense of relief we unlock the doors, happily breathing in the stuffy warmth of a boat locked up for the day. "Like I always say, the smellier the markets the more interesting the town. Based on this theory that's got to have been the most fascinating town of all!"

After an early and productive visit to the markets we are ready to head on. Within a mere two hours sailing, we drop anchor at Lengkuas Island, on the north-west corner of Belitung. A towering white lighthouse, built in the late 1800s graces the smooth round granite boulders, white sand, coconut palms and small patch of tropical forest that make up this pristine slice of heaven.

"Indonesia is certainly a land of extreme contrasts," says Carolyn as we bask in the warm afternoon sun having just enjoyed a refreshing snorkel in the remarkably clear water supporting much healthy reef. "I mean, one minute your in the thick of a seething mass of humanity and the next your in one of the most beautiful places on earth!"

"Yes, this place reminds me of the Seychelles, what a gem to have stumbled upon. Even so, Indonesia seems to make me feel uneasy, it's such a wild place, the way of life so unusual, the people so different. I often feel a little nervous, in case they might just decide to spring upon a handsome prize like *Fantasia,"* I reflect, dreamily contemplating a fleet of rickety fishing boats heading out to sea. "Look at them, the local fishermen and boats all look like pirates out of another century!"

"Oh Andrew, your imagination does run away with you sometimes. It's such a peaceful place, I feel safer here than most countries," chides Carolyn busily looking up new exotic fish in the identification book.

"Well, I just hope you're right!" I reply, mulling over the complex route that lies ahead. Our passports are now officially stamped out of Indonesia and *Fantasia's* cruising permit is expired. Even so we must pass through the many Indonesian islands which still lie between Belitung and the Malacca Straits, gateway to the enchanting Andaman Sea.

Across the South China Sea *Fantasia* voyages, smoothly guiding us through the doldrums, where the languid winds and heat mean we have to fend off a lazy stupor. Keeping us on our toes though, is the constant nervousness that a patrol boat will appear and demand our papers. Cutting between Lingga and Sebanka islands, way out in the 5 mile wide channel, we are amazed to come across a large wooden fishing house fitted with a huge complex net that lowers beneath the house.

"But how did they build it? It's 12m deep here? So those wooden poles must be like 20m plus to anchor into the ground and lift the house and net high over the sea like that!" As we slip gently along, converging with the equator, there are more and more of these strange fishing houses. Then we pass a large bay which opens up to reveal literally hundreds of these structures dominating the entire body of water. "Indonesia is just too amazing sometimes! I mean, just the sheer number of trees they needed to build all that. I count about 50 uprights for each structure, that's 10,000 trees!"

*

Our final day in Indonesia is to unfold packed full of the type of drama we had hoped to avoid. Leaving the more wild and traditional islands of the Riau archipelago, we sail north through the narrow channel between Batam and Bulan on route to the Singapore Strait. Every hour we sail brings us rapidly back into the 21st century. High speed ferries whiz by the local fishing craft plying these increasingly murky waters. The foreshore is thick with houses perched over the sea, rickety bare timber affairs capped in rusty tin, all with small wooden boats moored to the veranda as their means of transport.

Soon these quaint villages give way to bleak ship building and wrecking yards, miles of heavy industry and docks, lined with all manor of tugs, giant oil rigs, cranes, barges and ships. As the sun begins to fade to a dirty yellow in the smoggy air, our search for an anchorage becomes more desperate. Directly opposite this industrial jungle we find a remarkably quiet spot sheltered by mangrove rimmed islets thick with real tropical jungle. Just as we are celebrating this peaceful gem amid this overcrowded industrial sprawl, ready to crack a Bintang and relax after a demanding day, a small black speed boat races towards us.

"Looks like a police boat," I grumble standing in the cockpit, forcing a smile across my face to welcome our visitors. Three serious looking young Indonesians man the boat, dressed in random clothes, one's on a mobile phone, presumably talking to headquarters.

"Hello sir. I'm afraid you can't anchor here, it's too dangerous for you," begins the leader sporting a crew cut. It's almost dark now and in this reef strewn, poorly charted area, the idea of moving is distinctly unappealing. Our trio of 'police like' men tie up their boat so we invite them aboard, smiling and hoping to convince them we are nice people. Carolyn comes out with glasses of chilled cordial all round and our friends crack smiles of appreciation for the first time.

"Why is it so dangerous here? Really it is almost impossible for us to move from here now that it's getting dark." Carolyn offers around a plate of snacks and our friends are looking quite comfortable now.

"Oh yes sir, there are pirates operating in this area. They are based on the island through there," says our friend with the crew cut, motioning towards the mangrove lined passage leading off to the west. "Lately they have been raiding a lot of boats in this area!" This is not good news at all and I break into a cold sweat, studying the chartplotter for possible alternate anchorages, but generally feeling to move in the dark, on these waters would be courting disaster.

"Hey guys, we'd really rather not move now. More than likely we'd hit a reef and that would be really terrible!" I explain timidly, feeling very uncomfortable with our choices.

"Well if you want to remain here we'll have to stay aboard to protect you," suggests the leader with the crew cut whose name is Hery. We are happy to agree with this suggestion, even though a less than peaceful night is promised. Soon four more fellows arrive in another boat, all full of smiles now that they have a big comfortable boat to lounge on for the night. "Can you please put the front light on for us?" asks Hery, politely but firmly. Of course I oblige them even though our batteries are beginning to show signs of age and have been going flat lately.

We are very low on food yet Carolyn produces curry and rice for us all and our 'protectors' generally have a wonderful time lolling around on a fancy foreign yacht, in the warm equatorial evening.

Late into the night we do our best to chat with them as they joke and laugh, smoking their delicious smelling clove cigarettes. Of course we are a bit nervous least they ask for our ships papers and find us already cleared out.

Mara seems to possess the ability to sleep like a log regardless of disturbances in the night, yet Carolyn and I, used to being tuned in to any unusual noises, find deep rest very hard to come by. There's lots of coming and going in the night as our friends take it in shifts to go on patrol, they are carrying a rifle so we do feel fortunate to have them aboard.

Dawn creeps up and we find both boats gone with only two of our friends dozing on the trampoline. Carolyn puts the kettle on for coffee and while surveying the morning I notice a dark threatening mass of cloud moving towards us from the south-west. "Carolyn, look, I think there's another *Sumatra* coming. Sprat, better wake up!" Fresh in our minds is an experience from a few days ago, caught out by one in the open sea. Luckily we got our mainsail down in time, as it came in a sudden squall with the wind touching 50 knots, which could potentially have capsized us. Then it blew 30/40 knots for the next half hour, so we know what to expect and hastily pay out the anchor bridle as far as it will go. Within minutes the squall comes whistling over the mangroves, swinging *Fantasia* around so she is less than a boat length from the nasty looking reef edge.

To my horror the anchor seems to be failing us, dragging slowly on the unknown sea floor. "Quickly, can you two go forward and tend the bridle ropes. I'm going to motor forward to stop us dragging, so make sure the bridles don't get caught in the propellers!" I shout over the rising wind and now driving rain. Carolyn and Mara dash obediently forward while I rush to the helm. Hitting the start button there is only a distressingly feeble rumph, rumph, rumph. In a panic I hit the button for the port engine with despairingly the same result.

Having the deck light on all night has fattened the batteries! Looking behind, waves are already breaking on the reef just metres away and it seems that while we may have been saved attack by pirates, ending up on a reef could well destroy a boat like *Fantasia*. Adding to my worry is our lack of clearance which will make matters very difficult if we need to make repairs here. All this flashes through my mind in the brief seconds it takes in deciding to try the starboard motor again. Grumph, grumph, grump, Vroom and away she purrs, exciting the alternator and allowing the port motor to start. Now I can engage both engines and hold us against the building fury of wind, which is hurling rain at us so hard it hurts the skin. For what feels like an eternity the engines do battle with this tempest, while my girls, soaked to the skin, heads down against the full brunt of the stinging rain, diligently take up any slack on the bridles.

Eventually the *Sumatra* loses its puff and we re-anchor further away from the reef that threatened to swallow us up. As much as we'd love to be quit of this place we can't leave. We still have our two policemen huddled up in the cockpit, waiting for their friends to come and collect them.

Carolyn soon has us all sipping on welcome mugs of hot cocoa as we thank our lucky stars we're not in the same predicament as the nearby fishermen, whose large boat lays on its side, aground on the same reef. At least its sturdy, simple construction will allow it to haul off on the high tide with only minor scuffing. As we finish our drinks one of the police boats zooms up and they reluctantly allow us to head off. Just as they are leaving, Carolyn walks inside and finds their rifle stowed out of the rain on our lounge. She rushes out brandishing it to catch their attention and they return sheepishly to collect their weapon.

Even the business of crossing the world's busiest shipping super highway, the Singapore Straits seems a relaxing affair after the events of the last 12 hours. Now it's only a matter of dodging super-tankers weighing in at half a million tonnes doing 20 knots. Rain clouds have blown away, the sun is shinning, so we are all feeling very much relieved to have escaped that danger unscathed.

Just when one challenge is overcome a new one seems to take its place. *Fantasia* is now only two years old, yet already her batteries need replacing and her Dacron working sails have stretched out of shape, the screecher a failure, so it seems we have it all to do in the exotic far east if we expect our dreams to unfold. We've spent our Ambon winnings and our bank balance doesn't give us much leeway if things go wrong.

Are we doing the right thing having hauled Mara out of school, away from her friends and casting ourselves into this strange world? It feels we're gambling that wonders lie waiting for us, on the Thai/ Malay peninsular that reaches down to the equator out of the mighty Asian continent.

CHAPTER 21

FAR EAST FUN AND FIASCO'S

"I just don't know if we can do this Raja Muda Regatta! We'll need to get a new screecher made and somehow delivered. Then the whole business of arranging crew will have to come together." I'm feeling the financial squeeze, what with a new set of batteries to buy, deck paint, race entry fees, new anchor chain to be sourced, all in an unfamiliar country. *Fantasia* is merrily zooming north-west up the Malacca Straits, having to gybe downwind, zigzagging across the shipping lanes. "And then two weeks later there's the King's Cup out of Phuket. I mean, they sound wonderful and I'd love to do them, but a lot of things have to fall into place."

"I thought you said Gary Saxby's price for a new screecher was pretty good? His sails will be way better than those other ones! And aren't Glen and Karen Lyons keen to come, and Mike Hodges? Bill Donnelly and his family also seem set to do the King's Cup! Things will fall into place, you just watch out for that monstrous container ship that looks to be heading straight at us!" Carolyn is sitting at the saloon table helping Mara with her school-work, a little uncomfortable with us weaving through this busy shipping traffic of the Mallaca Straits.

"Oh yes, that ship, the *Zim Atlantic,* he's going to miss us by a good 4 cables!" Nevertheless I adjust our course a few degrees with the autopilot buttons to ease Carolyn's concerns.

"I can't wait to do those regattas Pup! Then I won't be doing this beastly school-work every day and missing out on all these amazing places we're passing!" Mara strikes an amusing pout, peeking up from her books to peer out at the hazy coastline of the Malay peninsular. She makes a fair point as it does seem silly to be travelling this exciting sea route, then spending so much time making her persist with uninteresting studies, which are not challenging her, when fascinating cultural experiences await ashore.

"We'll see how it all unfolds I suppose? It'll be nice to get past Port Klang and leave this highway of smoke belching tin boxes behind. OK, I think it's time to gybe Team *Fantasia,* get some practice for these regattas!"

On our first voyage around the world in 1996, we fell in love with Langkawi, the island of legends, with its lush tropical hills and distinct limestone ridges, a quiet and easy place to visit. Having sailed from Penang in very light winds, it's a midnight arrival and we carefully feel our way into commodious Bass Harbour, looking to anchor off the main town of Kuah. Our broadband radar shows a random spray of dots radiating out from the town waterfront so it seems this spot is more popular than ever.

"It's such a great anchorage, so calm and well protected," I enthuse, having dropped the hook in a safe area of water, peering around in the faint starlight at the ring of dark mountains which protect yachts from the capricious moods of the sea. "I can't wait to see it in the daylight."

Awaking early we eagerly dash outside into the warm morning air to find the sun peaking over the hills behind the town. " Oh look, they've got scaffolding around the giant eagle. They must be repainting him," says Carolyn, settling herself cross legged and breathing in the exotic view. "Look at that new building on the other side of town, it's like a fairytale castle with all those blue spires." Mara has dragged herself out of bed, unable to savour the longer sleep of a teenage youth with all this excited talk going on.

"Wow, what a strange place! There's a big Mosque there with a golden dome and what a big ferry terminal, and so many cruising yachts from all over the world! Look at that mega yacht over there and that huge square rigged ship!" She babbles on delightedly, finally getting to see this island we have told her so much about.

After breakfast we row ashore, leaving our dinghy on the white sandy beach which fronts the Legends Park, a well manicured botanical gardens, lush with such tropical specimens as the raintree, kapok, bael, black wattle and a magnificent avenue of the flamboyant flame trees of the forest.

Crunching over dry teak tree leaves we head for town which is actually something of a concrete sprawl. Devoid of the glorious greenery typical of the island, trekking through the streets is a sweltering affair. It's the duty free shops that attract sailors by the score though, all licking their lips at the prospect of stocking up on cheap alcohol. Yet the wide streets give an open feel and the shop assistants welcomingly un-pushy. Perhaps best of all are the well stocked hardware stores, crammed to the brim with a vast selection of goods including ships chandlery, a rare thing in Asian waters.

Our bags stuffed with rum and chocolates, sandpaper and paint brushes we trudge back in the thick heat of midday. Only yachtsman haunt the quiet streets at this time of day, your local being much wiser. Stopping at a busy Indian restaurant we point out the things we fancy, while a smiling Malay/Indian loads them onto our plates. Hungrily I hoe into saffron rice, crispy fried chicken, spinach with okra and chilli and squid curry, washed down with a tall glass of iced lemon tea.

"Wow, this is yummy!" says Mara, tucking into a roti. "So it cost 21 ringgets for all of us to have this fancy lunch? That's only $7

Australian, total! Back home you'd be lucky to get a piece of cake for that much! I like it here in Asia!" This is good, a lesson in culture and mathematics all in one.

"Yes, things are certainly looking up. Our new Kevlar laminate screecher should be arriving at the Royal Langkawi Yacht Club in a week or so and our crew are all organised. Too easy!" Yet I have spoken too soon. Within the week we are to be beset by a very trying incident.

Looking for a place to careen in order to make some repairs under the boat, we sail around to the west side of Langkawi, dropping anchor in Telaga harbour. It's a cruiser's heaven with two sandy islets offering protection from the south and a wild mountain range covering all other quarters. A magnificent sunset is blazing golden red hues across the fleet of anchored yachts and onto the coconut palm lined beach.

"Let's go ashore and stretch our legs me hearties!" I suggest feeling very happy with the world and of course they are both instantly ready for a shore party. We pull our dinghy high up the golden sandy beach and head off to explore. An elaborate lighthouse marks the entrance to the marina, so we head the other way, past a group of small squid boats where men tinker with large light bulbs preparing to head out to sea for the night. Further along the windows of an expensive resort reflect the magic evening light as wealthy families frolic on the beach. Veiled ladies sit delicately in beach chairs, keeping their skin pale, which is a sign of wealth here. Now the beach backs onto a wide grassy verge, shaded by java almonds, palms, pines and teak trees. Here locals sit by their cars eating take away meals and savouring the moment like us.

A group of lively young people wave merrily, calling us over to join them. They are a fine example of the movement in Malaysia to more western values, all dressed in trendy clothes and the girls without headscarf's. They offer us vodka shots and feeling relaxed we happily down a few, enjoying their warm company.

"Come with us for dinner. We're driving around to Padang Matsirat, there are some very good restaurants there. We have two cars so there's room for you all," suggests the most vocal fellow, sporting a goatee and tight jeans. It's an offer too good to refuse, we figure. Locals surely know the best places to eat out and of course we're always ready for adventure.

A winding road through jungle leads to the town, lit up Malay style with a somewhat gaudy selection of Christmas lights. The food is of course exceptional, although it does take a surprisingly long while to arrive. My stomach is feeling fully satisfied having just polished off an ABC desert, a meal in itself of shaved ice, sweet coloured syrup, condensed milk, corn, beans, grass jelly, peanuts, basil seeds and ice cream, when Carolyn suddenly remembers the dinghy.

"Andrew, the tide would be in now and we didn't tie up the dinghy! We'd better get back don't you think!" It's a little hard to get our friends to feel the urgency we are suddenly gripped by, but eventually we find ourselves running back down the beach looking for our dinghy. The tide is very high and with panic in our hearts we dash around but find no sign of it anywhere.

"Oh no, there's a light land breeze blowing off the beach, but perhaps it landed on the islets over there? I'll have to swim out to the boat and get over there on the surfboard!" An unwelcome mission is thrust upon me. Plunge into the tepid sea, swim through the jellyfish and anchored yachts, grab the surfboard, paddle over to *Brumby,* a friend's boat, awake them from sleep to tell them my girls are stranded ashore, paddle over to the islets to find no sign and notice the angle of the breeze would have blown the dinghy straight out through the entrance.

Back aboard I try to fire up an engine to set off in pursuit of the dinghy, only to find the batteries have gone flat! So it's all hands to hoist the mainsail and the heavy anchor by hand and sail carefully out of the crowded anchorage. After an hour the breeze dies and we are going nowhere so we drop sail and anchor in 14m, immediately noticing a strong tide running north-west. It's 2am.

Not long after sunrise, with a little sun on our solar panels, the engines fire up and we begin our search again. Carefully calculating the course it would have gone, we scan the horizon constantly. There are a great deal of fishing boats, any one of which could have seen our dinghy and picked it up. Often we spy hopeful looking white objects, which turn out to be large polystyrene fishing buoys. After sailing for 40 disappointing miles, we must concede it's lost and turn around to sail the 40 miles back to Langkawi, feeling very down. Our beautifully crafted strip-planked dinghy was such a vital part of our lives, for now we can barely get ashore.

On the return trip a simple dinghy is drawn up on the chart table. We will need to make a new one quickly if we are still to contest these regattas, only a few weeks away now. A boat is virtually unmanageable without a tender. Mara helps me make up a scale model out of cardboard, fending off the pain of our loss. Now we have it all to do, the holiday bubble burst.

Back in Telaga, just getting ashore is a mission. So taking advantage of a catamaran's ability to dry out on the beach at low tide, we leave Carolyn to mind the ship. Setting off in a rented car, new batteries are procured, glass cloth, epoxy resin and luckily honeycomb sheets are tracked down at a remote shop in the middle of the island. With the tide coming in to re-float *Fantasia,* the gear is loaded aboard and the work begins. Out on one of the islets we find a handy yachties camp and between tropical rain showers the new dinghy takes shape. One night we hear a party of French sailors making merry at the camp and in the morning find our partially tacked together dinghy crushed and splattered with red wine. It's a hard blow but we set to re-gluing the seams.

"It's more stable than the old dinghy, but not as pretty," remarks Carolyn a week later as we head back to the main town of Kuah to collect our new screecher. It's time to head for Port Klang some 230 miles back down the Malacca Straits to rendezvous with our crew and the start of the Raja Muda. Unable to find anything other than heavy hardwood to make a set of oars we cut some lengths of bamboo from the Legends Park to make a temporary set. Our new sail proves the best yet, strong and well shaped, its golden kevlar fibres driving us south-west with a half day to spare.

Approaching Port Klang the landscape is low and hazy, yet there is always romance and adventure even in the most polluted and industrial shipping centres. This being our first regatta we dock up full of nervous anticipation at the Selangor Marina. Mara is bursting to look at all the race boats so we take our leisure and wander the docks. Aboard one of the hottest yachts in the fleet, Neil Pryde's *Hi-*

Fi, we chat with a rather dry humoured Australian sailmaker, setting up a state of the art mainsail. Carolyn is looking surprised at the mass of garbage that is rapidly getting caught along the gleaming topsides. "Yes, the amount of rubbish is really bad this year! I've heard the catchment net broke in a flood so this is all pouring out of Kuala Lumpa. Anyway, we do say the 'Raja Muda is a race from the arsehole of Asia to paradise', so it gets better."

Glen and Karen Lyons, the parents of Nick our illustrious crewman, along with Mike Hodges, commodore of the Multihull Yacht Club of Queensland, arrive late in the afternoon, looking a bit shell shocked at their surroundings. We hurry them into *Fantasia's* saloon and regale them with rum cocktails, which soon adds a bit of colour to their cheeks.

Glen, a computer genius whose mind never slows down, heads into the cockpit to take some snaps of the stormy sunset. "What's that pungent aroma my nose is picking up? It's not a smell I'm used too," he comments. We are less than 100m downwind from a fleet of giant fishing boats and the pong is so powerful, we're surprised they aren't heading for the nearest hotel. "This camera's no good, I need a smellacam! The dull roar, the smell you could almost walk on, the weird juxtaposition of these modern race boats and those ancient fishing vessels, a warmth that feels like I could reach out and grab a handful. I feel so foreign, light-headed! Where's that rum!"

During the course of the next day the race committee employ teams of fishermen to net the huge islands of garbage floating down from Kaula Lumpa. They drag it over to the ramp and take it away on trucks, yet they have their work cut out as whole sections of grassy riverbank are appearing, these moving islands threatening navigation. It's a steamy eventful day, trying to acclimatise our crew. We do this by dragging them around town, lunching in a wild Malay eating house, letting them visit your classic Asian toilets and exposing them to the perils of purchasing phone sims. They love every minute but can't wait for the racing to begin.

To everyone's complete amazement I jump into the river of rotting KFC and McDonald's packaging, old tins, toothpaste tubes, coca-cola bottles, nappies, thongs, etc, and give the bottom a quick rub. It's a terrifying effort, my legs hitting lumps of submerged wood and getting tangled in large pieces of plastic. Even I begin to think I'm crazy and leap out before finishing my job to give myself a meticulous wash with soap and scrubbing brush. Motoring out towards the start line there's a terrible crunch as the propeller hits a lump of wood. The impact sounds so powerful, we feel sure the hull must be damaged, so I don my swimmers and dive in again, amazed to find not a scratch. Hoping to avoid this happening again we hoist the mainsail. It's an all girl team who hoist our heavy main, Karen enthusiastic to tally on the halyard with Carolyn and Mara. Meanwhile Glen, oblivious to the sailing at hand is busily re-wiring his videocam. Mike, whose own catamaran *Renaissance* is one of the most successful in Australia, studies the sailing instructions. It's all action aboard.

When the race starts, tacking into a light headwind, with the likes of *Hi-Fi* tearing past us, it's Mike who shows us some tricks with the sail trim, which improves our speed considerably. Even so we struggle against the monohulls who are in their element in these conditions. It's not until 2am in the morning we cross the finish line in 9th place, frustratingly pipped on the line by the last of the real high performance boats, *Kukukerchu* a state of the art Kerr 40. Feeling a bit discouraged we drop anchor in the south-west bay of Pangkor Island and lay into the rum. Mike's an experienced rum drinker, yet even so I notice he pours himself rather large shots of the golden brown liquid, tired out from the humid, sultry conditions.

"Are you awake Mike? Good morning Mike! Mike!" It's late morning, the hot sun is bathing everything in a steamy heat, and I've come down to bring Mike his morning coffee. "Hey Mike, it's a lovely day out. So, why are you sleeping on the floor of your cabin?"

"Ah, well, you see I got this far last night," he begins, bringing his eyes into focus, "and I thought to myself- this is far enough! I'll lay down and have a rest. So it looks as though I've been here all night." It seems perfectly natural to him and he takes a sip of his coffee, composing himself on the seat. Mike suffered a motor bike accident in his young days and sports an electrically stimulated foot, none of which slows his yachting adventures down in the slightest.

Diving into the clear green sea refreshes everyone's spirits amazingly and we all go ashore to explore. "This is more like it!"

says Glen, merrily strolling down the shaded beach snapping photos. "Coconut trees, verdant jungle, friendly natives and a harbour not full of floating islands of rubbish." Karen, her luxurious dark hair streaming down her back is shedding her cares by the minute. A mother to seven rewarding children, sensible, carefully spoken, the perfect balance for Glen's sometimes wild ideas. I too feel the lifting of concerns, after the busy weeks of preparing for this regatta. Mara and Carolyn, playing on a beach swing, laugh gaily while macaque monkeys look for mischief in the garden of a waterfront house. Further on that remarkable bird with its huge beak, the toucan enthrals us all, offering glimpses of its magnificent self, hiding in the leafy branches.

Bright pink minivans convey tourists around the island so we ride over to Pangkor town, whose ferry terminal is the island's gateway. "The shops are just full of these stinky baskets of dried fish and all these squid hung up to scare foreigners away!" complains Glen, while Karen gets him to try on a floral holiday shirt. "Karen I think this shirt makes me look touristy!" Glen is proving a wonderful laugh for us, on the loose in this bizarre Asian world.

The second race, from Pangkor to Penang gets off in very light airs, yet with our screecher sheeted hard in we are thrilled to find ourselves vying for the lead with *Hi-Fi*. In the halls and streets of the multihull world, the great dream of a fast multihull is that it would be able to beat a TP52. These are the state of the art monohull class, pure racing machines, with powered winches, retractable propellers, all carbon construction and the best sails and equipment available. Sunset sees *Hi-Fi* barely ahead of us but the breeze has worked around so that we can't point above the huge expanse of the shallow Kra bank.

"You know if we pull the centre-boards up a little we could keep on going across this Kra bank. Then, if that land breeze fills in again like it did in the first race we'd beat *Hi-Fi* home," I enthuse, excited by the prospect. Mike is a risk taker so he's also keen, along with Mara, who sees no reason why we can't beat them. Glen, on the other hand looks quite shocked at the idea.

"Your not serious are you?" he says, dashing over to inspect the chartplotter. "Andrew, the chart shows only 30cm depth, and there's 5 miles of it! It's not possible, it's crazy!"

"Well there's more than a metre of tide and these charts always exaggerate how shallow it really is. Although I have heard talk of old engine blocks and wrecks littering theses banks. We'll be OK, don"t worry Glen. Let's have a cup of tea." Feeling fairly nervous myself we take the gambit and begin a tense passage over this shallow body of water. All the time Glen paces about the wheelhouse, constantly glancing at the depth sounder, not looking at all relaxed in his touristy floral shirt. For a hair raising period we are whizzing along at rock bottom, 1.3m with not a mm to spare, yet after an an hour of suspense we drop back over the edge into deeper water and Glen collapses in a heap on the lounge to nurse his nerves.

"Now we just need that land breeze to fill in," says Mike looking doubtfully towards the low, hazy coastline, illuminated in the moonlight. Unfortunately it never eventuates and we have to beat all the way in. Approaching the finish, the two Malaysian Navy race boats, cream past and then like a recurring nightmare, *Kukukerchu* appears out of nowhere to pip us on the line again. It's 1am and now we have to motor 18 miles around to the northern end of Penang. Mike is brandishing a hard earned rum, "Cheer up you blokes, we still finished 5th over the line out of 40 boats. This is a great adventure fellas! Cheers!"

"Woah, this 12% alcohol beer is a bit nasty. No wonder it was so cheap," says Glen, shaking his head and looking a bit groggy. He had been so pleased with his purchase in Pangkor. We all enjoy the refreshing taste of grog, steaming along into a modest, cooling headwind. It's a testing bit of navigation, under the bridge from the mainland and past the bright lights of this famous island. Situated so snugly on the northern end of Mallacca Straits, it's vast natural anchorage offers protection from the Andaman Sea and tropical cyclones. Forest blossoms blend with scents of frying, detergent, spices, smog and all the aroma's of a thriving population.

Having docked up at the Straits Quay Marina and not managed to get into bed before 4am, we're beginning to think this regatta racing is pretty tough going and for us the real multihull racing hasn't even begun.

Stark, glaring tropical sunlight claws at our sleep deprived brains, yet there's too much action ahead to retreat back into the comforts of sleep. We lounge around drinking coffee while Carolyn chops up red pawpaw, mangoes and the bright red juicy dragon fruit to refresh our systems. She whips up lashings of toast and vegimite to cure 12% beer hangovers, which we all seem to have, even Mara, whose only grog was fresh juices. Grand apartments surround the marina on 3 sides with an expansive palm lined promenade so guests can wander around and look at exotic foreign yachts.

"Everyone coming up to join in the festivities?" says I, still feeling a bit lacklustre but hating to miss anything. Next thing I know a team of Penang flag pole balancers are offering us a chance to perch an 8m pole and giant flag on our heads. Glen and Mike are quick to decline so it's up to me. The fearful prospect of this challenge brings my senses into focus in a hurry. Surprisingly the pole is quite light and it's a matter of angling the huge waving flag into the fickle sea breeze, the minimally padded butt of the pole resting on my forehead. To my amazement the flag seems to keep it steady and thankfully I pass the test.

Rickshaw races are being organised which Mara is dead keen to join in, with me as the runner. "Hey look Pup, there's a catamaran coming in now!" she bursts out excitedly rushing over to watch it dock up.

"Oh wow, it's *Sidewinder* come down from Phuket, she's built by Alan Carwadine who runs Asia Catamarans. He's the chap who built *Cut Snake* then moved up to Thailand and started his own boat building factory. It looks light and fast!" The real multihull division only joins the regatta here so during the day we keenly inspect *Miss Siagon,* an all carbon Corsair 38 owned by an eccentric Englishman, David Liddell and *DaVinci* the Andaman Cabriolet, another ex-pat boatbuilding effort out of Phuket, led by Bob Mott and Grenville Fordam.

There's no escaping it, now I have to run, pulling Mara in a aluminium rickshaw around a short course. First she has to scull a glass of icy lemonade, being too young to scull the usual schooner of beer. Since it's quite hard to overtake, whoever finishes the drink first normally wins.

"Well you try sculling an long glass of icy, bubbling lemonade, it doesn't want to go down and it stings! We've been eliminated in our 2nd race and Mara is a bit cross at the injustice. I feel rather relieved, with enough challenges on my plate as the next day is *Fantasia's* first short course windward leeward racing. Luckily Mike's aboard, and his astute observations get us to the correct start line, where we mill about feeling nervous of the necessary quick hoisting and dropping of the spinnaker such racing entails.

Fortunately the wind is very light and we make an excellent start, engaging *Miss Siagon* on the first beat. *Sidewinder* streaks ahead, while we lead *DaVinci* and lag behind *Miss Saigon*. The wind being so light we run downwind with the screecher, completing our first race competitively. With a little more wind in race two we decide to use the spinnaker, but unfortunately there is some confusion on the foredeck caused by the addition of a man into our all girl team who had claimed this task as their own. Our 158 sqm sail goes up tangled so we have to drop it down and sort things out.

Each leg of a race is just over a mile long taking 10/15 minutes, so having lost 5 minutes already and concerned about another possible 5 minutes to get it down again safely we gloomily finish the run under jib alone. *DaVinci* are ahead of us but we see them arrive at the leeward mark still with their kite set and have to sail past while they struggle to drop it. The typical format of these races is two dead beats to windward and two dead downwind runs, so on the 2nd beat the afterguard is getting it together. Glen Lyons, himself a winner of the Brisbane to Gladstone Race, who has turned his interests towards cruising, with a vast family to entertain, is feeling a bit scathing of this whole racing caper.

"I don't understand why we're doing it? Sailing up to that bouy, then back down, and up, and down again. There's no point to it. I like to have a destination." Glen philosophises happily, fiddling with his videocam.

"Yes Glen, and think of all the amazing places we're getting to see and tonight we're going to the Buddhist temple for dinner! Now quick, be a good boy and winch up your side of the traveller when we tack." Cheerfully, like a well behaved boy, he applies himself to his task. *Fantasia* points higher into the wind at a good pace. As we round the last windward mark our trio of females have tamed the man, who is now obediently doing what he's told and our striking spinnaker is filling beautifully in excellent time.

Gybing the spinnaker from side to side is a delicate task, fraught with potential disaster, requiring the combined efforts of the after-guard and fore-deck crew. The synchronisation required is one of the great beauties and challenges of taming these powerful sails. Everyone rises to the task and we finish strongly, our crew work greatly improved, docking up feeling pleased with ourselves.

Late afternoon finds us dolled up in our best clothes, bussing through the old Georgetown streets headed for our evening destination. While the dinner parties at Selangor and Pangkor had been excellent, none of us are expecting the remarkable experience that lies in store. From the gated entrance of the Khoo Kongsi we stroll up a wide cobble-stoned alley, unaware we are walking into the heart of a 176 year old clan village formed by a square of over 60 houses with rustic terracotta roof tiles and faded cream walls. In the centre is Cannon Square, set up with white clothed tables for the entire fleet and entourage, surrounded by food stalls where chefs industriously create mouth watering aromas.

Most stunning of all is the clan-house, one of the most majestic in South-East Asia. The temple like roof is elaborately decorated with stucco sculptures, porcelain shardwork and ceramic figures. Huge colourful dragons play with a pearl, dragon-fish, men riding strange beasts, the intricacy of the work hard to comprehend. Under the eaves of this prayer pavilion are equally elaborate wood carvings, all richly gold gilded, decorating the entrance to the hilt. There are carved lions, dragons, elephants, deer, phoenix, eagles and a myriad of fascinating designs. We are in the heart of a truly remarkable place.

Garlic, ginger, tumeric, chilli and lemongrass sizzle in pans, the freshness of this food, prepared on the spot, heightens our senses. Satay chicken roasted over coals, tender baked lamb on a spit, expertly sliced by a humorous old Chinese lady. Sweet and sour fried fish, bean curd and mushroom, fresh crispy spring rolls and samosas, fried rice and curries all washed down with copious quantities of Tiger beer, a refreshing pale larger. "Wow, the food is really special. Have you tried any of the amazingly colourful cakes yet?" asks Karen, her eyes shinning happily. "Those Chinese men are certainly fussing a lot over those poles! They've spent ages setting them up and they keep wiping the dew off them every few minutes. What's it all in aid of I wonder?"

Next the usual roll call of podium winners is announced and crews get to collect their trophies on the dazzling temple veranda. A list of the results shows *Sidewinder* with two easy wins while *Miss Siagon* pips us by a minute in the first race and a mere 2 seconds in the 2nd, as calculated by the all important OMR rating, so we feel a trifle unlucky. Nevertheless, Mara's thrilled to bits with our Selangor pewter mugs for two 3rd's.

Suddenly a dancing lion prances through the startled crowd, manned by two men as the famous lion dance begins. His great eyes are blinking, mouth and ears working as he leaps up onto the high pole tops and begins his performance with exceptional martial arts skill, his comical antics played out in perfect time to cymbals, gongs and drums. The two men perform incredible jumps and manoeuvres in exact unison, while covered in the striking golden yellow lion costume. They seem to defy logic and there would be a considerable fear of them falling if not for the lions comical scratching, wiggling and arching. Even as this spectacular beast capers about his lofty perches, men on piggyback constantly wipe dew off the pole tops and a team hover below to break any fall. The crescendo, as he tosses a pearl ball about while executing death defying manoeuvres leaves us all stunned.

Next a group of the most exquisite women soothe us with elegant dances under the temple eaves, caressing our souls.

"Well, that fortune-teller was pretty interesting. He knew I'd just arrived in Asia and said we'll spend two years here having a very special time," reports Carolyn as the after dinner entertainment continues.

"Look at this portrait that artist man did of me. He was quite quick, and seemed to look deeply into my eyes. It's kind of unusual," says Mara brandishing her black ink brush caricature.

"That was amazing! Just that night alone has made this whole trip worthwhile," sighs Karen as we troupe back aboard, fully sated and ready for bed.

*

A glassed out sea, cut up only by the wash of yachts, fishing boats and ferries, devoid of the merest breath of wind means the start of the passage race to Langkawi is delayed. An hour later a fickle headwind floats down and the race committee waste no time in starting the various divisions. The IRC race boats are last to start and once again they are able to demonstrate their superior light air capabilities creaming along under huge specialised sails. *Sidewinder* is showing her excellent speed heading north-east, where a fresher breeze has been predicted to come from, while we have stolen a jump on *Miss Saigon* who shadows us to leeward and *DaVinci* have also headed well in towards the north-east shore.

Our dreams of taking line honours in one of these passage races, fired by our success in the Darwin to Ambon race have pretty much burnt out, seeing just how fast *Sidewinder* is proving, and seeing the pace of these state art mono-hulls like *Hi-Fi*.

When the wind starts to veer around to the north-east all the multis tack so that we are virtually all in a line. Suddenly and without warning the breeze picks up to a full 20 knots, catching everyone unaware. Out of the slothful peace of a tropical calm, Carolyn, Mara and Karen are thrust into action on the foredeck. *Fantasia* is instantly driving off on a power reach doing 16/18 knots, streaming spray off the leeward bow where the apparent wind has lifted to 31 knots.

Our valiant girls must tie down the screecher, dressed in lose light clothes to cope with the heat, the wind peeling their tops off as they are hosed with spray while they wrestle to sort any loose gear. Eventually they drag back the spinnaker, soaked to the skin, exhilarated and startled by the sudden change. Short sharp seas have built up very quickly, as they usually do when a strong wind fills in and *Fantasia* is hitting some seas pretty hard, so that while a multihull drag race has begun, it feels prudent to nurse our boat until these seas lengthen out. The wide beam of multihulls means they can hold a lot more sail power when the wind is strong so we are ripping up on the 70' Swan, *Silandra,* like it's anchored.

Suddenly there is a nerve shattering "BANG" and the boom is flogging wildly about. The shackle for the mainsheet block has worked loose, so while Mike takes the helm, the rest of us strive to tame the dangerous boom and re-attach the block. Even after our drama is mastered we have left *Silandra* in our wake. We winch on our sheets to tighten our leaches and power on with our main traveller right down for a short spell to calm everyone's nerves. *Fantasia's* foils are emitting a impressive, high pitched humming as she whizzes along, holding pace with the other multis.

"Look, it's *Hi-Fi*, away down to leeward, her mainsail is down and they are sailing with just a jib!" calls out Mara, excitedly. I feel a bit disappointed, sure we would have beat them in this wind anyway, but we still have plenty of competition. As we settle in I set our team to cranking up the main traveller and jib during the slight low spots in the wind as we try to hold onto *Miss Saigon,* who is proving the pace setter, while *Sidewinder* is just astern.

During our time in Penang, I learnt that the head of the North Sails loft in San Diego who made *Miss Saigon's* fancy black 3DL sails is aboard for these regattas, so there's no lack of skill aboard that boat. Mile upon mile quickly slips away as we fly on at 16/18 knots holding neck and neck with *Miss Saigon.* As we pass Paya Island, a popular diving destination, Langkawi is less than an hour away and surprisingly *Sidewinder* has fallen back. We are going hammer and tongs with *Miss Saigon,* both boats now really cranking up hard, each seriously trying to shake the other.

Aboard *Fantasia* we are regularly hitting 20 knots and the tension aboard is palpable as we eye our foe just down to leeward, blasting along in a ball of spray. Line honours here will mean the glory of a trophy while a close 2nd will be soon forgotten. Now I must put full confidence in this great mass of wood and fibreglass I have created and drive it for all it's worth. Concentrating hard I lay into the strong helm and engage the rig fully with the wind, striving to gain every Newton of force, while the crew trim the powerful sails enthusiastically.

Meanwhile, control centre at Langkawi Marina is in a panic. "Yes we can see two boats coming to the finish already! They've never finished this early before, we'll have to be very quick to get the finish boat out there in time. Hurry, let's go!"

"I can't stand the tension, it's too much!" says Glen looking unsettled but excited. Driving *Fantasia* pedal to the metal she begins to pull away from *Miss Saigon,* yet the slightest mistake will still cost us the race. There is considerable confusion in spotting the finish line as we blast along, spray flying off the leeward hull.

"I can see it, just down to leeward but virtually straight ahead, about mile away!" says Carolyn, returning from the forward deck drenched and exhilarated, even though race stress is not her thing. Within minutes we are flying over the finish line, cracking our top speed of 23 knots, the adrenalin rush of winning this tense race etched in our minds forever. Two minutes later *Miss Saigon* hurtles home, worthy opponents no doubt drenched and ready for a few drinks at the Langkawi Yacht Club.

In the morning's *Asian Yachting* wrap-up, Marty Rijikas writes- "It was the Australian catamaran *Fantasia* who took line honours, causing panic with the finish boat who did not expect such an early arrival. *Fantasia* crossed the line in spectacular fashion, flying a hull at over 20 knots." *Fantasia* has truly arrived in Asia, but we have to back up and head out for another race on the expansive waters of Bass Harbour, the very next day.

Milling about at the start we feel a bit weary, tucking in a reef with the breeze still blowing, yet it seems the others are even worse for wear. Practising with their spinnaker, *Miss Saigon* get in a nasty tangle, forced to retire before the start. We get off well with *Sidewinder*, while *DaVinci* seem caught unawares, nowhere near the line. On the short beat *Sidewinder* illogically drop their jib to change to a smaller one, giving us a handsome lead.

With all our competition dropping by the wayside we run downwind conservatively under the screecher hitting 18 knots at times, while *Sidewinder* catch and lead us around Intan Island having whizzed ahead by flying their big yellow spinnaker. Under the rating system, based on sail area and weight they need to beat us handsomely to win, so by simply hanging in with them on the breezy beat into the wind, we win our second race in a row and go into the final day tied on points for the lead.

We are to learn that winning regattas in South-East Asia is a great deal about surviving the constant parties. That night the Langkawi Yacht Club puts on a splendid buffet with a huge selection of stir fries, battered fish and prawns, Malaysian savoury pancakes, salads, potato bake, even steak to appease the western stomach. Dozens of huge round tables seat the entire fleet who tuck in with gusto, all the while glamorous ladies, looking like Miss World of Asia, sidle around our tables offering fresh glasses of Tiger beer. Then of course nothing can hold the Malaysians back from putting on a trippy light show for the after dinner disco. More beer, dancing, then merrily waltz back to the boat to have a few night cap rums. No wonder we awake on the final day feeling a bit fuzzy.

"Oh no! Quick sheet on, it looks like our race has started without us!" I cry out as we see the multihull division setting off and us still several minutes from the line. We only just beat *DaVinci* home, with *Sidewinder* clear winners on OMR and *DaVinci* 2nd. *Miss Saigon* are right out of sorts, not flying a spinnaker so things aren't looking good in the camp of the current King's Cup champion.   In the 2nd race of the day we miss the start again! Now Mike makes the discovery the race radio channel has moved to VHF 72, so we have been missing all the instructions. Now the *Fantasia* crew sail for all their worth, executing our tacks and gybes with nice timing, really lifting our game. We fall just 60 seconds short of winning the series.

*

"What will we do tomorrow with no racing on? says Mara, who at age 12 has already become the foredeck leader. She seems to have enjoyed the regatta more than anyone, not only the action of the races but the social opportunities of the parties.

"Yay, no more pointless sailing back and forth around buoys!" says Glen, even though he had truly begun to enjoy the racing. "We can do something really interesting. We'll hire a car and explore the island!" I for one am fairly relieved the racing is over, awesome experience that it's been. Day after day to rock up for such action, without the customary cruising kind of rest, lolling around in the way we had grown used too, proved quite testing. That night the Langkawi Yacht Club turn on the final presentation party, which ends in wild style with many of the fleet taking the party into the pool to seek relief from the hot tropical night.

"Thank you Puppi, that was the best!" says Mara, her smile radiant as she relaxes in the tepid pool water, amid the raucous laughter, singing and conversation of wild sailors partying with no restraint now that the racing is over. "I can't wait for the King's Cup now!" She dives under water, going into a long handstand. Our next regatta is only a week away now, and we must sail up to Phuket, clear in, get sorted and rendezvous with an all new crew. We'll need every minute of that week. Ah the joys of being captain of a sailing ship, I never thought having such fun would be so demanding.

CHAPTER 22

THAILAND FANTASY

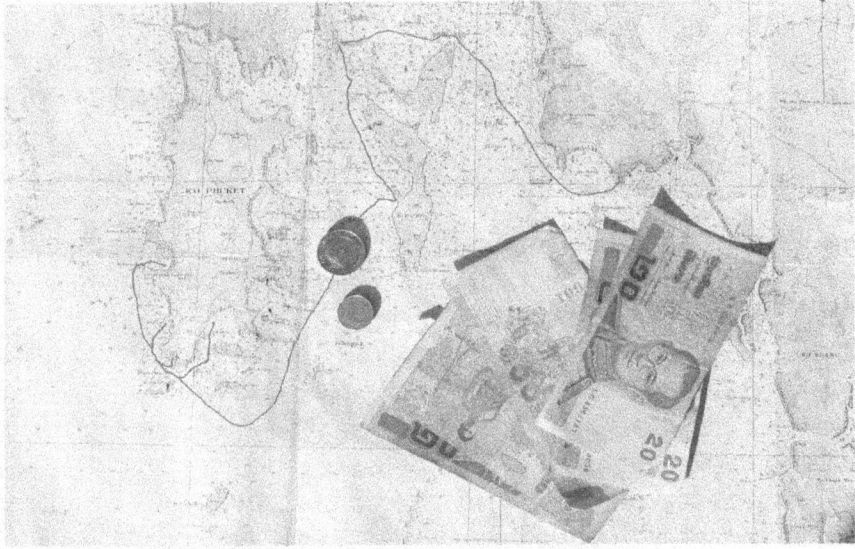

"It's a strange way we live, this sailing life of ours," says Carolyn as the three of us trudge down the pale dusty side road in Ao Chalong, Phuket Island, which leads to the Yacht Club. Each of us is loaded to the hilt with shopping from the early morning market, our hands straining on bag handles. We pass a field of coconut palms swaying in a fresh morning breeze, then on past some water buffaloes who peer with interest at these humans so laden down on this hot tropical morning, their animal smell in contrast to the sweet bush scents. "Most people just put their shopping in a car and drive home, where they need only carry it a few metres into the kitchen."

"Yes, but we have an adventure every time we just go shopping!" says Mara happily hauling her fair share. "Who'd want to live in a house! They're silly things! They cant float, always stuck in the same spot, square boxy things with way too many anchors! Why doesn't everyone live on a boat?" We've arrived at the yacht club pontoon and the tide has gone out leaving all the dinghies stranded on a layer of thick mud. While Ao Chalong lacks the white sandy beaches and clear water the island is famous for, it does offer excellent shopping and anchorage protected from all winds.

"Probably because they'd have to tackle this kind of thing whenever they want to go to the shops," I laugh as we load our shopping into the dinghy, hanging our legs over to push our feet in the soft squishy mud and slide our dinghy out to the water. Now with the dinghy loaded up we must clean the mud off our feet and row out into a stiff wind, striving not to take a wave aboard and wet all our shopping.

Finally we offload our prizes from the bucking dinghy and happily arrange them on the saloon table to savour our purchases. Delicate parrot-beak mangoes, bunches of wild red rambutans, clumps of longans, mangosteens, green prawns, squid, Chinese greens, red bean buns, pineapples, limes, red dragon fruit, crispy fried chicken, snake beans, with so much exotic fruit and vegetables our efforts seem more than worth while.

That afternoon our crew fly in from Australia. Once again our ace crewman Nick Lyons is able to join us along with Bill Donnelly, a Brisbane based orthopaedic surgeon, his wife Liz and two teenage sons, John and Tom. Phuket's King's Cup is a big international event, the 'one-to-win' in Asia, with more than 1000 sailors from 33 countries flocking to Kata, a beautiful long white sandy beach, lapped by the crystal clear waters of the Andaman Sea.

This year's multihull fleet has been billed as the best ever, so the Donnellys generously rent a room where we can offload our excess cruising gear. We lug bags full of charts of the world, books, computers, spare parts, diving equipment and more past the plethora of exotic tourists, lounging under beach umbrellas on a typically glorious tropical day.

Heading out for a practice sail, we discover the pleasing level of co-ordination attained at the end of the Raja Mudu has deserted us and must be worked up afresh. I feel a touch apprehensive at the prospect of mixing it with the 11 best multis in the land, with such little practice.

To officially open the regatta, all 100 yachts head out and in turn sail past the Royal Thai Navy patrol boats. Air-force planes fly over, showering us with flowers, highlighting the glamour of this event. Feeling blessed and a bit dazed we sail to the race course area, where the serious nature of the racing is evident. The hotshot IRC monohulls are demonstrating immaculate gybes and spinnaker drops, with ballerina style skill, their sails gleaming a crisp black, grey and gold. We feel a bit out of place with our low tech, dacron sails and round-top mainsail, when every other serious race boat, without fail, sports a square-top mainsail.

A windward leeward course of two laps is signalled, the start fiercely contested, all 11 boats hitting the line together. Our old foe *Sidewinder* is fast off the line, sailing through our lee with impressive pace. I learn too late the left hand side of the course has more wind and we open our account with a 5th, behind all the major players, although ahead of the trimaran *Cedar Swan* who won the Cup some years ago. Worse still, we have torn our spinnaker along the bottom, catching it on a deck cleat. Now we must sail the 2nd race using only the screecher, which is a reaching sail and not properly suited to these downwind legs. We slip down to 6th place, behind *Cedar Swan*. It seems *Miss Saigon* and *DaVinvi* have sorted out their equipment and crew issues, as they're right on the pace, with *Sidewinder* looking unbeatable.

After a few post race beers to cheer us up and a dip in the delightful crystal clear anchorage, Nick and I head off in a tuk-tuk taxi with the bulky spinnaker to the mammoth Tasker Sail loft. Five delightful Thai ladies, chattering happily away, rapidly replace the whole bottom panel as we watch in awe. Hundreds of other happy smiling Thais are busily employed building sails and yachting hardware in the moulding section. For under $100 our kite is all sorted.

Day 2 sees the race committee set a passage race around the islands, a welcome relief from the demanding short course windward/leeward racing, with more scope for strategy. It's a brilliant sunny day, with occasional cumulus decorating the vivid blue sky and a decent breeze allowing us to set our screecher on the reach down to Ko Yai in hot pursuit of *Miss Saigon*. As we pass Ko

Yai, a wild forested island with a prominent golden buddha, we roll up the screecher and begin beating into the breeze toward Ko Hi. *Sidewinder,* with yachting rockstar Joel Berg from Allyacht Spars helming and the Carwidine family pulling the strings, have built a handsome lead, while *Miss Saigon* benefit from local knowledge, short tacking out of the tide to pull away from us.

With the breeze beginning to die, we are struggling to hold off a charging *Skylight* and *Sweet Chariot,* both stripped out race machines, as we battle to round Ko Hi against the tide. At least *DaVinci* are a mile behind as we finally get around and set our kite for the run. With the tide now with us there is a collective sigh of relief aboard. Our elation to be pulling away from *Skylight* collapses in unison with our spinnaker, which flops down in a frustrating heap, the wind deserting us. Compounding our annoyance, *DaVinci* is now sailing along nicely across the channel, still in a decent wind. Feeling hot and annoyed as she passes us, we roll out the screecher, which sets much better in the very light wind.

Just as our hopes are being dashed, Mara, brandishing the binoculars, makes a discovery. "Hey, look! That's *Sidewinder* way back there! They must have followed the Fireflys to their windward mark. *Miss Saigon's* in the lead!" Now there's only two boats ahead of us, our enthusiasm is rekindled.

With the breeze filling in again, up goes our black kite with its distinctive yellow and orange star pattern. Pulling away from *Skylight* again, we fall in with two maxi Swan yachts, *Titania of Cowes* and the Chinese *Chao Ren Plus One,* both with massive crews and giant spinnakers. These mammoth monos blanket our wind as we struggle to pass them, losing our chance to catch up with *DaVinci,* yet it's a glorious way to finish, battling these multi million dollar yachts in our backyard built house.

Back at the anchorage off Kata beach, we savour the malty flavour of a few Singha beers to steady our nerves after the challenges of yacht racing. While I sit at the chart table enjoying a commanding view of the bustling anchorage, the results pop up on the internet. "Woohoo, we got a 3rd! Our first podium finish!" This is a good boost for our moral and we head off to the evening party bolstered by this modest success.

Tonight it's the Katathani resort that welcomes us into their sophisticated grounds. Glamorous Thai ladies constantly ply us with trays of delicate canapés as we mingle with crews from all over the world. "Wow, I'm really having to up my beer drinking skills doing these Asian regattas, with all this free alcohol!" I say to Bill, happily accepting another Singha beer from a smiling Thai beauty. In the food hall I load up my plate with finely cooked meats, gingerly dab on a few exotic sauces, then select a generous helping of fresh, crisp salad. Mmmm, I could get used to this!

"Puppi, have you seen the amazing fruit displays! Look at these melons, somebody has carved complex flowers all over them. So much work and just for this night!" says Mara, who is drinking in the beauty of Thai culture. After giving me a pep talk about how we'll do even better tomorrow, she heads off to mingle, a talent I'm delighted to observe she is taking to with gusto.

Soothing moonlight shines down through the gently swaying palms, as a Thai reggae band starts pumping out cool reggae rhythms. Carolyn hands me a glass of Mount Claire champagne, guiding me out onto the dance floor and a few sips of the heady liquid soon persuade my body to cut loose. The mesmerising, peaceful beat lifts us close to heaven. Our hard won, stylish acrylic 3rd place trophy sits on a table nearby, reminding us of the racing ahead. Mara is off happily chatting with the only sober people, the Malaysian navy team, who follow the somewhat sensible Islamic custom of abstaining from alcohol. Back in Australia, we'd be paying through the nose for beer, wouldn't be able to afford dinner and trophy's would only be awarded for the regatta winners, not the winners of each day. I savour the moment, feeling irie with the world, zoned out on the dance floor.

It's easy to get carried away, party too hard, drink a little too much and in a way you'd be missing out if you didn't make the most of such lavish affairs. Nevertheless it does make it hard to drag everyone out of bed, manage a relaxing breakfast and have the team revved up and raring to go out on the start line by 9am. With a nice 10/12 knots blowing we work hard and improve with every tack and gybe. A windward leeward race is very demanding, almost frantic work for the foredeck crew, who are constantly wrestling with our very heavy spinnaker and adjusting *Fantasia's* huge centreboards. When a third straight windward leeward race is signalled by the race committee, there are sad groans and mutinous talk from the foredeck union.

Of course they soon settle down as race excitement gets their blood flowing again. After we cross the finish line in the final race and they pack away the kite, bodies drenched with sweat, there's no doubt in their minds, sailing is a demanding sport. Nevertheless we return to the anchorage feeling very pleased with our performances.

A refreshing swim in the pristine aquamarine sea, feels like the best medicine in the world. Drying our bodies in the warm Phuket sunshine, Carolyn brings out plates of snacks and cans of Singha beer. We all loll about, gazing at the crowd of beach-goers, gradually unwinding after the hectic thrill of yacht racing. Before long the results pop up on the Internet, where to our disappointment we score 3rd, 4th, 4th with mere seconds in 2 races holding us out of the podium.

Yet there's no time to feel low. We have to get ourselves ready for another glamour evening party. It's like we are in something of a dream, welcomed into the foyer of the Orchid Beach Resort by 4 beautiful Thai ladies, sleek in gold thread dresses, who bow and smile so warmly, guiding us into the party. Lush tropical gardens surround a huge complex pool, where model boats swan about in honour of the racers, who stand about chatting in groups.

Carolyn's eyes are wide in admiration. "All these amazing statues! Dragons, a phoenix and that giant Buddha head with a waterfall coming out of his mouth! Thais take life into another dimension! Look at the flower display around the stage, perfect peonies and chrysanthemums."

We mill about with the hundreds and hundreds of crew who have elected to attend tonight's party, a huge gathering but well short of the full 1000 crew involved in the racing as not everyone likes to party. Amongst the sailors are some of the most successful people in Asia. People like Hong Kong's steel magnate, Frank Pong who is campaigning one of his fleet of maxi yachts, that all sail under the name of *Jelik*, with a crew of over 22 or Neil Pryde, one of the world's most successful sailmakers, with the slick *Hi-Fi*. It's a world of successful ex-pats and people attracted to the exotic freedoms of Asian life, so it feels satisfying to hear how impressed many of them are with *Fantasia,* the family boat, being such a strong contender.

Standing in something of a daze, I take in the raw power of an inspired Thai rock band, pumping out the big hits booming out of every disco in the fast lane of Asia. The music hits me, Pit Bull's *Mr Worldwide,* David Guetta *Titanium,* and now the Black Eyed Peas, "*I Gotta feeling that tonight's gunna be a good, good night*" we're leaping up and down for the joy of life. Carolyn has dragged up Mara, the reluctant dancer and even she can't help but be blown away by the energy of the band.

"This is it girls, we're there! We've made it to party heaven!" The band's going off, "*Let's do it, let's do it, let's paint the town, we'll shut it down, let's burn the roof then we'll do it again!*" It's one of those moments you feel anything's possible, an alcohol driven moment of enlightenment. When we're all danced out, Mara drags me off to admire the fruit display.

"There's like 12 carved melons there, watermelons, honeydew melons, canary melons, giant papaws, they're so intricate! Look, magnificent bird of paradise flowers and angels wings carved out of ice. Thailand is just so cool!

Fortunately there's a lay day to balance out the frantic action, so while the rest of the crew head off to ride elephants and go white water rafting, Carolyn and I spend the day catching up on repairs. A nasty tummy bug has been running rampant amongst the crew, gripping Nick earlier in the week and now it's my turn to battle nausea, diarrhoea and headache. All night long I writhe in the uncomfortable grips of this foreign bug, sleeping poorly, worrying whether I'll be fit for racing in the morning.

Phuket is blessed with yet another spectacular sunny day, yet even my customary dip in the sea to wipe clean the bottom, fails to ease my nausea. The crew are praying for a more relaxing around the islands race and whimper when the race committee signal more windward-leewards.

Up on the foredeck, the girls have the spinnaker tamed by now, and it's up and drawing within boat lengths of rounding the mark. Nearing the leeward mark I feel confident in keeping it up as long as

WINDWARD TO FANTASIA

possible, knowing they can get it down and stowed quickly. The smaller boats are able to carry their kites right up to the mark and whip them down professional style as they round, while we need 100m or so to pull down our sock and get it all packed away.

Beating back to the anchorage, Nick hands me a beer, relieving me of the helm. "Seems you came good Andy, fended off that tummy bug. We sailed well today, our teamwork was spot on mostly. It was cool how we got the better of *DaVinci* in both races and we were so close to *Miss Saigon* we surely beat them on OMR. I don't know about *Sidewinder* though, they are so fast in this light wind and flat water stuff, we need more breeze to beat them it seems, but we got closer to them today!" He's proved spot on as the eagerly awaited results spring to life online, showing a 2nd in race 7 and a 2nd in race 8 for *Fantasia,* just a minute behind *Sidewinder* in both.

"Woohoo! That puts us only one point behind *Miss Saigon* now!" announces an excited Mara. "And tomorrow the forecast is for stronger winds and surely they'll give us another passage race!"

At the Centura Grand resort a troupe of Thai drummers build up to a powerful, high speed crescendo. Awe-struck, we pound out the rapid rhythm, our spirits soaring and full of hope for the last day of racing.

Out on the start line it's blowing north-east 20knots, the perfect breeze for *Fantasia* to show how she performs in the rougher weather she is built for. Reaching back and forth before the start she's raring to go, throwing up spray, speeding about effortlessly in the building seas. Hitting the line within seconds of the gun, cranked up hard on the wind, we head up the first short beat, looking forward to rounding the mark and setting off on a speed reach towards the islands. Suddenly there's a heart stopping 'BANG' and the mainsail falls down, forming a messy flake on the boom.

The meagre piece of aluminium our first sailmaker had deemed strong enough for the job has pulled right through, just when we needed it most, leaving our main halyard at the top of the mast. Hastily we re-hoist the main on the topping lift rope and set off again, still on the pace. As we begin to crank on the mainsheet I begin to realise how much of this load goes straight onto the halyard. Thinking of our meagre 10mm polyester braided rope we go easy on the winching, but the load is way too much for this low tech rope and moments later "POW" down it comes again.

Nick is quick to volunteer and sets off up the mast, hoisted on the fractional spinnaker halyard. With the mast whipping around in the waves, he is unable to free climb the last section, getting thrown about and bruised for his efforts.

"King's Cup race control, this is *Fantasia,* just to notify you we are retiring from from today's race." Mara is in tears with the frustration and pain of defeat, which we are all feeling as we limp back to the empty anchorage. "We should have got Saxbys to build all our sails and not gone for the cheap and beastly loft!" In fact none of the budget equipment I bought is proving up to the job, with lots of our blocks beginning to grind out and spit metal filings and our traveller cars jamming up under load. I should have known the sea would eat up all but the best gear.

Hundreds of international tourists frolic joyously along Kata beach, lounging under beach umbrellas, playing ball and swimming. Wafts of coconut tanning lotion float out to us mixing with the fresh sea air. The holiday vibe is catchy. Casting our disappointment aside, we are soon enjoying the vast swimming pool that surrounds *Fantasia.*

There is something about clear blue sea, how its clarity soothes one's soul. Even Mara is getting over our loss as she challenges Nick to shinny up the bowsprit bob-stay, the bar tight dyneema as hard as steel making it a painful business, but Nick is up for it. I dive down, deep into the quiet world below where only the distant roar of longtails and jetskis penetrates, taking in the eerie peace. Bursting through the surface, I feel full of positivity once again.

Bill Donnelly is floating happily in the shade of *Fantasia's* vast bridgedeck with his family around him, the surgeon's cares lifted for now. "Well Andrew, 4th place in the King's Cup isn't too bad, especially for a home built boat with dacron sails and a crew who hadn't sailed together before." He's so right, we have everything to be thankful for!

The final presentation ceremony highlights the sophistication and class of this event. At the door, anyone not wearing appropriate clothing is turned away by poker faced Thai security guards. Tshirted Aussies and Russians are barred without exception. The King's personal representative presents the trophies and so important is this man, it is forbidden to turn one's back on him once he gives you this coveted prize. As I sit watching famous yachtsmen from all over the globe, back away respectfully, the pomp and ceremony adds so much glamour and meaning to gaining a podium position. Strolling dreamily out of the lavish gardens of the Centura Grand I feel quite inspired to return next year.

"Considering that I really don't like the stress of racing that much," says Carolyn as we pause under a stand of coconut trees, gazing out at the bay filled with yachts. "I've got to say that was a most wonderful experience. I'm so glad we did it." She gives me a big hug and we walk down onto the pristine white sand of Kata beach.

"It was rather hectic, I've got to admit, but now we can relax and look forward to months of cruising in this magic place!"

*

Thus December 2011 rolls on. We take the Donnellys on a week long cruise, for which they pay us handsomely, allaying our financial concerns for the time being at least.

After the hectic pace of the last few months we're happy to hang out in Phuket's best cruising anchorage Nai Harn, a deep bay on the island's SW. A gentle swell, virtually unnoticeable at anchor, can make landing a dinghy on the beach challenging, as it surges in to form a pleasant churn of white water, full of gambolling tourists. Landing close to the Nai Harn resort seems to be the calmest spot and we drag our dinghy past sun baking Russians, obliviously burning lobster red, dodging a Frisbee we leave our dinghy near the beach chairs where a pale English family lounge happily under blue beach umbrellas.

Luxuriating our feet in the warm white sand, we weave past the world of international tourists, all enjoying the magic of this place, exuding powerful aromas of sun-creams plastered over deodorants and perfumes. At the back of the beach the local Thais loll around in their permanent rickety stalls, selling bottled drinks, fruit smoothies, chilled sliced fruit, prawn crisps, ice creams and massages, all smiling happily in the delightful Thai way. Behind them a low sandstone wall leads up to a park backed by dozens of local restaurants and massage houses, offering a satisfied belly and a relaxed body.

There is a particularly peaceful feel about the place, a relaxed calm vibe. We purchase some mangosteens from the fruit stalls and walk down the road. Savouring the soft sweet fruit, we come across the Buddist temple grounds, hidden amongst trees behind the busy beach front. Stray dogs lounge happily about the roads and temple grounds, looked after by the monks. Beyond the temple is an extensive lake and it feels the combination of the calming temple and peaceful lake, spread a dreamy vibe over the Nai Harn area.

"Can we spend Christmas here Andrew, please? I love it here," Carolyn pleads, and I don't need much persuading to agree. We're not the only ones, as the bay is full of yachts all enjoying the jetski free anchorage.

Just over two years after launching *Fantasia* we find ourselves spending a relaxing Christmas in one of the most beautiful places on earth. The tolerant Buddhist religion of Thailand allows the Thais to seize on Christmas as a chance to party and celebrate life. We're happy to enjoy a simple time, drinking in the beauty and savouring the moment. Mara sets up our tiny tree, decorating it with our host of trophies and a few presents. She's had a wonderful year, as we decided to abandon her official school, which was failing to challenge her. Now we just encourage her to read and cover a maths course, allowing her to fully take in the culture around her.

Near the northern entrance to Nai Harn bay is the wonderful little beach of Ao Sane. Backed by shady trees, quaint bungalows and a tasty local restaurant, looking out over a boulder decorated beach. On Christmas day we walk along the quiet foreshore road, grass seed and wild-flowers scenting the hot afternoon air, to attend a smorgasbord dinner. Along with a troupe of international cruising yachtsman, we tuck in heartily, gazing out over the tranquil bay. After even the most hungry of sailors is sated with good food, a reggae band strikes up on a temporary wooden platform, perched over the coarse sand and random rocks. We groove around to help burn off a few excess calories, occasionally flopping down amid the crowd and sipping on bottles of Chang beer. "It's nice how you can drink beer in a public place here!" says Carolyn as she polishes off her bottle and leaps up to dance some more.

Allowing the strong alcohol content of the Chang beer to wash over me, the relaxing reggae rhythms are soothing, so I lie back to take in the final moments of vivid sunset over the Andaman Sea. It's been a long journey to arrive here and be savouring this special period of life. Not so many years ago I had been in the Med, unable to afford even a jacket to ward off the icy cold of winter. Now with some mighty testing hard yards behind me, we have a yacht competitive on the world stage, an amazingly comfortable machine to continue this wonderful lifestyle, my small family enjoying every moment. Yes, I've truly landed on my feet.

Whoosh, a powerful firework fires off only a few metres away, pulling me out of this pleasant reverie. Cheerful Thai men balance pyrotechnic mortars on the beach sand and they blast off into the clear night sky, bursting into those brilliant colours that have excited man's soul for thousands of years. One of the cardboard tubes falls over to a drunken angle and the explosive trail whizzes close over the crowd of party-goers. Now I'm really back in the moment. The Thai men laugh and keep on letting off fireworks. This is Thailand, a land where people can still light fires, drink in public, let off fireworks, fun things whose banning in western countries has made life that bit more sterile.

*

2011 draws to a close. No, the world is not coming to a cataclysmic end like the media and popular movies seem to need portray in order to sell. The world is beset with problems, but for now the vast ocean sends in a gentle swell as we sail along the coast of Phuket to the largest bay, the commodious Ao Patong. Here, behind the long white sandy beach lies one of the most popular nightclub hubs in all of Thailand, famed for its lively New Years Eve celebrations.

We're back in the fast lane now, after our peaceful hiatus in Nai Harn. Jetskis and speedboats whiz about the bay, leaving oily rainbows in our pristine backyard, the strong aroma of petrol overpowering the subtle scents of bush blossoms from the surrounding hills. Rowing ashore to see in the new year, Patong

Beach style, the sun sets over a fiery red ocean, where a huge cruise ship is lit up like a Christmas tree.

Dozens of venues pump out the latest pop hits, which merge together into a crazy high energy cacophony of sound booming out over the entire bay. The beach is already crowded with revellers, drinking in the building excitement as a continual parade of floating lanterns take off into the night sky. Hawkers ply the beach with stacks of folded lanterns on their backs and for 100 baht you can have the pleasure of lighting the small wax candle inside the tall paper cylinder. Now think of a wish as it builds up hot air, then let it float off into the night sky, where it rises above the bay and sails out beyond the crowded anchorage, 10 minutes of enchanting pleasure. Along the waterfront boulevard a host of stalls sell trinkets, alcohol and mouth watering foods. One of the more alarming stalls offers an array of deep fried crickets, small grubs and even crispy cockroaches in its selection of popular Thai insect snacks.

Cocktail vendors juggle bottles of rum, vodka and whisky to attract custom. We buy a Margarita and a Thailand Fantasy, just to watch the flying glass and long streams of tequila, rum, triple sec and juices as our artful barman works his magic. Mara sips a pina colada mocktail, decorated with a purple orchid and pineapple slice, eyes wide to the marvels that surround her. The crowd is thick everywhere, grooving *Gangnum Style*, building with every hour closer to midnight.

We join the flow of humanity swirling through the town, the occasional firework bursting like heavenly flowers in the clear night sky above the crowded rooves and the random chaos of Thai electrical wiring. Every bar and nightclub strives to outdo the other with artistic, sensational and gaudy glamour, dazzling neon lights, strings of incandescent globes, colourful LEDS and fairy lights. All hoping to ensnare wealthy westerners, who wander these wild streets in search of the forbidden delights of Asia. Glamorous, partly naked pole dancers strut their stuff for all to see, beaconing to this mass flood of humanity to enter. Glorious ladies tout their nightclub's attractions; the sex shows, bar girls and cheap drinks, where you never know if your smiling beauty is one of the ubiquitous lady boys.

Bankla Road is cut off to all traffic and tonight it's elbow room only, an adventure just taking in the sights. The surreal *New Tiger Discotheque* is built like a bizarre cave with a huge brightly painted tiger and hooded cobra dominating its street front, hung with strings of flowers to bless the night. "Hey, it's the *Fantasians,* come have a drink with us!" Rob Azzapardi generously shouts us Heinekens and Sprite for Mara. Under a cloud of balloons, we sit with our friends, watching the flowing street party build up to near frenzy pitch.

"They used to hawk fireworks in the street, but the smoke got so thick people couldn't find their way to the bars, which was bad for business, so now we have cans of silly string," say Matt McGrath, buying a box of cans from a 10 year old boy. Soon we are all covered in tangles of coloured paper string and passers by are so cool they just enjoy being sprayed. There's no sense of 'us and them' in the vast international crowd, it's like we're all in this together to have fun. There's burly Russians, some of them no doubt part of the Russian mafia rife in Phuket, rough looking Aussies, wild looking Europeans, it seems there's someone from every nation in the world here tonight, all co-existing in the most remarkable harmony.

After a few beers with our friends we join the flood tide of humanity heading back to the beach. There's no push and shove in the crowd, it's as though the Thai's have cast a spell of peace over everyone. We pass the police who have a temporary house set up. "Wow, look at this," says Carolyn, "*Resting place for drunk people.* Haha, the Thai's are so sensible and loving!"

As it gets closer to midnight and the beginning of 2012, more and more paper lanterns lift off into the night sky, everyone excited to send off a wish for the new year. It's really a self funded extravaganza, with tourists also buying fireworks which are going off all over the beach. When the new year rolls up there are literally 1000 lanterns filling the sky and now all the big resorts around the bay begin to let off their salvos of fireworks, the high vibe of the people is a tangible beautiful feeling. This cascade of colourful explosions filling the night sky seems like a celebration of how amazing the world truly is. The three of us embrace, a tiny family feeling part of the whole world.

"This is an education hey Sprat! Better than beastly school work!" I call out to Mara over the buzz of the crowd, the explosions and music, as there seems no end to this incredible display, it just roars on with great joy and momentum. "What an epic year we've had! What would you like to do in 2012?" Mara is beaming, bright eyed and innocent, in awe of what she is experiencing.

"Thank you Puppi, for all the amazing things we did, it's been so wonderful! Let's do more racing in 2012, maybe we can improve *Fantasia* a bit more, make our crew work even better. Let's win some regattas!"

"Haha, yes I think that can happen!" says I giving her a big hug.

"And what about you Carolyn, my glorious partner of so many adventures, what do you desire for 2012?"

"Well, I'd be greedy to want a more wonderful year than the one we just had. I'm really looking forward to spending time exploring this amazing coastline, getting off the beaten track and savouring the simple beauty of nature."

Returning to *Fantasia* we're relieved to find our ship unscathed by burning lanterns crashing onto her deck. Everyone drops straight into sleep, yet I lie awake taking in the immense stillness and peace that envelopes *Fantasia* so snugly anchored in Patong Bay.

It's been a fine year, but no magnificent finale like I had hoped, no spectacular victory in the King's Cup, a crowning glory to rest my laurels on. As I begin to drift off into the ecstasy of sleep a deep realisation washes over me. Life is a endless series of challenges, it's the never ending story where *Fantasia* found her name. Hurdle after hurdle must be tackled, each one the opportunity to grow and experience wonders. For all we've learnt from our years of sailing and building our boat, still the coming year looms a difficult challenge. We'll need to scrape together the money for new sails and equipment, ship them to the far east and fit them. Yet it seems our destiny to follow this path and as my life motto seems to go, "nothing ventured, nothing gained", we'll play our hand, hope for the best and enjoy the thrill of life unfolding.

CHAPTER 23

EPILOGUE

"So wait a minute! You mean the story's going to end like that? We get a 4th in the King's Cup, not even making the podium! You need to finish with a win, a resounding victory of some kind Pup!" exclaims Mara indignantly. Two months have passed and we're anchored in one of the most beautiful places on earth, off Phra Nang beach, jewel of the Railay Peninsula. This is the heart of Krabi province, mysterious land of towering karst monoliths. Limestone wonders dripping in stalactites, jut out of the azure sea and lush jungled shoreline. *Fantasia* is surrounded by these monstrous menhir-like marvels, undercut by the sea's movement, as they mushroom up into a rock climbers heaven.

"So you're not even going to cover how we got the record for the Champagne Run, or how we won every race at the Langkawi International Regatta!" Mara has taken to the regatta world with a passion. It's easy to understand why, with every night a glamorous party, packed full of interesting people, who all seem to adore her. Having just turned thirteen, she is confounding the world's best crews with her ability to free climb our main halyard, 20m to the top of the rig, just like a monkey. It's a feat that makes us cringe with nervousness that we let her do such a thing, yet it seems wrong to curb her abilities. Right now she's cart-wheeling down the topside of the boat in the bosun's chair, releasing some of her boat-bound energy.

"Well, yes, I know it's a wonderful feeling to win and when I began writing this book I did kind of imagine finishing it on some spectacular note. Like winning the King's Cup or the Brisbane to Gladstone Race. Yet somehow that doesn't seem right, it's implying life is only wonderful for those who win. To me the real victory is getting here and the amazing experiences we're having every day.

Fantasia has proved to be a spectacular sailing boat that has carried us to these magic lands. That is the achievement to satisfy my soul. Living on a sailing boat and travelling to foreign lands is one of the last true freedoms man can experience." I philosophise contentedly, staring at the cliff face where calcium stalactites reach downwards like giants hands, the red rock riddled with bat caves, glowing in the golden hue of a magnificent Phang Nga Bay sunset.

"Couldn't you just cover how we beat the 13 best multihulls in Asia, including *Sidewinder* in the Phang Nga Bay Regatta? That was an amazing win for *Fantasia,* a family cruising boat, with only us and your mum and dad for crew, beating all the stripped out racers in the fickle and light airs of the most incredible bay in all the world! You could talk about your light air sailing skills, honed on the Lane Cove River and Sydney Harbour. It was an epic victory, especially since all the locals know that bay much better than you. You need to talk yourself up Pup, make up stories like everyone else! I think the best moment was when we picked up that new north-east breeze and shot off at 14 knots while all the others boats were still becalmed. I'll never forget that!"

I take a swig from my glass of Chang beer, amused by Mara's determination that I end my novel on a victorious note. "Yes, but that's not my way Sprat. I've always loved competition, but only for the game's sake. When I was a kid I loved to play board games, any games with my cousins. They often accused me of being too competitive, even cheating! I simply loved to play well, and concentrated so hard on the games I often won. The thing is I really didn't care who won, it was just for the thrill of playing. Winning doesn't make you the better person, testing your skills does however make you a more capable animal to survive and enjoy this complex world we live in. Am I making sense you guys?"

Carolyn has produced a plate of freshly sliced mangoes diced on the skin and peeled mangosteens, which she puts on the cabin roof, sitting back to take in this enchanting spectacle. Back in 1996 we had anchored *Longnose* in this very spot, thrilled to be discovering the world, amazed by its splendour. Sixteen years later, an eternity in our lives, very little has changed here. Still the romantic wooden sailing junk graces its mooring, a timeless craft dating back to 200 AD. The Railay Peninsula can only be reached by boat, as steep limestone cliffs rule out access by car. Now that the regular daily roar of unmuffled longtail boats has died off, a glorious peace has fallen over this ancient landscape formed more than 200 million years ago, making one feel an insignificant blip in time, but grateful for the experience.

"Yes, that's all very well Pup, but where's the finale? The gang busting pirate attack or the glorious sound of the winning canon as we cross the line first, bringing home a bounty of trophies! How are your readers going to know *Fantasia* is now the leading multihull on the Asia Yachting Grand Prix pointscore? I don't see how your finish works?"

"Well, think of where *Fantasia* got her name, *The Never Ending Story*. That's what this is really about. It's a story about the amazing adventures along the way and enjoying every minute. No story ever really finishes, how can it? There's always going to be ramifications from any event that lead on. Does the Universe have a start or finish? I mean, what would be on the other side if this Universe finished? Could there just be nothing at all?" This fairy-tail location is going to my head, but we are all feeling so relaxed, under the spell of this eternal landscape, peopled by incredibly creative artisans who are so in touch with the earth.

"It's just the beginning for our adventures on *Fantasia,* there'll be many exciting moments to celebrate. There'll always be the eternal battle between good and evil. During periods where the light of positivity gains the upper hand over the dark forces of negativity, you have the golden ages. Of course when the black energies of negitivity pervade, that's the dark ages." I'm having a wonderful rant, so eat some mango to fuel my ideas. "It's the great challenge of living things to push towards the light of goodness. That's Fantasia, the creative force of positivity."

"It's a battle royal at the moment, what with the forces of greed flourishing in our luxurious modern world. People are jealous of each other's wealth, made dissatisfied by the cunning hard sell of our capitalistic religion. We battle each other for supremacy, destroying the land in the process. Huge multinational companies led by ridiculously rich people, who sell off the world's natural wonders. They have so much money they don't know what to do with it!"

"Oh, but that's a grim picture, what can we do about this?" cries Mara, feeling sad at the thought of this dire situation, which always brings doubt into one's future. She springs off the bow and flies through the air, 10m towards the back of the boat, running the momentum to the stern to free herself from dark thoughts.

"Don't despair my Sprat, the world is an amazing place. We do what we can I suppose. Follow our destiny, focus our attention on what we can do for mother nature and she will reward us. We'll go where we think we can do the best and push for a positive world, where sensible ideas prevail which benefit everybody and everything. When I freed myself of university, disillusioned with becoming another brick in the system's wall, I wanted to find a real purpose for my life, rather than just working for a dodgy multinational company. I followed my intuition, the path of my heart and inner guidance, read books on religion and spiritual growth. One day I did a meditation, which was supposed to show me my purpose in life. I saw myself working with sail as a wonderful means of transport. A vague and broad image for sure, but it did galvanise my sense of direction, which has led me to this beautiful moment."

Mara unhooks herself from the bosun's chair and sets to, busily devouring fresh tropical fruit, while Carolyn sits cross legged on the trampoline, breathing in the warm night air. Spiders and crickets break the quiet evening peace, while a lone owl hoots high on the hill as the gentle tinkle of wavelets caresses the beach. For the moment we have found our own Shanghai-la, a place one would love to stay forever, but I know things will change and there will be many more challenges to overcome.

"It's so special here in Asia, I could live here forever," says Carolyn giving herself a luxurious stretch. "I don't suppose we will be able to just hang around here, enjoying the beauty of Phang Nga

Bay, you'll have itchy feet soon and want to head off adventuring some new place, I'll bet!"

"Well, funny you should say that. I was thinking we could sail around to the Gulf of Siam, do the Top of the Gulf Regatta and the Samui Regatta, explore the east coast of Malaysia along the way. What do you say to that me hearties?"

"Woohoo! Yes that will be awesome! We could win the Asian Grand Prix Championships! I'm sure there'll be no end of adventures along the way. Thanks Puppi, at least if your book doesn't end with a magnificent finale, it ends with the promise of one!"

"Haha! Fiddlesticks to your finale Sprat! I can't fit the entire *Fantasia* story into one book! We'll get you that sailing dinghy to help burn up that abounding energy of yours hey! Maybe we could pick up a cheap Optimist in Singapore on our way around."

"Yes! Yes, yes to the sailing dinghy! I think I'm too big for an Oppi though! Couldn't I just get a Laser like you had?" She's looking sharp as a cat now, ears pricked up, whole body poised to pounce on the idea of buying a sailing dinghy. "Maybe if I practice a lot I'll be able to campaign for the Olympics and win a medal at the games!"

"Dinner should be ready now, you two mad things. Roast fish and veggies will fuel us up for our next challenge!" We head inside, leaving the subtle lights glimmering through the trees ashore, the sheer cliffs bathed in starlight. Out in the bay the sea mirrors the heavens above, as the reader finds themselves floating away from the adventures aboard *Fantasia*. Rising up, Ao Nang and Krabi town become tiny clusters of light. The vastness of surrounding bushland, heart warming when viewed from such heights. The world is such a magic place, what are we waiting for, bring on the horizon.

THE END

About the Author

Andrew Stransky has spent his entire life adventuring the world on sailing boats. Born in England in 1965, the first 8 years of his life encompass a family sailing odyssey on a 35' steel sloop. His intrepid family voyage more than half way around the world, returning to their homeland of Australia. This experience leaves him deeply in love with the magic of cruising far flung destinations. He spent his teenage years dinghy racing on Sydney Harbour and contesting Sydney Hobart races on his fathers yacht. Foregoing specialised tertiary education to adventure the world, led him to become a masterful Jack of all trades, a most handy skill for a sea captain. After several voyages into the South Pacific, he circumnavigated the world over 4 years with his mate Carolyn. On his return to Australia he summoned all his acquired knowledge to design and build a 50' composite catamaran. *Fantasia* proved a highly successful international ocean racer, which he lives on and races to this day with Carolyn and his daughter Mara. He is a regular contributor to Australian Multihull Magazine, passionate about sharing the thrill of exploring exotic locations with everyone.

www.ingramcontent.com/pod-product-compliance
Lightning Source LLC
Chambersburg PA
CBHW021501090426
42739CB00007B/412